To my g[...]

Roberta Faulkner Sund

twin #2

ROBERTA *and* ROGENE

ROBERTA *and* ROGENE

The Intrepid Faulkner Twins

from Texas

Roberta Sund and Rogene Henderson

Fort Worth, Texas

Library of Congress Cataloging-in-Publication Data

Names: Sund, Roberta, 1933- author. | Henderson, Rogene, author.
Title: Roberta and Rogene : the intrepid Faulkner twins from
Texas / Roberta Sund and Rogene Henderson.
Description: Fort Worth, Texas : TCU Press, [2017]
Identifiers: LCCN 2017045573 (print) | LCCN 2017053015 (ebook) |
        ISBN 9780875656830 | ISBN 9780875656724
Subjects: LCSH: Sund, Roberta, 1933- | Henderson, Rogene. | Twin
        sisters--Texas--Biography. | Sisters--Texas--Biography. |
        Women scientists--Texas--Biography. | Scientists--Texas
--   Biography. | Women travelers--Texas--Biography--Anecdotes. |
        Travelers--Texas--Biography--Anecdotes. | LCGFT:
        Autobiographies.
Classification: LCC F385 (ebook) | LCC F385 .S87 2017 (print) |
        DDC 917.6404--dc23
LC record available at
 https://urldefense.proofpoint.com/v2/url?u=https-
3A__lccn.loc.gov_2017045573&d=DwIFAg&c=7Q-
FWLBTAxn3T_E3HWrzGYJrC4RvUoWDrzTlitGRH_A&r=O2eiy819IcwTGuw-
vrBGiVdmhQxMh2yxeggw9qlTUDE&m=goLdIDCmD2Dplbbam U5n-qdeXd3cwj-
ARv9ZJICT55A&s=9w-h6D8mdKSKZdTXwQWTTU8uzn_6Ad8BUM2A0h2f9qQ&e=

TCU Press
TCU Box 298300
Fort Worth, Texas 76129
817.257.7822
www.prs.tcu.edu
To order books: 1.800.826.8911

CONTENTS

P. M. Faulkner, 1924

Lenoma Rogers, 1924

INTRODUCTION

"Don't drop me. I'll have another one!" our mother is quoted as saying to the attending nurse. Rogene was the first to leave the womb; Roberta followed six minutes later, and in some ways, to be explained in the stories that follow, that seniority claimed by Rogene set the tone of our relationship. Although she was the dominant twin, our energies merged to produce exponential levels of mischief and adventure in the places we lived. More than the tucked-in womb-mates we had been before birth, we quickly began to move like a small, busy tornado across the Texas landscape, then to places near and far. The events narrated here show not only how our lives unfolded but also provide a window to a time and place that now belong to folklore.

Our arrival in the Texas oil boomtown of Breckenridge in 1933 caused a stir. It was a day of excitement, and for once it was not about an oil well coming in or the Breckenridge Buckaroos winning a ball game. Lenoma Faulkner, our mother, had given birth to identical twin girls. Twins were rare. Our parents already had two daughters and no doubt were hoping for a son. Without sonograms, unavailable at this time, two baby girls in a row must have been quite a surprise.

That we arrived at all is something of a miracle, considering the factors working against us. Our father, Philander Moulden Faulkner, P. M. for short, worked at a bank in Breckenridge. He had planned to marry his longtime sweetheart Callie as soon as she was free of her obligation to care for her ailing mother. (It was the custom at that time for the youngest daughter in a family to forego marriage if her parents needed her to care for them.) Daddy was in his forties. He finally decided to wait no longer and began to court our mother, Lenoma Rogers, who was a home economics teacher at the local high school.

Lenoma lived in the teacherage where all female teachers were housed. Female teachers were not allowed to date. Indeed, the policy at that time dictated that there be no married female teachers, so Lenoma and P. M. had to be sneaky. They met at the First Christian Church, where Lenoma's father, the Reverend A. D. Rogers, had once been pastor. Reverend Rogers objected to the budding romance. He thought P. M. was too old for Lenoma, so the couple decided to elope. Going back even earlier in our family history, the marriage that produced Lenoma almost didn't happen, either. Rev. A. D. Rogers started out as a circuit rider with his older brother, the Reverend E. H. Rogers. They carried the mail and the gospel to the people in the hills of Tennessee. The two brothers married sisters, Lou Ella and Sally Spearman, over the strong objections of the girls' brother, Robert Spearman, Assistant Attorney General under presidents Cleveland and Wilson. He announced, "I'll not have my sisters marry a couple of itinerant preachers!"

If he had won the argument, the Faulkner twins would not have come to be. The preacher brothers later parted ways over the use of musical instruments in church services. A. D. sided with the Disciples of Christ, which approved the use of instruments; E. H. went with the Church of Christ, which did not.

Lou Ella and A. D. had a son and four daughters, Vivion, Edith, Lenoma, Fay, and Roberta. E. H. and Sally had a son and a daughter, Sam and Maggie. Robert Spearman was handsome and had many girlfriends. He married a lovely lady named Fanny. They had two daughters: Winnie, described as snooty and aloof, and Rogene, her father's favorite. Rogene died at a young age of diphtheria.

Although we were unlikely arrivals, we were nevertheless full-term babies, each weighing more than six pounds. There was much discussion over appropriate names for us. The local newspaper solicited suggestions. A letter written by our father early on refers to us as Number One and Number Two. In the end it was our maternal grandfather, the Reverend Amonel Davis Rogers, who named us. He considered himself a clever bestower of names. After all, he had

E. H. and A. D. Rogers, circuit riders

The Rogers family

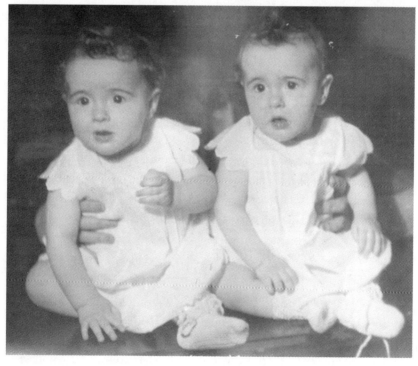

Number Two, left, and Number One

named our mother Lenoma, his own name spelled backwards, and he had named his only son Vivion. He named Number One Rogene after Rogene Spearman. He named Number Two Roberta after his youngest daughter. We are grateful that whoever named our father Philander Moulden did not have a hand in naming us.

Our two older sisters were named Martha Lou after the two grandmothers, Martha Francis Pigg Faulkner and Lou Ella Spearman Rogers; and Callie Fay after Daddy's former sweetheart and Aunt Fay, who died of acute leukemia shortly before she was to be married. Apparently Lenoma agreed to name her second daughter after P. M.'s former girlfriend, but she always called the child Fay, never Callie Fay. The older Callie eventually married and moved to California. We received Christmas cards with pictures of her and her family. When we asked, "Who is this family that sends us Christmas cards every year?" Mother would say, "A friend of your father, someone he knew before you were born."

Our names were not put to much use until we were adults because we looked so much alike that it was easier to refer to each of us as "Twinie" or "this twin" or "that twin." Otherwise, our dresses had to be pulled up to see which of us had the birthmark on her back and was therefore Roberta. Having our dresses pulled up to check our identity is one of our earliest memories. We formed a special bond with each other, perhaps because we were the only ones who knew for sure who was who. Lenoma called Rogene "Genie" and Roberta "Buddo." We turned "Genie" into "Neany," and that's what we called each other until we figured out we did not have the same name. Then "Buddo" turned into "Buzzy," and from then on we were Neany and Buzzy.

Our birth necessitated a larger home. Since there was no air-conditioning back then, Daddy bought a house on a hill that would catch the breeze on hot summer days. The front lawn was terraced. When we were older we used to lie down, stretch out, and roll down the hills that formed the terraces (good pre-TV entertainment!). The house

Twins, 1935

had four bedrooms and two baths plus a living room, dining room, butler's pantry, kitchen, and breakfast room. It was on a double lot running from one street through the back lot to the next street behind us. Daddy installed a cow, chickens, and a garden in the back lot. There was a garage with a small apartment at the back of it.

Now, we would like to introduce you to some people, places, and events from our formative years that helped shape our lives.

1

CHILDHOOD *and* YOUTH

M. B.

MOTHER AND DADDY hired a combination housekeeper and nanny to look after us. She was referred to as a "colored" lady at that time, rather than the current term of African American lady. During the week she lived in the little apartment at the back of our garage. Only on weekends did she spend time with her own family across town. At that time many middle-class homes in Breckenridge had these small apartments known as "servants' quarters." M. B., as she was called, was warm and caring. She was sincerely devoted to the newborn twins, and being in charge of the Faulkner twins gave her additional standing in our small town. Sitting on her spacious lap as she dressed us was a pleasure. She also bathed us, fed us, combed our hair, and directed our play.

Neany remembers with chagrin the time we may have hurt M. B.'s feelings. Our parents told us that M. B. would be spending the night with us while they were out of town. We screamed in terror, "We can't see her in the dark! She is black." We hope M. B. forgave us.

When we were about three, M. B. became gravely ill. As it became clear that she would not last much longer, our father took the unprecedented step of bringing us to her home in the black section of town so she could say good-bye to us. The scene is still vivid—the overheated room, M. B. lying under piles of blankets, her relatives standing silently by as Daddy lifted two wiggly little girls up to kiss her good-bye. It was a wrenching time. Buzzy remembers feeling totally abandoned. She had no idea that Mother was capable of taking care of us.

Miss Jennie

Another woman who was very important to us was Miss Jennie Lauderdale, the preschool Sunday-school teacher at the First Christian Church in Breckenridge. We loved her dearly and wanted to please her. When we arrived each Sunday morning, dressed in our pale pink silk coats embroidered with flowers, she would have us hang up our coats on the little pegs along the wall and go stand in a circle with all the other children to sing, "We're all in our places with sunshiny faces / Oh, this is the way to start a new day." Miss Jennie accompanied us on the piano. Buzzy, taking the song literally, was troubled when it was a cloudy day with no sunshine coming through the windows to shine on her face. She feared she was singing a lie.

Grandpa Rogers

A. D. Rogers, our preacher grandfather, was a tall, portly figure who loved to talk and eat. As children, when we visited his home in Denton, Texas, he always managed to sit close to us twins at the dining room table because we didn't eat very much. He could reach over and get our extra food. Sometimes he was premature and grabbed a favorite morsel, leading to loud wails from us twins. He ate raw, sweet onions as if they were apples and always had large, red apples on hand for us to eat. "Only the biggest and best apples are good enough for my grandchildren," he'd say. We had a hard time getting those huge apples eaten and often resorted to dropping half-eaten apples behind the hedge outdoors.

On those visits to our maternal grandparents, our mother, grandmother, aunt, and all four of us girls retreated to the back room where wonderful stories of our mother's childhood were told. We children loved to sit and listen. This back room was the location of the infamous "hemorrhoid" chair, an office chair that had been a gift from a parishioner. It had a sagging cane seat that had disintegrated to form a hole in the center. We were much older before we knew the significance of the name, but from all the giggling when it was mentioned, we sensed it was something naughty.

Our departure to the back room left our father all alone with grandfather, who talked and talked and talked. One of the few times our father showed anger was when he declared to our mother, "I am NOT going to sit alone in the front room with your father anymore."

When we twins were older, it was thought that we might have a talent for writing, so we should be the ones left alone with our grandfather. We could later record his stories for posterity. Woe! We felt like sacrificial lambs. We do not remember any of what he said to us, only the misery of missing out on the good stuff in the back room.

On these visits we considered it a great treat if Daddy invited us to walk with him early Sunday morning to get the Sunday paper at a shop down the street. We would skip alongside our father in anticipation of getting to see, and later to read, the Sunday comics. Our father taught us to read by pointing to the words in the comics as he read them to us while we sat on his lap. Sometimes after church we went for lunch at the local boarding house. It was the custom then for people to go for Sunday lunch to a boarding house much as many people today go to a restaurant. Grandpa would take us by the hand and lead us to various tables to introduce us. We felt very special. He never knew which one of us was which, but that did not seem to matter. We were quite shy and would tuck our heads and smile.

The Bathtub

"It is just not safe for women!" Grandpa was sure of it. The new-fangled bathtubs, in which the whole body was submerged in water, would be too debilitating for the weaker sex. As an upstanding minister in the town, he waited a long time before he even considered buying one. He did not want to appear wanton in satisfying his earthly desires by purchasing something that might be considered frivolous. But now he had done it. The bathtub was installed in the parsonage in an old closet. An unvented, coal-fired stove was added to the small room to stave off the cold. Before antibiotics, the fear of pneumonia was great in those days. Grandpa declared that he personally would test the safety of the tub by taking the first bath. The room was heated to a suffocating level. Grandma warmed the water on the stove and mixed it with cold water to get just the right temperature for a bath. The family waited anxiously outside as Grandpa entered the small, unventilated room. In time, he staggered out, almost too weak to stand. He declared that baths were definitely too debilitating for the womenfolk, and only he and his son would be allowed to take them. A little carbon monoxide goes a long way.

On another occasion Grandpa "raised his Ebenezer" as our family would say, that is, he took a stand just as the prophet Samuel did when he raised a rock to acknowledge God's help in defeating the Philistines in the Old Testament. Grandpa had been taken to the local hospital with symptoms of appendicitis. While lying in bed awaiting surgery he began to feel better. He arose, got dressed, and walked home.

Brush Arbor Meetings

It was fun driving with our dad to brush arbor meetings in Caddo, Texas, to hear Grandpa preach at summer revivals. Caddo is a small town just down the road from Breckenridge. It had been much larger. Our father said there used to be five banks in Caddo at the height of the oil boom. Now there were barely five houses. There was no air conditioner in the Caddo church, so the preaching was held outside in the evenings under a brush arbor to catch the breeze. We twins enjoyed sitting on the wooden benches and destroying pill-bug traps with our toes in the sandy floor. One memorable evening our grandfather began to recruit an impromptu choir from the congregation, calling on our mother to lead the way. Mother loved to sing old hymns and even pop tunes as she cooked in the kitchen, but we children knew that Mother could not carry a tune. She turned familiar tunes into strange-sounding songs, but she could not refuse her father. She went forward. The choir sang beautifully—over the giggling of us children.

Grandpa also preached on occasion in a small wooden church in Caddo. We twins would run to sit on the front row, where no one else seemed to sit. One time we were entertaining ourselves with much giggling during Grandpa's sermon. Grandpa stopped preaching and called us down in front of the whole congregation, saying, "If my granddaughters will settle down, I will continue." We were mortified and never acted up in church again.

Lenoma, Our Mother

Mother loved to laugh and tell stories. As a preacher's daughter, she was raised to be refined. She never referred to the postman as the *mailman* for fear someone would think she was saying *male man,* and proper young women did not use the terms *male* or *female* in public. She told us of her moral dilemma as a young teacher when she was teaching children to read. One lesson centered on the oo sound, and the lesson in the reading book was about a little rabbit named Sir Peter Poot. If you knew our mother you would know that a vulgar word such as *poot* would never cross her lips. So what to do? Maintain her dignity and teach the children the wrong sound or deign to utter the correct pronunciation and suffer the inner humiliation? Mother chose the former and the children learned about Sir Peter Poat. To this day Rogene uses "Sir Peter Poat" to describe anyone whose actions smack of needless propriety.

Mother liked to tell the story of how she outwitted her parents and the nosy parishioners of her father's church. Young ladies were supposed to come to church wearing the proper number of petticoats under their dresses. Some of the older ladies took it upon themselves to check the young girls to be sure they were wearing the requisite number of petticoats. Mother knew she'd be checked, so if she had not managed to wash and iron a sufficient number of petticoats, she would put on what she had and sit on the front porch of the parsonage, which was located next to the church. Her parents left earlier and assumed she would follow. When they came home after the church service, Mother would tell them she had beat them home, although, in truth, she had never left the front porch.

Mother majored in home economics and got her degree from CIA (College of Industrial Arts) in Denton, Texas, later named Texas Women's University. She loved to wear beautiful dresses, a trait inherited by Buzzy. She sewed, repaired, and altered many of our clothes.

Our mother was an excellent cook. She was proud that Daddy always drove home from his office for lunch. He expected to find there a good meal, a clean house, beds made, and everyone dressed. No lolling around in pjs during the summer months.

The kitchen was where our mother shone. She was a powerhouse there, often singing CIA songs as she cooked. We girls helped, and it was there we learned the facts of life from the chatter of Mom and our older sisters. It was there we learned to churn butter during World War II when Daddy bought a cow to keep in the back lot, so we would not have to go without milk and butter. It was there that we learned on the radio that Harry S. Truman would be Roosevelt's running partner.

Mother had all her shiny tools displayed in the kitchen and was expert in the use of them. Her china and silver were precious to her, and she loved to get them out for company. Polishing the silver was a major task that we children were enlisted to do. Daddy supplied Mother with everything she wanted for the kitchen, including a large hotel-style stove with eight burners, two ovens, a griddle, and a warming oven. She reigned over this stove like a queen, especially for major meals at Thanksgiving and Christmas. We had a refrigerator, though many others in town still used iceboxes—chests made of wood. The ice man made regular deliveries to put large chunks of ice in the metal-lined top compartment to keep the contents of the lower compartment cool.

Mother's Thanksgiving dinners were a delight. She had the usual turkey and dressing, mashed potatoes, peas, giblet gravy, and an orange jello salad containing chopped pecans and carrots. She liked to put oysters in the dressing, but this did not go over well with most of the family.

The highlight of Sunday dinners was often barbecued chicken. Everyone got half a chicken except big sister Martha, who ate a whole chicken. Our father was very pleased that he could provide such sumptuous meals for his family and that his daughter could eat a whole chicken. He would laugh, slap his knee, and exclaim, "She ate the whole chicken!" One wonders if his pleasure had to do with being the eleventh child in a poor farmer's family. Daddy gave Mother's good cooking credit for his living well into his nineties.

Church potlucks were a chance for the women of the church to show off their culinary expertise, and competition was fierce. You didn't want to miss out on these affairs. Mother's beef noodle casserole was always a hit.

One such potluck seemed to us a major tragedy. It was October, and all the children were asked to come in Halloween costumes, with prizes being given for the best ones. We were five years old. Mother had sewn elaborate costumes to make us look like little mice, complete with ears and long tails. We felt sure we'd get a prize. Just before we were to march across the stage in front of the judges, two boys chased us and pulled off our tails. We had no brothers to prepare us for such boyish antics and were crushed. No prize for us!

At mealtime Mother insisted we clean our plates. "The starving Armenians would love to have that food!" she'd say. We didn't know who the starving Armenians were, but we would have gladly packaged up the food we didn't like and sent it on if we just knew how. When Roberta was older and visiting New York City, a cab driver told her he was Armenian. Of course, she had to tell him the story. He wondered how Mother had known that the Armenians were starving back then.

Many dinner parties were held at our house to entertain friends, businessmen, relatives, or members of the many boards on which Daddy served. We could tell the status of the guests by the menu. Ordinary people got chicken spaghetti. Special people got barbecued chicken. On such occasions, we twins were introduced, admired by the guests, then told to take our baths and go to bed. One night when we were about four years old, we forgot to take our pajamas with us into the bathroom. Neany wrapped up in a towel and went through the kitchen as told. Buzzy decided she would entertain the guests by dashing stark naked through the room where they were sitting to reach the alternate door to our bedroom. It did not go over well. Some of the guests were amused, but our father was very angry. This was the beginning and the end of Buzzy's streaking career.

When we were about seven we inadvertently embarrassed Mother at one of her parties. She was giving a bridal shower for an old friend who had taught with her. The whole week before the shower we heard Mother and our sisters talking about the fact that Miss B was finally getting married. We twins adorned the back of a box in our rudimentary printing with this great piece of news: MISS B IS FINALLY GETTING MARRIED. This box turned out to be the one in which a gift was later wrapped. Mother had not noticed what was written on the back of the box. Unfortunately, Miss B did!

Mother delighted in making wine sauces, but Daddy didn't allow alcohol in the house, so Mother, undeterred, hid the cooking wine in a special spot in the back of the pantry. We knew where it was, but we didn't dare tell.

Mother was often on a diet and at such times was known to eat on the sly. Rogene remembers she had a very special piece of chocolate candy she wanted to save until later. She knew she did not have much chance of saving it from her three sisters unless she saved it in a secret spot. With much glee she told Mother she was hiding it under the celery in the refrigerator. She thought this a very clever idea; unfortunately, Mother was on a diet and very hungry. Rogene never saw the candy again.

Mother woke us each morning with "Rise up, O Sons of Belchazzar! Rise up and Greet the Day!" followed by her rendition of the hymn, "Rise Up, O Men of God./ Have Done with Lesser Things."

This method of awaking children has been passed on to later generations. When Mother did the laundry and wanted us to bring her our
dirty clothes, she would sing out, "Bring out your dead!" as per
bubonic plague times.

Mother was excitable. One day we twins decided to climb to the
top of the chicken shed to get a better view of our surroundings. Rogene slipped and grabbed for the corrugated tin roof, cutting her hands
rather badly. With bloody hands she ran screaming into the house
causing Mother to run to the front porch and scream, "P. M.! P. M.!"
over and over in a vain attempt to fetch Daddy from his business a
mile away. Fortunately, the household help we had at the time calmly
went to the phone and called Daddy. After a visit to the doctor and
many stitches, all was well again.

Mother had been too upset to use the phone. Phones were so different then. When you picked the receiver up, an operator asked,
"Number, please?" This operator, almost always a woman, was sitting
in the telephone office in downtown Breckenridge. She knew almost
everyone by name and certainly knew what was going on in the area.
The number she asked for was just three digits. Our home number
was 510. The operator would connect each call by hand. A long distance call was very expensive and not used except to report a death
or an emergency.

Mother did not like to go into the back lot where the cow and
chickens were. When Daddy once had to be gone overnight, he asked
mother to feed the chickens. "Why, P. M.," she said, "I don't think I
could recognize the chicken feed. I might feed them the wrong thing
and poison them." We were amazed that Mother didn't know which
was the chicken feed until it dawned on us that she just did not want
to do this chore. We proudly stepped forward and volunteered for the
job.

Once, when our pregnant older sister stayed with us for six weeks
while her husband was on a geologic field trip, she spent most of her
time sitting in front of the TV set. She developed bad backaches and
visited the doctor to ask what to do. The doctor, not knowing our sis-

ter's daily routine, suggested she was exercising too much and should cut back. Our mother smiled and asked, "Which should be cut, the trip from the bed to the TV or the trip from the TV back to the bed?"

The Peppered Ham

Our mother was generally a good-natured sort, but one time she became really annoyed at a local small grocer when he failed to deliver the groceries she had ordered in a timely manner. When we twins came home from college to visit, Mother kept exclaiming how wonderful it would be to have for supper one of those peppered hams that the local grocer kept in stock, but she was mad at him and did not want to give him any business. Throughout the day, she repeated this same message, adding that she did not want us to drive to his shop and buy anything. Finally, after many repetitions of the same message, it dawned on us that she really wanted us to go buy that peppered ham. As we left the house on our errand, she cautioned us that, if we should happen to go to that store, we should not reveal our identity, because she did not want the grocer to know her family was shopping there again. When we arrived at the store, the grocer welcomed us with open arms, asking about each member of our family and saying how nice it was to see us again. It is pretty hard to hide the identity of identical twins in a small town!

Christmas Eve Gift

A lovely Christmas custom came to us from Mother's side of the family. On Christmas Eve one of us phones or visits another member of the family and quickly says, "Christmas Eve Gift!" The first one to say it wins, that is, the other person is now obligated to give them a Christmas Eve gift. No one actually gives a gift—well, maybe a hug or such. It's competitive fun and a way to keep up communication among all family members.

Mother's Vote

Women had not had the right to vote for all that long when we were children, so it was a touchy subject. When our Daddy was mayor, he wanted to get one of the bridges in town repaired and needed to have a bond issue approved by the voters to do it. Mother wasn't that keen on voting, but Daddy said she must because this was an important project and the vote might be close. The issue failed by one vote. Daddy was crushed. Then Mother explained how she voted, and it became clear she had not understood the wording and had voted against rather than for the project. There was silence in the household for days after that.

Our mother, with her culinary skills and her refined manners, gave a gift to her family of incalculable value. She brought nurturing love and stability to our home. And she brought humor. She was the only one who could make our father laugh. We all loved to sit around the family table after dinner and tell family stories full of fun and joy. We still miss the opportunity to tell her all our new stories, small successes, and little joys.

More about P. M., Our Daddy

P. M., born in 1884, grew up in Oklahoma in what was then called Indian Territory. He was one of eleven children born to Issac Green Faulkner, who fought with the Confederate cavalry in the Civil War. Daddy recalled riding bareback on a horse and being warned if he saw Indians to slide down the side of the horse so it looked riderless.

From his pictures Daddy was a very handsome young man. Since he did not marry until his forties, he was almost fifty when we twins were born. We never thought he was older than other fathers, only quite a bit wiser.

P. M. started out as a bank clerk in Breckenridge and eventually set up his own savings and loan business. We children loved to go visit his office and play with the different types of business machines. His office had a certain special smell that seemed to represent the mystery of the business world. There was a clever check-writing machine—just punch in numbers, pull the lever, and out came the check. A box of two-cent stamps, first-class postage at the time, stood ready for any letters that needed to be mailed.

Daddy had a car agency, first for Oldsmobile, then Mercury. The first cars had running boards along the sides to make it easier to step into a car. Some nifty cars had rumble seats that folded out of the back of a two-seater. When we twins learned to drive, Daddy would let us drive his used cars. We remember paying twenty cents a gallon for gasoline.

When our family took trips in our car to see relatives or to go shopping in Fort Worth, my father always drove, because Mother could not. With four feisty girls under the age of ten in the car, our father was very clear on one rule: Thou shall not touch the rearview mirror. This rule was so embedded in Neany's brain that when she grew up and started to drive, she still followed the rule. She thought that the mirror was so delicately in place that if it was moved, one could never get it back in just the right spot again. Finally, in late high school, Neany discovered, by trial and error, that it was actually quite easy to adjust the rearview mirror.

After World War II, cars were much in demand and very scarce. Dealerships competed fiercely for their share of the new cars. On top of this problem, our father was considered too old by Lincoln-Mercury to hold down a dealership. So our older sister's husband joined the firm to add the required youthfulness.

Daddy liked to recall buying his first car. Cars had just come on the market in 1902. There was a dealer in Graham, Texas. Daddy paid him his money. The dealer drove with Daddy around the block and gave him the keys. Daddy drove home! No lessons or driver's license required.

Father, unlike Mother, took everything done at church very seriously. If the church doors were open, whether for worship services, domino games, or board meetings, he was there. He served on the church board and was extremely loyal to every pastor. Once, without telling the church of his condition, the regional office sent us a pastor who was an alcoholic. Soon, rumors began to fly concerning the pastor being inebriated on various occasions. Father remained staunchly supportive until the night the pastor, who was performing the wedding ceremony for the church secretary and her fiancé, became so drunk he kept falling out of the pulpit. After that, Father was the leader in sending the man on his way.

We never heard our father use a curse word. His strongest expletive was "Sam Hill" as in "What the Sam Hill are you doing?" There was a grocer in our town who was actually named Sam Hill, and as children we thought there must be a connection between the expletive and the grocer. When we asked our father about it, he just smiled a little and said he would have to tell the grocer about our question.

Daddy dressed conservatively. He always wore a white shirt and dark tie with a dark suit and dress shoes. He was color-blind and sometimes asked us girls to advise him on the choice of ties. He never entered the kitchen except to walk through it to the dining area. When we were older and came home from college for a visit, we were startled to see our father go into the kitchen to get a drink of water. Always before, he had gotten his water by asking Mother to bring it to him in the sitting room. The other change we observed in father at about this time was that he started wearing dress shirts with tiny blue stripes, instead of the totally white shirts he had always worn before. The times they were a-changin'!

Daddy was tolerant of our noisy household until it came time for the evening news on the radio. Then we knew we'd better be absolutely quiet or suffer Daddy's wrath. There was no TV, but after the radio news there were exciting radio programs—the comedy *Fibber McGee and Molly*, *Inner Sanctum Mystery*, and *Your Hit Parade*, which played the top ten songs of that week. On Saturday mornings we heard *Let's Pretend* stories.

There was a time we nearly lost Daddy. He had cleaned out the henhouse and afterward came down with a severe respiratory illness. We twins were preschoolers and naïve as to what was happening. We thought Daddy just had a cold and had to stay isolated in his bed, like we had to on such occasions. Dr. Gwin, the doctor who had delivered us and who still made house calls, came to our house and told Mother this was very serious, and that Daddy might very well die.

We had to hope that his body could fight this off and that his fever would drop. There was nothing more to be done. Mother's sisters, Aunt Bob and Aunt Edith, came to be with Mother during this ordeal. As far as we twins were concerned, it was a momentous occasion to have a visit from these two aunts who always made over us. We were showing off and vying for attention when Aunt Bob, who had always been so sweet to us, suddenly screamed, "Behave! Don't you know your father is dying? Your mother has enough on her mind without you misbehaving!" We were stunned! This was the first we knew that Daddy might die, might never again be there for us. Could that be? Now we were scared, bewildered. Aunt Edith chastised Aunt Bob for upsetting us.

Then came the miracle! Dr. Gwin called to say there was a new wonder drug called penicillin. He didn't have any but he knew where he could get some in Dallas. He was willing to drive there and bring this drug back for Daddy. This would take the better part of a day. He made the journey, came to our house, and administered the shot. Daddy quickly recovered.

Daddy's only other serious illness came when we twins were in college. He had surgery to remove a tumor on his kidney. According to the surgeon, the survival rate for such tumors was quite poor, so we were worried. To our great joy Daddy survived and lived on into his nineties before he died of old age. We were grateful to the surgeon for his competent work, but Daddy complained that the surgeon had charged what to him was an exorbitant fee of five thousand dollars. Daddy lost quite a bit of weight and was much skinnier than his usual consistently slim self. Mother was insulted when someone remarked to her that Daddy was such a slender man they wondered if he ate well at home. Mother took this as a suggestion that her culinary arts were not good enough to entice Daddy to feast on her cooking. She decided to fatten him up a bit by pouring whipping cream on his morning oatmeal in place of plain milk. After some time Daddy developed a little potbelly. Not what Mother had hoped for. Back to plain milk!

One of Neany's last memories of our father was when he was in his early nineties, and she had come home to visit. He wanted to show her that he could still drive. He suggested they take a drive into the country, and she agreed. She soon discovered that he could not see well. He drove seventy miles per hour right down the middle of a local country road following the center yellow stripe. Fortunately, the road was not heavily used, and only occasionally did they meet someone coming in the opposite direction. When Father saw a car approaching, he slowed to about ten miles per hour and pulled off to the shoulder on the right side. When the car had passed, Daddy was off again—seventy miles per hour—in the center of the road. Rogene had seldom been so frightened. She prayed that if the good Lord would get her safely home, she would never ride with Daddy again, and she did not.

We girls went down to the county courthouse and asked that they take away our father's license to drive. The officials were shocked. They would not do that. In fact, they found it hard to believe that P. M.'s daughters would make such a request. They knew when P. M. drove to his office and when he drove home. They watched him. And they were not about to heed what his disloyal daughters were saying. The daughters only hoped no tourist happened to pass through the town when Daddy was driving.

Daddy lived to the age of ninety-five. Mother lived alone in that house with various housekeepers for another ten years. She spent the last two years of her life in Rolling Meadows, a retirement community in Wichita Falls, where Buzzy lived.

Breckenridge

Breckenridge was a small West Texas oil boomtown of about six thousand souls. To say this is West Texas is a bit of a stretch, but Breckenridge is over one hundred miles west of Fort Worth, whose slogan is "Where the West Begins." The tallest building in town was the Burch Hotel. It had maybe ten stories and was rumored to be the scene of illicit rendezvous and the home of the local bootlegger. We were told not to go into it.

Oil and ranching were the major sources of income. The job of mayor was passed around among the top businessmen. When asked, Daddy took his turn. This same group, along with the ranch owners, were members of the Country Club and did much of their major shopping in Dallas-Fort Worth. This was a source of conflict between Lenoma and P. M. Daddy thought we should buy locally to support the hometown merchants. Mother had her favorite stores in Dallas-Fort Worth. She even had her favorite clerks who knew her taste and her size. It was a special treat for us when Daddy drove us to Fort Worth each fall to get our new school clothes. The shoe department X-ray machine that determined what size shoes we should buy was especially exciting because we could see the bones in our feet.

Farmers and ranch hands came into Breckenridge on Saturday and parked along the main street, hoping to get the best parking spaces in front of the two movie theaters. You could recognize the cowboys by the cowboy boots and hats they wore. Unlike today, they always removed those big hats when they went inside a building. They shopped and tended to business during the day, then returned to their vehicles in the evening, sitting on fenders or in truck beds to visit with friends and watch the world go by. Some went to the movies. At that time there was a pause in the middle of the movie while someone changed reels. During that pause a number of things might happen. A pianist might play, a local dance studio might perform, or a school or church choir might sing. If you were black, you had to sit in the balcony at the movies, and you even had a separate drinking fountain.

Once Buzzy drank from the "colored only" fountain. She did not turn black as some of her friends predicted. The schools were also segregated. Trains, both passenger and freight, ran through Breckenridge at that time. We remember going with Daddy to meet a train where someone arrived to present the town with some sort of commemorative plaque. Daddy, as mayor, received it and made a brief speech. Trains were a safety hazard in our little town. After a child was run over trying to cross in front of a train on his bicycle, we were repeatedly cautioned about the dangers of crossing the tracks without first looking to see if a train was coming.

There were two Jewish families in Breckenridge. They had set up businesses there after fleeing Nazi Germany. The Benders ran a department store on Main Street. It was the only store in town with a pneumatic system for paying. A clerk would stuff your money into a small glass container, which was whisked on a conveyer belt up to an office on the second floor. Shortly your change was returned in the same little container. It seemed like a miracle to us as small children.

The second family operated a jewelry store. Daddy took us there to buy us a wristwatch in honor of our graduation from junior high. It was a big event. There were no battery-operated wristwatches then. They were all wind-ups. Wearing a wristwatch made you special. Buzzy still has that watch.

When Lyndon Johnson ran for the US Senate in 1948, our little town of Breckenridge was included in his helicopter tour of the state. Just about everybody who could make it, including Daddy and us twins, came to the vacant lot beside a car dealership to gaze with awe as LBJ's helicopter came to a landing, the first helicopter we had ever seen.

The Bostonian

We did not realize how provincial we were until the Bostonian came to town. There was a wealthy ranching couple who were blessed with a single child, a daughter. Everyone in town knew she would inherit the large ranch belonging to the family, and she was hard as nails.

She roped and rode as well as any cowhand. When it came time for college, the family thought she might need a little refinement, so she was sent to Boston for finishing school. Well, as you might guess, she ended up marrying a Bostonian, and that poor guy had to move to our rough-and-ready town to manage the ranch. The first observation by townspeople was that he had manicured nails! Can you believe it? He actually had clear nail polish on his fingernails. The second habit he had, most unusual to our town folk, was that he carried an umbrella when it rained! Now in West Texas, men do not carry umbrellas. If it rains, they just get wet. The kiss of death for him from our father's viewpoint was an innocent question he asked Father. At the time our older sister, Martha Lou Faulkner McGaughy, who lived in the same town, was about nine months pregnant or appeared so. It was pretty obvious to everyone that she was soon to deliver. The Bostonian had the unmitigated gall to ask Father when his new grandchild was to arrive. Father exclaimed to us later, "Why, the nerve of him asking such a personal thing! I just pretended I did not understand what he was talking about." After Daddy left the room, my mother and we girls all laughed and said the Bostonian must have thought Daddy was deaf!

Aunt Fay

We did not get to meet Aunt Fay. She was Mom's younger sister and the tomboy. In the family portrait one can see she is the only one of her siblings not to have inherited her mother's curly hair. She has her father's straight brown hair, cut in a bob with bangs. She excelled in sports. Her yearbook shows her playing volleyball and basketball in the bloomers female athletes wore back then. After college she got a job teaching in the town of Electra. From the letters she wrote our mother, it is apparent the two of them were very close. She addresses Mother as "Nomsie" or "Pullett."

She returned to live with the family during one summer and wrote a plaintiff letter about cleaning the family bathroom. She tells of scrubbing, with a cleaning cloth the "size of a lady's handkerchief," every tile and fixture and even under the "long unexplored area beneath the bathtub." She retired to the dining room to rest and "before the perspiration dried from my brow," little sister Bob hung her wash in the bathroom, leaving a mess. When remonstrated, Bob replied, "Do it again if I want to." Fay continues, "To cap it all off, a letter came from Mary Jane (Vivion's wife) saying Mama should make me work, as Edith and Bob have been there all winter working, and I have just been resting (paying forty dollars a month to rest). I do love her because she is my sister-in-law, but somehow I just can't like her."

Her later letters from Electra describe meeting a handsome young rancher. "Can you believe it? He thinks I'm pretty!" she enthuses. They are going to marry and have begun to build a home on a ranch he owns, a "House on Sunshine Hill." Fay seems blissfully happy in her letters.

Then leukemia strikes. Letters now come from Seton Infirmary in Austin. Blood transfusions are needed. Grandmother's blood is a match and brings forth a brief rally and hope, but not for long. Fay dies close to what was to have been her wedding day.

In Grandfather's letters to the Faulkner family, he writes of losing his best friend, his sports partner, the bravest and best of the family. He adds that all we can do is submit and help each other and that God must have had some most important work for Fay, to call her just when He did.

When Buzzy visited Mother shortly before she died, Mother asked her if she believed in an afterlife, and then with tears in her eyes, she asked, "Why did that sweet girl have to die?" Buzzy believed she was hoping to see her beloved little sister Fay in heaven.

Aunt Bob, Our Favorite Aunt

Mother's youngest sister, Roberta Rogers, nicknamed Bob, lived with Grandma and Grandpa. She had been engaged, but our grandfather refused to agree to the marriage. He felt she should stay single to look after him and grandmother, as was the custom. We twins thought this very sad. She had our sympathy. She taught first grade in Denton, Texas, for many years until our oldest sister Martha Lou and husband, W. B. McGaughy, moved to Denton with their adorable daughter, Rebecca Ann, who was ready for second grade. Aunt Bob requested and was granted a change of assignment to second grade so she could teach Miss Becky. Since Aunt Bob had no children of her own, she was eager to adopt Becky as her godchild. Aunt Bob had a favorite joke. She would say, "A B C D goldfish? L M N O goldfish!" This was thought by my parents to be a little rough for us children to hear.

Aunt Bob wanted dearly to be a member of the Daughters of the American Revolution because several of her friends were members. As such they got to go to some very nice teas at the college. To be a member, she had to present evidence that a family relative had taken part in the American Revolution. She set out to research the family history to find some such relative. Aunt Bob was a confirmed teetotaler, of the "lips that touch wine will never touch mine" variety, but the only relative she could find that was associated with the American Revolution was a bootlegger who had supplied whiskey to the troops. She decided that some of that whiskey must have been used for medicinal purposes and thereby managed with a clear conscience to get into the DAR and attend the teas with her friends.

Aunt Bob liked to visit the Baker Hotel in Mineral Wells, Texas. It was a beautiful building where weekend ballroom dances took place, attended by officers from the nearby army base. Seeing those handsome cavalry officers in their leather boots and riding breeches come down the long outdoor staircase leading to the third-floor entrance was romantic and stunning.

A smaller hotel in the same town hosted an early morning radio show, "The Light Crust Doughboys," broadcast from their dining room. They sang "Good morning, breakfast lovers! We're glad to see you." We thought it would be wonderful to be there for breakfast and see them in person. Daddy was not persuaded.

Aunt Bob made many efforts to make herself beloved by her nieces. We adored her. When our family arrived for a visit with the Rogers, Aunt Bob always grabbed us twins to give us a hug and a wet kiss. We didn't like that kiss, and Neany would find a way to disappear when she saw it coming, leaving Buzzy to get a double portion. Buzzy never figured out how Neany managed that. Aunt Bob gave us beautiful dolls from Neiman-Marcus at Christmas and played silly games with us. She would hold seances with a Ouija board and seemed to take the activity seriously. Aunt Bob would let us sit in her lap while she drove the car. She never drove above forty-five miles per hour. Freeways were not for her. She had a back-road path to get to a Dallas teahouse from Denton without getting on the freeway. When she left the house in the car she would toot the horn "Good-bye," and upon returning she would toot the horn "I'm back!" so as not to frighten her parents.

Mother never got along too well with her sister Roberta. Maybe it was because of the jealousy Mom sensed from Aunt Bob, who had not been allowed to marry while Mother had. The tension between Mother and Aunt Bob was still in evidence late in Mother's life. When Mom was living at Rolling Meadows retirement home in Wichita Falls, Aunt Bob sent her many greeting cards. Aunt Bob was a believer in the power of prayers given by radio-TV evangelists in return for a donation. Whenever Mother was ill and got better, Aunt Bob would inform her that the cure came because of the donation she had sent to a certain evangelist.

While at Rolling Meadows Mother never asked us to go out of our way to take her anywhere until one day she asked Buzzy and her husband Eldon to take her to Denton to visit Aunt Bob, who was in a retirement home there. They went the next weekend. The two visited amicably; then Buzzy and her husband drove Mother around to see her old haunts and the parsonage that had once been her home, now occupied by university students. On the way back to Wichita Falls, Mother asked if Buzzy thought she had set things right with Aunt Bob, if they had parted friends. "Yes," Buzzy assured her. "You did." The very next weekend they were back in Denton to bury Mother in the family plot in Roselawn Cemetery. Mother must have had a premonition of her own death and wanted to make up with her sister.

Growing Up

We twins shared one major failing. We could not pronounce the letter r. People would often stop and ask us our names and we could not pronounce them correctly. Rogene would say, "Whoa Gene" and Roberta would say, "Whoa Butta." The inquirer would look puzzled and ask over and over again, "Tell me your name." We hated that. With each reply we spoke softer and softer. Roberta remembers hiding behind Mother's skirt hoping the inquirer would disappear. "The twins are so shy," people commented. We weren't shy. We just could not pronounce our names. If only we had been named Ann or Sue or anything we could pronounce. Why didn't we just lie? The thought never occurred to us.

Our older sister Fay would call in her friends to watch the show as she had us try to pronounce words containing r. We were the source of much amusement. They especially liked to hear us say "bird" and then "board" which we pronounced exactly alike. These performances ceased when Mother caught on to what was happening.

Plans were made for us to be baptized by our grandfather when we were considered old enough to make our confession of faith and join the Christian Church in Breckenridge. Grandpa, who had been the minister of the Breckenridge church years earlier, would come over as a guest minister to receive our confession and to baptize us. The trouble was that no one told us about that plan. So one Sunday when we were about seven and the minister made a plea for anyone who believed that Jesus was their Lord and Savior should come down the aisle and say so and be baptized, we looked at each other and decided that would be the right thing to do. Without consulting our parents, off we went down the aisle, much to the chagrin of the rest of the family.

About that same time, we began having revival meetings for all the dogs and cats we could round up in our driveway. We would preach to them the way we heard our grandfather and our hometown minister preach. Our congregation usually either wandered off or fell asleep. One time we decided to baptize some of the cats. We were not acquainted with the sprinkling type of baptism and quickly learned that cats are ferociously opposed to the full immersion method. Wounded and weary of cat scratches, we ended our brief career as evangelists.

Buzzy conducted her first scientific experiment about this time. Neany had been declared allergic to hedge flowers and taken to a specialist in Oklahoma City for advice, leaving Buzzy at home to ponder how this could be. She could smell the hedge flowers with no bad effects. Could Neany just be playing a game for attention? When Neany got back, Buzzy was waiting with a handful of hedge flowers to push up against Neany's nose. The result was not pretty. Neany was definitely not playing a game! Buzzy repented.

Horned toads were fun to watch as they ate the red ants in the ant beds in the back lot. Buzzy remembers stroking their tummies to make them spit out dark goo. We didn't realize we would someday be TCU horned frogs.

We were allowed to go to the movies twice a week. The price was only twelve cents, much cheaper than a babysitter, and we loved to go. We were sometimes given an extra nickel for popcorn but never a dime for those high-priced candy bars. We were skinny little girls and once an obese lady sat down on top of Neany, thinking the seat was empty. Buzzy proclaimed over and over, "You're sitting on my sister!" but the lady ignored her until Neany managed to wiggle a little under the weight above her. Still, no action. Finally, Neany managed to pinch the lady and she arose. She did not apologize.

School Days

When it came time for us to enter first grade, Mother bought identical school clothes for us—cotton dresses for warm weather, corduroy coveralls for cold weather, and a raincoat for rainy weather. Alas! It was the beginning of a seven-year drought. The rainy weather never came. We didn't get a chance to wear those adorable raincoats before we outgrew them.

We were six and happy to have finally gotten old enough to go to school. We loved it—the sweet smell of erasers and pencils, the seemingly endless sources of papers and crayons. For the first time we twins had our very own books. And we were allowed to walk the five blocks to school all by ourselves. What joy! An adventure! At that time almost every child walked to school. There were no lines of cars waiting to pick up children after school as one sees today.

First grade brought new friends. One was Jerry, who agreed to play the role of "father" during recess when we played "house." When his father got wind of this he forbade Jerry's playing with girls for fear it would make him a sissy. We were sad to become "fatherless."

Another friend was a girl named Jackie. We didn't play a trick on Jackie, but it seemed that way. We loved to play on the monkey bars on the school playground. We'd hang our legs over the bar and let go with our hands so our bodies hung swinging in the wind. Jackie said she couldn't do that. We said, "Yes you can! We'll teach you." We lifted her up and hung her legs over the bar. When we let go, she threw her legs straight up in the air and came crashing down on her head. That must have really hurt, but she didn't say a word. We walked home with her to be sure she was all right. As soon as she saw her mother she let out a scream that would wake the dead. We were in trouble but still wondered why she had thrown her legs up the way she did.

Jackie's birthday was July 14, 1933, one day after ours. She insisted that since fourteen is a larger number than thirteen, she was one day older than we. We never convinced her otherwise. We learned a lot in first grade, including a way of expressing ourselves that angered our father. Many of our new friends used the word *git* for *get* and *ain't* for *isn't*. We copied this until our father heard us. He said firmly, "No child of mine will speak like that. I'll beat the socks off you if I hear it again!" Father never ever hit us, but this threat caused us to contemplate how hard you'd have to hit someone to have their socks fly off. Needless to say we went back to *get* and *isn't*. Another somewhat local expression was the word *wart* used as a verb to mean *pester* as in "Stop warting me to get you a candy bar." Roberta's Yankee husband insists this is not a word used in Standard English.

The Texas legislature had just passed a law that said Spanish should be taught to Texas school children at least every other year. Our teacher did not know Spanish, but she did the best she could. She taught us to sing *"Ay donde, ay donde seva mi perro"* ("Oh where, oh where has my little dog gone?"). She sang it with a nasal twang and we copied her. For a long time after that we thought Spanish was a nasal language.

The principal of our elementary school was very fond of woodworking. He thought every child should learn to use a lathe, so we all had to take shop. We glued together flat pieces of wood, using a lathe to fashion the wood into a jewelry box. Wood chips flew everywhere. It was really scary. We don't recall having safety goggles. Using Mother's sewing machine, which we were not allowed to do, was tame in comparison.

Sex Education

One thing we didn't learn in grade school was sex education. It was forbidden then and may still be. We had no brother, and our father was very modest, so our sex education came from these sources: Old Testament stories in the Bible, a little book we found hidden in Daddy's dresser, the conversations of our mother and older sisters, and the soap opera *Stella Dallas*. We figured out that the Biblical expression "He knew her" meant more than a passing acquaintance and "to lie with a woman" didn't mean just to nap together. The rest we tried to surmise from that little book we discovered in Daddy's dresser. We weren't supposed to listen to *Stella Dallas* on the radio when Mother had it on, but we listened on the sly and gave ourselves away when we asked Mother what PG meant.

Years later, when Roberta was teaching German in the local high school in Wichita Falls, Texas, she received a package of materials from the German Education Authority. It had been mistakenly sent to her and was meant to go to the little German school on the local air force base to teach children of German pilots training there. In the packet for first-grade students was a poster showing a naked man and woman with all their body parts correctly labeled. One wonders whether American students, had they been given this information at such an early age, might not have giggled and blushed and used nicknames for body parts later in life. It certainly would have enlightened the Faulkner twins and others on a subject that would have been helpful and useful. Our schools educate children in many, many areas, some of which may never be useful to a particular student, but the areas that would most probably be of use to all students—that is, sex and child rearing—seem woefully neglected. That makes no sense.

Death

Our first encounter with death came when we started school. One boy named Danny had fair skin and freckles. His face was almost always beet-red from running about on the playground. In class he was so full of energy he could hardly sit still. Danny began to miss school a lot, and his mother visited our class to get homework so that Danny could keep up with the class. Summer with all of its glorious fun came and seemed to last forever. In the fall, it was as if we had never been to school at all and were starting afresh. But Danny was no longer with us. Perhaps he had moved. In late fall we learned that Danny had had his last adventure. He was dead from leukemia. What was death? We did not really know. We did know that Danny would not be returning to our class. But where was he? Had they put him in the ground as we had seen happen to other, older people in the nearby cemetery?

At his funeral service, which was open casket, we saw a small greyish-white face that was supposed to be Danny. "That is not Danny," Neany thought. "That is just the bag of skin where Danny used to live. Danny would never be that still and pale." This first encounter with death taught Neany a lesson she has never forgotten. There is more to life than the body.

In second grade we were asked by our teacher to be flower girls at her wedding. We were very excited. Life doesn't get much better than that! Rogene remembers chewing on the flower baskets, which were embroidery stiffened with sugar. Talk about a sweet tooth!

In third grade we were introduced to cursive writing with ink. Every desk had its own inkwell. Ballpoint pens hadn't been invented yet. We used wooden pens into which we put a pointed metal nib that we dipped into the inkwell. We had to make lots of circles in an effort to improve our penmanship. We often wore our hair in pigtails, and it was not uncommon for mischievous students to dip the pigtails of the students seated in front of them into the inkwell on their desks. We kept our pigtails short. Our friend Jerry got in trouble for drinking the ink.

When the school photographer came to take each child's picture, Mother took pains to comb our hair in perfect curls just like those of Shirley Temple. On the walk to school we destroyed those curls, thinking they made us look like sissies. Poor Mother!

Childhood Terrors

There were no air conditioners when we were very young, so in the summer when the temperature headed toward one hundred degrees Fahrenheit, we took lots of cold showers and sat in front of fans that were in every room. Buzzy remembers going to sleep with the cool breeze blowing over her from the open windows beside the bed in the side bedroom, hearing the reassuring chime of the clock on the shelf and the howl of coyotes not too far away. She could see the moon and sometimes imagined men with knives sailing down the moonbeams to get her. Very scary! She vowed never to stare at the moon.

Scorpions were a problem. We had a few painful encounters that taught us always to check between the sheets for scorpions before getting into bed, and also to check before putting on our shoes to see if any scorpions had taken up residence. Buzzy remembers one night after turning off the light to sleep, she heard a faint "plop" on her pillow. She turned on the bedside lamp to discover a mama scorpion and a bunch of baby scorpions on her pillow. Apparently they had fallen from the ceiling air vent.

Another terror of our young lives was the regular visits to the dentist. Our parents had lost most of their teeth and wanted a better fate for their children. This was before fluoride, so there was usually at least one cavity to be filled per visit. Our dentist did not believe in deadening the tooth before drilling into it to stuff it with amalgam. The pain was the worst we ever encountered. Buzzy used to gaze out the window at the people on the sidewalk outside and think how wonderful it would be to exchange places with them. The dentist said, "If you don't like the pain, you should do a better job of brushing your teeth." Children today cannot possibly realize how grateful they should be for the introduction of fluoride in the water.

Depression Times

We were definitely children of the Depression. Mother sewed most of our clothes. Daddy kept chickens as a source of eggs and fried chicken. A cow on the back lot supplied milk. When it was time to go to the feed store to buy feed for the chickens, we girls got to go along to pick out the feed sacks, which were made of colorful cloth with floral designs. They would eventually be made into our pajamas by our seamstress mother. When we outgrew our dresses,

Mother would sew a ruffle around the bottom edge to lengthen the dress.

We had fried chicken every Sunday from the flock of chickens kept in our back lot. First, our father would wring the heads off the chickens, which then flopped around the yard squirting blood. A horrific sight! When the birds lay still, we brought them in for mother to dip in boiling water to loosen the feathers. We had the job of plucking off the feathers, a job we deplored. The smell of the wet feathers was enough to make us gag.

At Christmastime we were each given twenty-five cents to buy presents for the other five members of the family. Woolworth's Five and Dime was where we shopped. One Christmas Neany bought a rubber duck as a present for Buzzy. On Christmas Day she discovered Buzzy had bought the same duck for her.

One cold winter morning we were warming our feet by holding them close to a space heater in our bedroom. Our father came by and said for us to take our shoes off as they might catch fire. "It costs money to replace shoes," he said. "Burned toes grow back for free." We learned to be very frugal.

Soft drinks were out of the question. They cost too much, and Mother considered them unhealthy. A doctor had once shown her what carbonated beverages did to the stomach. He poured coke over a piece of meat in a glass and pointed out the bubbles as a sign of damage.

When we went to ball games we were never allowed to buy so-called "hot dogs," but that didn't keep us from asking. One time it seemed to Buzzy that a miracle occurred. Her plea to Daddy for a hot dog met with an affirmative answer plus a dime to pay for it. She could hardly believe her good fortune. She ran to the hot dog stand, paid her money and was given a sizzling hot dog on a bun. Just the fragrance sent her into ecstasy! When she raised it to her mouth to take a big bite, the hot dog flew out of the bun and landed in the dirt in front of the bleachers! Just as the world seemed perfect, disaster raised its ugly head.

Grandpa's Silver Dollar

Grandpa Rogers presented us each a silver dollar when we started school. He said we must not spend it but rather save it for when we went to college. It would help pay our expenses. The next summer, when the Depression was at its worst, people often rang our front doorbell and asked for food or money. If they asked for food, Mother would always give them a plate of food to be eaten on the back-door steps. One Monday morning in summertime Mother was in the back lot washing clothes when the doorbell rang. We answered. A raggedy man said, "My children are starving. Can you give me money so I can buy them food?" This was a moral question. Should we give the man our silver dollars to feed his hungry children, as Jesus said we should, or should we mind Grandpa and keep the dollars for our education? Neany gave the man her dollar. Buzzy kept hers.

A man often pushed a cart through our neighborhood selling homemade tamales. Mother said she wouldn't buy from him because the tamales may not have been made under sanitary conditions. Actually, Mother didn't like tamales. We never saw her eat one.

We had a dog named Bob after our Aunt Bob. He was a small brown-and-white wirehaired terrier and our constant companion. We loved him. Our parents would not hear of letting him in the house, so he lived in the backyard. Unfortunately, he had a bad habit of chewing up newspapers, and not just ours but all around the neighborhood. We didn't know how to stop that. He would dig under the backyard fence to roam the neighborhood. Someone poisoned him. Daddy said we didn't have enough money to take him to the vet, so we sat with him as he died. He looked at us with pleading eyes. We were young, innocent creatures learning a big lesson about the transience of life. We learned there were some things over which we had no control. It was so painful to watch, but there was nothing we could do to help. It cured us of ever wanting another pet. Buzzy would experience that same helpless, hopeless feeling later in life when her son Phillip was diagnosed with incurable brain cancer.

As children we loved to read. We went to "Story Time" at the local library every week until we learned to read for ourselves. We read *The Wizard of Oz, Snow White, Alice in Wonderland,* and all the Nancy Drew mysteries we could get our hands on. We read every book in the East Ward School Library and many in the town library.

Sometimes we played Indians with Billy, a neighbor friend, and an older boy named Freddy. We made a tent out of an old sheet and said that was our wigwam. One day when we were inside the wigwam, Freddy put his hands in Buzzy's pants. She jumped up and reported his behavior to Mother, who told Daddy. We never saw Freddy again.

The Backyard

A giant live oak tree dominated our backyard. It was huge, taller than the house, and its branches spread out to form a canopy over the whole area. It provided cool, dark shade even on the hottest of days and was the scene of many happy hours of play. We learned to climb it and lolled along its sturdy branches like the leopards we would later see on a trip to Africa. Its acorns provided decorations for many mudpies. Loud cicadas serenaded us with background music. It was the site of great adventures for us children, as we dared to climb higher and higher in its branches.

Many a game of hide-and-seek was played in that backyard. A sulking child might take refuge there from some parental confrontation or a petty argument with siblings. It was like a giant theater where our everyday dramas were performed.

On hot summer days we loved to make ice cream on the back steps of our home. We would do this before there was Blue Bell ice cream in the grocery store or ice cream parlors in the town. Mother mixed the ingredients and poured the mix into the ice cream maker. Around it Daddy poured the ice mixed with salt to lower the freezing point. We took turns doing the cranking, turning the handle until it was too hard to move. Each child had to take a turn at the handle. When we could no longer turn it, we let Daddy have a try. When he

The backyard tree

could no longer turn it, the time had come to take the ice cream out. Great care was taken to lift the frozen ice cream container without getting salt water in it. It was hard work but so refreshing to eat the ice cream inside. Yum! Did it ever taste good!

Also in that yard was a large cistern that collected rainwater from the roof. Mother thought the town water was too harsh to use in washing her daughters' hair. Only the cistern water was pure enough to make the girls' hair shine. Mother had her own hair done at the local beauty parlor.

In the summer we went to the YMCA for swimming lessons and then for free swim time. In the lessons we were first taught to put our faces in the water and blow bubbles. When we could do that well, we were promoted to the next group where we learned to float face down in the water. When we could shove off and float face down clear across the pool we were promoted to the flutter kickers, and so on. Buzzy remembers Neany always being one group ahead of her. Try as she might, she could never catch up. This continued the pattern that began when Neany was the first to be born and would continue right into adulthood. If Buzzy studied really hard for a test in school and made 95, Neany made 100. The only skill Buzzy managed to accomplish before Neany was whistling, so she whistled a lot until our father got fed up with the constant whistling and said, "A whistling girl and a cackling hen, both will come to no good end." That shut Buzzy up.

Wartime

December 7, 1941, brought war, and everything changed. It was a Sunday afternoon. Daddy had driven us out into the country to look for mistletoe in the mesquite trees so we could use it to decorate the house for Christmas. Mother stayed in the car with the radio on while we gathered the mistletoe. All of a sudden Mother screamed, "P. M., we're at war!" The Japanese had bombed Pearl Harbor.

All the young men were soon drafted. Daddy said he was glad to have only daughters. We were glad to have a father too old for the draft. Roberta worried that there would be no young men left when she was old enough to marry. We asked Daddy who would win the war. Daddy could almost always predict who would win the football games that were an important part of our hometown social life. But now he just said, "I don't know." That was really scary.

Before, during the Depression years, it was thought that married women should not work because they would be taking a job away from a man who needed it. It was only fair to have one income per household. Now because so many men were being drafted, women were needed and encouraged to join the workforce.

Soldiers from the army camp in Mineral Wells came to Breckenridge on Saturday nights, to the USO (United Service Organizations) located in the YMCA building. USOs were set up in towns near military bases to give a place for soldiers to go for entertainment. They had snack bars and held dances. Local girls were encouraged to attend and be dance partners. Our older sisters went, but we were too young. Breckenridge was the closest "wet" town where one could buy beer, a situation that attracted many soldiers. If any soldiers showed up at the First Christian Church on Sunday morning, Daddy invited them to Sunday dinner at our house. We loved that. We vied for their attention often to the point of becoming annoying.

Gasoline was rationed, so there were no more summer family road trips. Shoes were rationed to two pair per year. Our mother bought our shoes a size too large for fear we'd outgrow them. We did a lot of clomping around. When the weather was warm, many children wore sandals made of cardboard and fabric. We preferred to go barefoot except to school and church.

When the army base in Mineral Wells just east of Breckenridge decided to move troops to the west of us, a siren would sound that night to indicate a blackout. We had to turn off all lights and pull the window shades down until a second siren gave the "all clear" signal. If someone didn't cooperate, an air raid warden came to their house to enforce the rules. We listened to the roar of the trucks hauling the troops rumbling by in the night on the highway a few blocks from our darkened home.

If a family had a son drafted into the military, it put a little flag in the front window with a blue star on a white background with a red border. If a family got a telegram saying the son was killed in battle, it would change the star to gold. To save gasoline, the *Breckenridge American* newspaper advertised for young people willing to deliver those telegrams by bicycle. We wanted to volunteer, but our mother said it would be too sad.

Propaganda posters went up everywhere, including in our elementary school. There was a distorted picture of a scary-looking Japanese soldier with huge ears. Underneath him were printed the words, "Loose Lips Sink Ships." We were told this meant we should not divulge any knowledge we had of troop movements. The school janitor had a son who helped him. The son had Down's Syndrome and looked very much like the Japanese soldier on the poster. We were very careful not to speak when he was within earshot. How easily we succumb to propaganda!

Another wartime assignment for us students was to collect scrap iron for the war effort. It was a time of great patriotism, and we truly wanted to do our best. One item wanted was metal lipstick tubes. Our poor older sisters suffered from the diligence of their twin sisters, who felt it was their duty to collect all the lipstick tubes they could find for the cause. Once we thought we had a real coup. We saw that our neighbor had a large backhoe in his back lot. We bravely went over and asked if we could have it for our scrap-iron drive. The suggestion was not well received.

Before the advent of the automatic washer and dryer, Mother and a helper washed our clothes in a wringer washer located in a shed on the back lot. This task happened every Monday. Mother dreaded it. Even with a hired helper, the workload was horrendous. The water for washing was heated by building a wood fire under a water-filled iron pot located outside the shed. That iron pot disappeared during one of the scrap-iron drives.

In the hot summer months when there was no school, we twins were delegated the task of hanging the freshly washed sheets up to dry on the clothesline in the back lot. There is nothing quite so lovely as having damp sheets slap you in the face in the burning heat of a Texas summer. By the time we got all the sheets hung up, the first ones were dry and we could take them down and fold them. Before the invention of wrinkle-free wash-and-wear fabrics, everything had to be ironed, even the sheets. Mother had a mangle to help with that. A mangle is a machine with large heated revolving rollers through which the semi-damp sheets are fed. The sheets come out flat and dry. This was before the arrival of fitted sheets on the market, so all sheets were flat. We changed sheets on the beds once a week, so to save on washing sheets, we put the bottom sheet in the laundry and moved the top sheet to the bottom. A fresh sheet was then used for the top sheet.

Everyone who could was asked to plant a "victory garden." Daddy planted a big one. Mother canned the excess, and Daddy hid the excess in a space dug out under the garage floor. This precaution would help feed us if the Germans took over. We pictured the Nazis coming up our driveway on motorcycles while our family hid in that hidey-hole under the garage.

Mother sent us to the garden one day to look for squash to cook for supper. After boiling the "squash," she decided to splurge, putting the whole week's butter ration on them. We made faces when we tried to eat it that evening. What we had picked as squash turned out to be gourds. There went a week's worth of butter ration! Good thing we had a cow and a churn!

Students were asked to bring money to school to buy stamps to support the troops fighting in the war. We all participated, except for one girl whose religion forbade it. Each stamp cost a dime and would be licked and pasted in a little book. When the book was full, the student got to ride with the principal to the post office where the book would be exchanged for a $25 War Bond, a very exciting adventure for a third grader! How proud we were when we licked the last stamp to fill our books and were told to go to the principal's office. When we got to the post office and presented our filled books, the postmaster asked the fatal question, "What is your name?" We replied "Whoa Butta" and "Whoa Gene" loudly and proudly and then ever softer as the man asked us to repeat. Finally the man said, "Aren't y'all P.M. Faulkner's girls? I'll just call him." Oh, how quickly a moment of triumph can deteriorate into humiliation!

Finally, about fourth grade, after much effort on the part of our speech teacher and much trilling of the tongue, we could say our names. Hallelujah!

Our favorite cousin by far was Daddy's nephew, Frank Morgan. He was handsome and charming and taught at the local high school.

We were in elementary school with freckles and pigtails and not much going for us except for our handsome cousin. He gave us a bit of status. We heard plenty about our good-looking cousin and how all the girls had a crush on him. We were very proud to be his kin. We couldn't wait to be old enough to be in his class. He was drafted and looked great in his uniform, but he died in the service, and then the war didn't seem like such a glorious adventure anymore.

At the age of twelve, we twins suffered some rather dramatic changes in our lives. It was 1945, and the only US president we had ever known, Franklin Delano Roosevelt, died. What would happen to us? Could Truman really handle the complications of war? Also, in the same year, the only pastor we had ever known in our church left for another church. What else could happen? Our world was turning topsy-turvy. Then the atomic bomb was dropped on Hiroshima. We were frightened by this awesome power. The newsreels at the movies and the pictures in both the morning and evening newspapers showed the absolute devastation of this bomb. You might think we would be sad, sympathetic for those unfortunate enough to be victims, but all Buzzy remembers is a feeling of great joy that this would bring an end to this horrible war.

Finally, the physiological changes that occur in girls at that age struck us, and we had to adapt to still more changes. It just did not seem fair to Neany. Bemoaning the fact that she had not been born a boy, Neany became reconciled to her feminine nature when she realized that she could conceive and bear children in a way that men could not. And she could achieve many of the professional skills that were dominated by men if she stuck with her studies. Buzzy looked upon this change as an exciting adventure. Now she was a woman!

Hijinks in Junior High

As we came into junior high, the war, World War II, was ending but still uppermost in our minds. We had seen POW (prisoners of war) buses loaded with young Germans heading down the main street of

Breckenridge going to South Texas POW camps. The movies we saw and the games we played were about war. There was no TV then, but the movie houses showed newsreels about the war after the feature film. One of the movies we saw was about American prisoners of war outsmarting their German captors, who were portrayed as dumb and mean. We had this film in mind when we got into real trouble one day. In junior high, the cafeteria was in a separate building. When we were let out for lunch, we didn't have to come back into the main building for an hour. One lunchtime we decided to pretend we were prisoners of war and had escaped our captors, that is, the principal and teachers. We got a little carried away. We got together with some of our chums and made signs saying, "Free the prisoners!" and marched around the building holding these. Much to our amazement, many other students joined our parade. We slipped inside the principal's office while he was at lunch, opened his desk drawer, and put in an empty coke bottle with a string of licorice candy stuffed inside. We wrapped a note around it saying "This is a bomb," in case he didn't catch on. Meanwhile our parade had grown so that most of the students had joined us. When the bell rang signaling the end of lunch, we were supposed to go back to class. We did, but most of the students continued to march. The principal found our note and called the fire department. Someone snitched on us, and we got in deep trouble for being the organizers. It is a good thing Daddy was on the school board, or we might have been expelled.

Years later when we were Fulbright scholars in Germany, we saw a similar movie, only this time the roles were reversed. Clever German prisoners outwitted the stupid American soldiers guarding them.

A Memorable Piano Recital

When the local piano teacher's son borrowed money from Daddy and didn't pay it back, his mom said she would teach us to play the piano for free as a way of repaying Daddy. During the Depression this

The twins at twelve

type of bartering was very common. If you owed someone money and could not repay it, you offered to repay with services or items of value. That is how we came to have a baby grand piano in our living room. Alas! We had no talent. After many years of lessons we were still on the most elementary level. In one unforgettable recital, the teacher thought it would be charming to have us twins play a duet. We played a piece that had about four repeated phrases at the end and a final finish with a resounding chord. Well, one of us repeated the phrase five times instead of four, causing the other one to start the whole sequence of repeated phrases all over again. Thus the piece went on and on and on with an occasional resounding end chord by one of us, but never at the same time as the other one played it. The audience grew restless. There was much shuffling of feet. Finally our teacher arose and asked if we could end the piece starting at the first of the repeated phrases. The end finally came, to the relief of everyone involved. Our parents said we didn't have to take any more lessons after that. We missed getting a new dress every spring for the recital but were otherwise very happy.

Our lack of talent in playing the piano did not mean we didn't enjoy listening to music. Although we grew up in a town with no symphony orchestra and in a home with no classical music available, the movies introduced us to Tchaikovsky in Song of Russia, and other movies brought us Chopin, Rimsky-Korsakov, and others, still among our favorites today.

We wanted desperately to get a chemistry set one Christmas. We had seen one in the store for five dollars and tried to sell Daddy on the advantages of such a set. We described in detail all the wonderful reactions we could create with it. Maybe we overdid it. On Christmas morning we found under the tree a one-dollar chemistry set. We did the only thing we could do with such a cheap set—that was to make a big stink. Daddy explained he was afraid we might blow ourselves up with the more expensive set.

M. E. Daniel

It was considered a great feat among the neighborhood children to roller-skate down the long, steep driveway leading up to the hilltop mansion of M. E. Daniel, the richest man in town. The former Daniel-Meyer Coliseum at TCU was named for him and for Dutch Meyer. Milton Daniel's driveway was so steep that by the time a roller-skater got to the bottom, he'd be going too fast to stop for any passing cars which, fortunately, were few. We sustained many skinned knees from those attempts—a badge of honor. Some of our friends had broken limbs.

Mr. Daniel was well loved by the children of Breckenridge, both for his exciting driveway and because he held a gigantic Easter egg hunt with lots of neat prizes every year on the beautiful green lawn of his home.

Dancing Lessons

When we were in junior high we were sent to dancing lessons to polish our social skills. There was a special dance party at the end of lessons. Most of the girls at that age were taller than the boys. There was only one tall boy, and Buzzy longed for him to ask her to dance. At last he did, and off they sailed across the dance floor. She was in heaven! Unfortunately, elastic was hard to come by during the war, so Mother had sewn panties for us and used buttons to fasten them instead of elastic. Oh, that she had used two buttons instead of only one! As Roberta and her handsome partner danced, the button popped off her panties, which fell to the floor. With a quick flick of her foot Buzzy sent those panties sailing across the room. One wonders what the chaperone thought when she found the unoccupied panties.

On Being a Twin

We were a twosome from conception. What one might never have the nerve to try alone, two together would not hesitate to attempt. Individually, we were timid. Together we faced the world without fear! There may have been a bully or two in our schools, but that was of no consequence to us. We had each other.

Having an identical twin carries the advantage of always having a companion, a coconspirator in any scheme that might be thought up. The first time we got a phone call from a girlfriend asking us to go to the movies with her, we told Mother we thought it strange. If she wanted to go to the movie, why didn't she just go? Mother pointed out that not everyone has a twin as a built-in companion.

A disadvantage to having a twin is that there is always the fear that your twin will do something embarrassing and everyone will think it was you. Neany was always pleading with Buzzy to get her school assignments in on time for fear any tardiness would reflect on her. Buzzy was horrified one summer when Neany, after reading Kipling's *The Jungle Boy*, decided to be a jungle girl. She walked on all fours, grunted, and refused to bathe, comb her hair, or brush her teeth for several days. This was right about the time Buzzy had been awakened to amorous love when the lifeguard at the swimming pool kissed the hurt finger she had scratched on the wooden deck. The feel of his rough beard made her blush, and she dove into the water to hide it. Being a jungle girl was far from her mind. She was more interested in getting rid of her freckles, maybe using make-up, maybe staying out in the sun to see if the freckles coalesced. She wanted to look like an attractive young lady capable of catching the attention of a young man. About this time we twins decided to stop dressing exactly alike, to help people know for sure which twin was which. Heaven knows, each of us did not want to be mistaken for our goofy twin sister, especially not by a prospective boyfriend.

Summer Camp

We loved going to summer camp, both church camp and Girl Scout camp. We went to the small country town of Buffalo Gap south of Breckenridge for our first church camp. Our sister Fay went as well, and Mother went along as a chaperone. It was Mom's first and only time to accompany us to camp. She was not an outdoorsy person. We loved the swimming pool, staying in it as much as possible until our skin shriveled like prunes. We slept on cots in a long army-type barracks.

One morning when we had devotions we were told to take our Bibles and find a secluded spot to meditate on the assigned scripture. Buzzy crossed the road that ran by the camp and sat in a grove of trees. There was an army base nearby. At that time pilots were a part of the army. The Army Air Corps must have been training pilots in the art of dropping bombs on targets with some accuracy. As Buzzy sat meditating, she was startled by the loud sound of a low flying airplane, then a sudden "whoosh" as a sack of flour came through the trees and burst "kapow" near her feet. She nearly jumped out of her skin. You can be sure she never crossed that road again.

Another church camp we went to was in Mineral Wells. At the end of the week there was a swimming race. Neany won for the girls, and a boy from Albany won for the boys. Someone suggested that the two winners race. Neany beat the boy quite easily. His mother was there as a girls' counselor. That night as we had evening devotions, the boy's mom told us, "We must avoid the sin of pride. No one should congratulate Neany on winning the swim race today for fear it will inspire pride in her." This was an epiphany for us. We learned that church camp counselors are not always saintly.

At Girl Scout camp we were sitting on a fence on parents' visitation day when a couple of ladies walked by. They stopped and looked at us. One said, "They must be identical twins. You know that means each has only half a brain. So sad!" We jumped down and followed the ladies down the path, limping and grunting, trying to act as brainless as we could.

One summer we went with our sister Fay for a six-week stay at Camp Arrowhead in the beautiful Hill Country of Texas while our parents took a well-deserved vacation. The camp put on an operetta, and everyone was encouraged to try out for the various roles. Fay and Neany were asked to be in the chorus. When Buzzy tried out, the music counselor said, "You know, what we really need is a curtain puller." Buzzy remembered her first grade teacher had asked her to "just mouth the words" when the class sang at the PTA program. Apparently, her vocal talent was limited to being a good listener.

We took horseback riding instruction at Camp Arrowhead. We were town girls and hadn't ridden horses much at all. We learned a lot that summer but were ranked near the bottom of the class. Some of the girls had been coming to this camp for years and were quite proficient. The final week included a horse show, complete with judges sitting at a table in the middle of the show ring. We had to draw for horses. When Buzzy drew the name of the meanest, most unmanageable horse of the bunch, a look of horror came over our counselor's face. She told Buzzy just to do the best she could. As we trotted around the ring, Buzzy's horse suddenly took off across the ring and jumped over the judges' stand. The judges ran for cover. Buzzy was disqualified. We thought she deserved a medal for staying on the horse!

For two summers during our high school years we went to New Mexico to take part in an archeological dig cosponsored by the Girl Scouts and the Museum of New Mexico. The leader was Dr. Bertha Dutton of the Museum of New Mexico. She was a tough taskmaster. She taught us how digs were done and also made sure we conserved water. We lived in tents, and if we brushed our teeth we were required to spit on some green plant. The dig was on a ranch. As instructed, we cautiously dug dirt out with a trowel a few millimeters at a time and recorded the exact location of any pottery fragment we found.

Daddy at the beauty pageant

After a few days of careful excavating, the ranch owner drove up in his pick-up and saw what we were doing. He said, "Hell, I can help you with that!" He got a shovel out of his truck and shoveled up a big chunk of dirt. He commented, "That will make the job go faster." Dr. Dutton was not pleased.

That year we had with us a visiting artist from Philadelphia. Someone found a rattlesnake and shot it. The artist was horrified and insisted on hiding behind a small hill before the snake was shot. She was convinced that the snake's mate would come back to bite in revenge. We believe she went back to Philadelphia the next day.

We were so happy when the town of Breckenridge decided to build a swimming pool in the park. Neany and Buzzy signed up for synchronized swimming and spent many happy times swimming with a group of girls in a circle with one leg up in the air and the rest of the body underwater. It was our only successful sport.

One year there was a beauty contest at the Breckenridge swimming pool. Several of our friends entered and paraded past the judges in their swimsuits. We didn't enter because we knew freckles would prevent our winning, and besides that, our father was mayor and therefore one of the judges. We were shocked when our friend Nancy won. We felt sure Treva Jean would win. She had the face of an angel. When we asked Daddy why Nancy won, he said they liked her big bosom. This was another epiphany. Freckles and faces are not as important as breasts in a beauty pageant.

High School

Our sister Fay drove us to the high school across town until we were juniors. After Fay left for TCU, since our mother didn't drive, it was left to Daddy to drive us to high school. We were fourteen, still too young to get a regular driver's license, but Daddy decided it would be okay for us to drive ourselves to school if we stuck to the back roads. After all, there were special considerations given when a family had urgent reasons for a fourteen-year-old to drive. The back road took us by way of a narrow wooden bridge over a small stream. There were two wooden planks across the main floor of the bridge to serve as guides for wheels of vehicles driving over. One morning we were startled to see a rough-looking man standing on the bridge leaning over the outside rail looking down into the river. Most mornings we managed to cross on the planks, but this time we were distracted and missed the planks and so drove on the bridge floor, dangerously close to the man. We felt no thump and heard no splash but still feared for the man's safety. When we looked back, we couldn't see him anywhere. Another moral decision. Should we stop? He was scary looking. We'd be tardy for school. We went on. There was great relief later when we heard no news reports of a body found in the river.

Learning to drive was a bit different then. Cars had no turn signals, so you had to use your left arm to indicate turns or stops. The arm was pointed straight out to indicate a left turn, straight up from the elbow for a right turn, and straight down for a stop.

We twins were always running a bit late. Two of Fay's chums who lived nearby were astonished that Rogene would sometimes leave the house wearing socks that didn't match. Rogene was never concerned about how she looked. If she couldn't find socks that matched, she just wore ones that did not. This habit carried over to later life until her boss suggested she dress more professionally.

When we left the house we would dash out the door, jump into whatever car we had, fling it into reverse and, without looking much, back down the long driveway beside our house. One day, the cleaning lady parked in our usual path and we collided. We felt so guilty! Fortunately, the car could be repaired at Daddy's car business.

Later in high school, we twins were responsible for the demise of a social club for girls. The club was called the Tri Hi Y and caused a lot of pain. A girl had to be voted into the club, and even one person could blackball an incoming prospect. The club was supposed to encourage moral uprightness among the members, but we thought it was an elitist clique. Our older sister had been hurt by not being admitted. We got voted in and ran for officer positions. We won. At the first

Twins and friend at 1951 crowning of the Buckaroo Queen.

meeting we held a discussion about what pain was sometimes caused by the club. We proposed to do away with the club. A vote was taken and the club dissolved, much to the dismay of the teacher sponsor.

We were not good at typing. The typing teacher called us aside after the first semester and said she knew we had a straight "A" average and she did not wish to ruin that, so she would give us a passing grade in typing only if we would agree not to sign up for the second semester. We agreed.

Daddy asked us to talk to his Lion's Club. We decided to talk about the new wonder tonic called Geritol, which we thought was a big joke. One of us spoke while the other did tricks. We had a large fake sunflower in a pot with a hole in the bottom. The stem of the flower went through the hole and into a space below the podium. One of us poured Geritol into the pot while the other pushed the stem of the flower upwards, so it looked like the Geritol made the flower grow. Most of the Lions caught on to our skullduggery and thought it funny, but one man came up afterward to tell us how Geritol had worked wonders for him.

A Missed Senior Prom

We took up two competitive high school activities. One was Ready Writing, sponsored by the English teacher Mrs. Bailey, wife of the superintendent. The other was debate, sponsored by Miss Ratliff, the drama teacher. By the time we were seniors we were pretty good at debate. We made perfect partners. That year the question being debated was "Should the Electoral College be Abolished?" We had to defend both pro and con. Mr. Squires was the new Civics teacher and was very helpful. We went to State that year. The competition took place in Austin on the same weekend as the senior prom. Someone had talked David Buchanan and Dickie Phillips into being our dates for the prom at our high school. No one expected us to go very far in the debate competition because the big schools in Houston, Dallas, and Fort Worth always took the top prizes. We felt sure we'd be home in time for the prom. Lo and behold, we kept winning. We got to the semifinals and debated one of the Houston schools. The judges seemed ecstatic that we won. They came over afterwards and gave us pointers on how to do even better. The final debate was to be at the Saturday night banquet, so there went the senior prom. We were exhausted and lost the finals, but we were very proud to be second in the state. The next Monday it was announced that there would be a special assembly at our school. We thought our second-place win was to be announced and we would be honored. Instead, we found it was to comfort the football team, which had lost its Friday night game. The team got the cheers and words of encouragement. Football was king in those days, and maybe still is. More than one businessman had commented that it was a shame we twins were not boys. We would make a great passing duo.

We liked chemistry, and Breckenridge High School had an excellent chemistry teacher named Mrs. Maxwell. Unfortunately, she retired the year we needed her. Our teacher was Mr. Harwell, who was a new teacher and a music major. He had had only one semester of chemistry in college and did not take the second semester because he didn't like the first. His solution to his predicament was to assign reading in the text, then write questions from the teacher's manual on one board with the answers on the other board. The test questions always came from those board questions.

In the athletic sports arena, we were not so great. The only group sport available for girls was softball. We learned about humility when captains chose teams. We were almost always the last to be chosen. We then proceeded to left field, the position we always played. At least two things contributed to our failure to perform well in the field. First, we did not own a glove, so we had to catch balls in our bare hands. Second, we wore glasses. In our family, one of the worst things you could do was break your glasses. Our father was "not made of

Twins and their mother at Lion's Club Convention banquet in my city.

money" as he liked to say. So when a ball was hit into the field, we considered it our job to dodge it, not catch it. Roberta remembers hiding behind a mesquite tree in hopes she wouldn't be noticed.

At high school graduation Neany was named valedictorian. Buzzy came in third, following Rogene, as was her habit.

We had now reached the point of our next big adventure.

2

COLLEGE

When the time came for our sister Martha to go to college, our parents decided on a finishing school in Nashville, Tennessee, called Ward-Belmont. Ward-Belmont was picky about the applicants they accepted, so a woman was sent to interview the family. Mother told us to mind our manners and to sit quietly without crossing our legs, as that was not ladylike. When the woman arrived, she sat down and immediately crossed her legs. We got the giggles and had to leave the room. When we visited the campus that fall we were amazed by the dorm bathrooms that had toilets with chains above our heads to be pulled to flush the toilet. That was scary! Martha was told she would not be allowed to leave the campus without wearing heels, hat, hose, and gloves.

Texas Christian University

We were relieved and pleased when our parents decided to send us to Texas Christian University in Fort Worth, Texas. Our father wanted to send us to a school where he could be sure we would be well supervised for social activities. TCU turned out to be a fortuitous choice and one that pleased both Daddy and us twins. TCU had already played an important role in our family, being associated with the Disciples of Christ, a denomination in which Grandfather had been a minister. In a letter dated March 25, 1913, our grandfather, the Reverend A. D. Rogers, had been appointed to the Advisory Board in a fundraising campaign for a BIGGER AND BETTER TCU. Our cousin, Cleta Rogers, began her drama career at TCU, and our sister Fay was then a junior there. Eventually, Roberta's daughter, Nancy, would graduate from TCU and marry a TCU graduate.

We twins looked forward to college with great anticipation, thinking we could take many interesting classes compared to what was available at our small high school. We wanted an academically challenging school. Daddy considered it his responsibility to pay for college for all four of his daughters. He mentioned that had we been boys, we would have been expected to work and earn our own way through college, just as he had.

Roberta remembers a wonderful sense of freedom at TCU. No longer did she have to tell her parents where she was going or what she was doing. She was free to decide everything for herself. Rogene remembers being in awe of the wide variety of classes we could take.

At registration entering freshmen were told where to find the office of their adviser, who would be a professor in the field in which they had chosen to major. We had not decided on a major. This was frowned upon. "You are grown-ups now. You must make up your mind," we were told. We liked creative writing and loved to tell stories like Mother. This interest pulled us toward an English major. On the other hand, we were very curious. We had lots of "why" questions. "Why did our skin shrivel up like prunes when we stayed in the pool for a long time? How was it possible for the speedometer on the car to read zero when the car was moving slowly across the pasture to get to the brush arbor where Grandpa was to preach? How could a headless chicken flop around the yard so vigorously when Daddy had wrung its neck? Why did adding salt to water make the water freeze at a lower temperature?" We wanted to know how things happened. This interest in causality pulled us toward science. We considered, too, that science jobs might pay better than literary jobs.

Undecided

We were put with a group called "undecideds" and sent to professors who didn't have many advisees—in our case, to Dr. Irene

Huber, the one and only German professor. It was soon after World War II. Germany was still regarded as the enemy, so almost no one was majoring in German. Dr. Huber, who was Swiss, had plenty of time to talk to us, a situation that turned out to have a big influence on our future. She looked at our high school records and decided we were smart and therefore able to take an overload of courses. She signed us up for three lab courses—physics, chemistry, and biology, plus English, physical education, German, and math, a total of twenty-three hours, whereas seventeen was the limit. When we sought the approval of our instructors, they noted that we were way over the limit and insisted we drop something. That turned out to be physics.

Dr. Huber asked us if we'd like to travel abroad. We said we sure would, but we didn't have any way to pay for it. She mentioned Fulbright Scholarships that paid for overseas study. She cautioned that getting a Fulbright to an English-speaking country was difficult, because so many people applied for those, but if we would minor in German and keep up our grades, she would recommend us for a Fulbright Scholarship to study in Germany for one year after we graduated TCU, all expenses paid. How exciting this sounded to two young girls from a small Texas town! We did as she suggested, and she was true to her word. What a deal! She needed students and we wanted to travel. How grateful we are that there was a Dr. Huber at TCU when we needed guidance. She set us on our way to a fulfilling future: Fulbright Awards, graduate studies, and exciting careers.

Later, we went for advisement to the vice president of the university, D. Ray Lindley, so that he could help us decide on a major. Rogene said she thought she would like to get a PhD in science. This was 1951, and Dr. Lindley advised her that ladies should not try for a PhD. Of course, she was then determined to get one and eventually did. We dreamed of going to medical school so we could be like Dr. Gwin who saved Daddy's life, but women physicians were unheard of in our area at that time. We both chose double majors in biology and chemistry and double minors in German and mathematics.

English Class

Freshmen were placed in English classes according to how well they did on an entrance exam. Lower-level classes emphasized grammar, whereas upper-level concentrated on composition. As usual, Neany beat Buzzy out. Neany was placed in the "smart" class, taught by Ms. Major, and Buzzy was placed in the "not so smart" class, taught by Ms. Bryson. The first day of class Ms. Bryson asked the young man sitting in front of Buzzy, "In the sentence, 'The boy hit the red ball,' what part of speech is the word *red?*" The boy thought for a long time. Mrs. Bryson hinted, "Is it a noun, a verb, an adjective?" The boy said in a confident voice, "Verb!" Roberta collapsed in disbelief. She had some very good English teachers in high school and couldn't believe this young man's obvious lack of knowledge. Mrs. Bryson said, "Miss Faulkner, I'd like to speak to you after class." Roberta feared she had done herself in and prepared for a reproof. Fortunately, Mrs. Bryson just wanted to tell her she might be happier in the upper-level class and offered to transfer her. Saved! Thank you, Professor Bryson! Roberta redeemed herself when one of her short stories, "Amonel Spelled Backwards," was published in the Freshman Literary Contest publication called Spring Harvest, along with a story by Rogene entitled "Six Feet Under."

We worried that our enrollment at TCU was costing Daddy a lot of money. We heard other students talking about scholarships for students with good grades, so we made an appointment to talk to TCU president Dr. Sadler to ask for such a scholarship. He told us that he expected our father to donate money to TCU, not the other way around. Roberta decided we'd have to get jobs after graduation to pay Daddy back. Tuition was then $13.50 per credit hour.

Physics Class

Which class to drop our freshman year turned out to be an easy decision. The first physics professor we had was near retirement and obviously tired of freshman physics. He announced on the first day that he believed we had all had physics in high school and would therefore be bored with the same old stuff, so he got out his guitar and started singing Russian folk songs, a hobby of his. We fled the class, which we took the next year under Dr. Morgan, an excellent teacher.

At that time there were no calculators. Slide rules were the preferred method of doing calculations. Roberta had never used one, so she trusted doing the calculations only by hand. Dr. Morgan saw this practice and asked Roberta why. She replied that she did not trust that slide rule. At the next physics lab he came and stood by her, insisting she use the slide rule without checking the calculations by hand. The pressure worked, and she switched to the slide rule.

German Class

We chose German as our language to study because of the influence of Dr. Huber and because we thought it was the best language for science. Dr. Huber was a tall, stately maiden lady who was an inspiration for us. She told us that she had never lived a traditional life. In Switzerland, it was the job of her brothers to find all their sisters a husband, but they had given up on her. She attended college, which was unusual for women at that time, where she was told not to attend the class on the sex life of the bee, a comment that insulted her, so she read every book she could find in the library on the subject, making the best score given on the test.

In our German class one day Dr. Huber told us she could yodel. After that revelation the class would not give up until she yodeled for us. We had to promise that we would not laugh. But when she began to yodel, it was just too much. The whole class went into hysterics. She did not yodel for us again.

Math Class

We liked the cleanliness of mathematics. It was like solving puzzles. Our math professors at TCU, Professor Charles R. Scherer and Dr. Landon Colquitt, were excellent. Professor Scherer was an older man who was department head and had unfortunately missed getting his doctorate because someone else published on his thesis topic just before he submitted his work. We students thought that practice was unfair.

We also liked Dr. Colquitt, who was young and handsome. All the girls had a crush on him, but he up and married a lovely English professor named Betsy. Miss Bramblett, another math teacher, was more difficult to understand. Both Professor Scherer and Dr. Colquitt were interested in the social development of their students as well as in their academic success, so they formed a math club. We met once a month, sometimes in a professor's home, had refreshments, and played board games. It was fun because all of the people there were nerds like us. Roberta had her eye on a handsome young math major from Maine. We twins were playing Scrabble with him one evening; he was winning until Rogene put down the word "anus." He said that wasn't a word, so Rogene made him look it up in the dictionary. Roberta was mortified. There went her chances of getting a date with him! Rogene never seemed to understand that there were things more important than winning!

When we were freshmen, the math club planned a party at a shrimp restaurant. We twins complained that we had never eaten shrimp and didn't think we'd like them. Much to the chagrin of the seniors, the party was shifted to Cattleman's Cafe, mainly because Professor Scherer thought freshmen should have a say. We later learned to love shrimp.

Biology Class

Biology was a descriptive science at the time, involving a lot of memorization. It was fascinating but did not fully satisfy our curiosity about what made things work. We had majored in both biology and chemistry to find the biochemical basis for human life. Currently, the field of molecular biology would have met our needs, but that field was in its infancy at the time. Dr. Hewitt was head of the biology department and also the premed adviser at TCU. On the first day of his Comparative Anatomy course there were not enough chairs for all the students. He told us not to worry, because after the first test there would be plenty of seats. He was right.

We had to dissect a cat in that class. Dr. Hewitt said we were fortunate, because only a few years earlier students were required to bring in their own cats. The neighborhoods around TCU had learned to keep their cats indoors at the beginning of each fall semester. In our senior year we studied the lobster in Dr. Hewitt's invertebrate course. At the end of that class we boiled our lobster specimens and ate them. Very tasty!

As biology majors we were required to be assistants in freshman laboratories. These labs usually involved a lot of work with the microscope. There was one excellent student who had visual problems and could not see well through a microscope. One day we were showing the students amoebas growing in pond water. Students had to move a slide with a drop of pond water on it around under the scope until they saw an amoeba, a small one-celled organism. The student with visual problems worked very hard and became increasingly frustrated as the lab wore on, because she could not find an amoeba. Just as the lab ended she squealed in delight and called us over to show us that she had found an amoeba. It was an air bubble! She began to revise her life goals to a career that did not require microscopic work.

Most of the biology majors at TCU were headed for medical school, and Dr. Hewitt was responsible for writing recommendation letters for their admission. Dr. Hewitt was interested in invertebrate zoology and taught a great course on the subject. The class was full of premed students for two reasons. First, they wanted to make good impressions on Dr. Hewitt, and second, the course included a fun trip to Port Aransas on the Texas Gulf Coast to collect and identify invertebrate specimens. We twins were excited about the field trip, too, but we ended up causing quite a commotion.

As soon as we arrived at the coast and dropped our things off at the motel across the road from the ocean, we and most others went straight into the waves to look for specimens. When it got dark, people started heading back to the motel. A reporter from the *Fort Worth Star-Telegram* had come along to report on the trip. He asked if anyone would like to drive with him to Corpus Christi to telegraph in his report to the paper. We twins volunteered. We thought we might see more specimens there. We told the only two people left on the beach where we were going, so no one would worry. These students were a young married couple who had a separate cabin from all the rest of us. Off we went with the reporter. After he sent off the report, we stopped at a café for a cup of coffee. It was quite late when we returned to the beach at Port Aransas, where a search was going on, which turned out to be for the Faulkner twins who had not been present for bed check. Dr. Hewitt was frantic and about to call the Coast Guard and our parents to report us missing. The leaders had questioned all the other students except the married couple. Fortunately, Dr. Hewitt had not made the call to the Coast Guard. Many years later, we saw a write-up of that night's adventures in the *Star-Telegram* by the same reporter, telling about one of the more stressful moments in his career as a journalist.

Roberta discovered one skill she absolutely could not master. Dr. Forsyth's course in histology concerned learning to identify various tissues as seen under a microscope. Try as she might, Roberta just could not distinguish between heart and gut tissues or even human versus cat. She passed the course, just barely. What she learned for sure was that she would never be a pathologist.

Chemistry Class

Chemistry was always exciting to us, as shown by our early yearning for a chemistry set. We found the subject to be challenging and fun. The head of the department was Dr. Hardt, who taught our first class in chemistry. It was at 8:00 a.m., bringing forth many moans from students about the early hour. Dr. Hardt told us how lucky we were to have an 8:00 a.m. class that got us up early enough to have an extra hour in the day compared to other students! The first assignment he gave us was to write an essay about all that was known about the chemistry of water. At first, Rogene thought it could be done on one page, even in one paragraph. But the deeper Rogene went into the subject, the more she realized that the properties of water were complex and that a good deal of biochemistry was governed by the properties of water. It was an eye-opening assignment.

Dr. Hardt thought we had all had chemistry in high school and therefore knew how to do the basic math problems of first-year chemistry. He said to come see him if we had any trouble with the first chapter math problems, because he didn't want to bore the class by going over them. He didn't realize that some of us had had a music major as our high school chemistry teacher. Roberta did not go to see Dr. Hardt about this. The first chemistry test contained lots of those problems, and she failed it miserably. Woe! When she did go to see him, he agreed to drop that grade if she did well on the subsequent tests. She did. Thank you, Dr. Hardt!

As with biology, we were required to be chemistry lab assistants for the freshmen and sophomores. This was at a time when many young men had returned from World War II and were going to school on the GI Bill. They were different from the students coming right out of high school. They were there to learn and prepare for jobs, and they put up with no nonsense. In one lab, we were teaching students to precipitate metals out as sulfides by bubbling hydrogen sulfide gas through a solution containing metal ions. The byproduct of this reaction was hydrogen gas, which is highly explosive. We had many safety precautions, including that all of the stills had to be covered with wet cotton towels. Despite all our efforts, one still blew up. No one was hurt, because the wet towels protected the students from the explosion. We gave an additional lecture on the safety precautions, and the lab continued. It was not too long before a second explosion occurred. This time we got Dr. Hardt, whose office was nearby, to come and give the safety talk. Finally, a third explosion was heard. At this point, one of the veterans came up and announced, "One explosion can be an accident. A second explosion can be a coincidence. But a third explosion—that's a pattern. Something's wrong. I'm going home." He was so right.

Another chemistry professor who was important to us and an excellent teacher was Dr. Alexander. He taught analytical chemistry. He was very precise and careful in all he did. One day Rogene saw him drop his car keys. After he retrieved them, he quickly dropped them again. As he reached down to get them a second time, he was heard to mutter, "And I call myself a scientist!" Rogene felt sorry for him and wanted to tell him it was okay to drop your keys twice in a row. When Dr. Alexander had gallbladder surgery, he came back to TCU eager to show his scar to anyone he could convince to stop while he pulled down his pants—a circumstance we thought was a hoot!

Plumbing Problem

An accident occurred with a middle-aged man who worked as a janitor in the chemistry stockroom. One day he was found covered with water, trembling, and crouching under a sink in the chemistry stockroom. The poor guy was cleaning up the stockroom when he found a bottle with metal flakes covered by oil. This looked to him like debris that needed to be cleaned up, so he opened the bottle and put it under an open faucet to wash the contents down the sink. As any chemist would recognize, metal flakes stored under oil were most likely sodium metal, which is highly explosive in water. The janitor had caused a huge explosion that left him uninjured, but shaken, under the sink. It blew out all the plumbing. There were tales of startled people who had been sitting on toilets at the time.

Dr. Hogan was the professor who taught us organic chemistry, which was mainly memorization. He rarely gave a grade higher than a B. We twins were accustomed to getting an A, so we had to be prepared for the lower grade. We were not asked to assist in his laboratory classes. He used a wheelchair and reminded us of Perry Mason as portrayed by Raymond Burr on TV.

We learned mountains of knowledge at TCU, not always in the classroom. Both TCU and Fort Worth were awash with cultural activities that we small-town girls had never experienced. We went to every guest lecture, special convocation, theatrical performance, sports event, and chapel service for which we could find time. The sermons by Dr. Rout at chapel services were especially inspiring and made a real difference in our understanding of morality and Christianity. One professor remarked, "You twins are really getting a good return on your parents' investment. I see you at every event on campus."

A very special moment for us was when M. E. Sadler, the TCU President, presented us with the M. E. Sadler Brotherhood Award for

Sadler Brotherhood Award

"outstanding contributions in the fields of inter- faith, interracial, and intercultural understanding" to advance better relations with groups and individuals on and off campus. We regularly attended church at the University Christian Church and participated in the college youth group there.

Football was a major sport at TCU. Since we had come from a high school where football was king, we attended all the games at TCU. We had only to walk down the hill from Waits Hall to get to the stadium. As freshmen we always wore our purple beanies. One week the Horned Frogs were playing Texas A&M. Someone arranged for us twins to have dates with Aggies for the game. Well, we thought that was quite exciting until we learned that you had to stand up the whole game if you sat with the Aggies. That took all the thrill out of having the dates. Especially after the Aggies lost, our dates were miserable companions.

Our father was excited to come to a football game when we were at TCU. After the game we stood in the parking lot as he exclaimed about the amazing plays. When he illustrated with his arms how a pass was caught, he accidentally knocked his glasses off. The lenses broke into several pieces when they hit the ground. "What in tarnation was I thinking, to do a tomfool thing like that!" Daddy hollered. We had to tape the pieces together so he could see to drive back home to Breckenridge.

We twins were not very athletic and took only the required physical education classes. In one such class the instructor had all of us girls pair up and hold hands across our waists to do a "hop-skip" folk dance in a circle around the gym. Of course we twins were one couple. We were skinny, scrawny girls, and we must have looked like two grasshoppers skipping about. We glanced over at the instructors and saw that they were looking at us and collapsing in laughter. At least we were entertaining!

We were on a committee to bring programs to the TCU campus. Breckenridge had a splendid boys' choir conducted by Gwen James, so we suggested they be brought to TCU for a concert. We were thrilled that our suggestion was accepted and so proud when the concert in Ed Landreth Auditorium was a rousing success.

We lived in Waits Hall in a suite with two other girls. Each pair had a bedroom with a shared bath between. Our suitemates were Shirley Root and Joan Leimer. There were no phones in the rooms, only one at the end of each hall. There was a buzzer button on the wall of each room, so if you got a phone call, whoever was at the front desk would buzz you to let you know to go to the hall phone to get your call. The method everyone used, to know if they had missed a call, was to hang a pop bottle cap on a thread and perch it on the button. If the button buzzed, the cap would fall off, signifying a missed call. What a contrast to the mobile cell phones of today's world!

Joan Leimer introduced us to symphony music. She knew we could get in free to the Fort Worth Symphony Orchestra performances if we volunteered to usher. We had a car for transportation to the symphony hall at Will Rogers Auditorium, and Joan did not. She talked us into going. We sometimes slept through part of the performance, but, even so, we absorbed a lot of musical knowledge.

We volunteered to teach swimming for the Red Cross in Fort Worth, where we taught a class of adult women. One was terrified. We finally got her to put her face in the water and to float face down right next to the edge of the pool. When the class members got to the point at which most were ready to move on, we asked the ready ones to line up and jump in the water, then come to the surface face down and swim across the pool or just stand up in the waist high water if they felt afraid. All went well until the fearful lady decided she could do this, much to our surprise. She jumped in and came to the surface floating face down, stiff as a board, and never moved. We had to jump in and stand her upright!

Dean Shelburne was Dean of Students. She was prim and expected us to be the same. Girls were not allowed to wear shorts in public unless they were headed to the tennis courts with a tennis racquet in hand. The dorm doors were locked at 10 p.m. sharp, and you'd better be in your room. Despite the lack of air conditioning, we were told to keep the shades down at night, so no one could see into our rooms. The shades blocked what little breeze there was on hot, steamy nights. Also, we were to have no food in our rooms. Kitchens where food could be kept were on each floor.

The basement held a washing machine, dryer, and Coke machine. The first time Roberta used the washing machine, she put in too much detergent. When she came down later, she found the whole basement filled with suds.

Late at night we often went to the basement to get a Coke to keep awake for studying. We were not supposed to be out of our rooms at that hour, so we tried to be sneaky. When we put money in the machine, the Coke bottle made an astonishing amount of noise banging down as it came out. We thought for sure we'd be caught and reprimanded, but never were.

Dead Cat under Bed

The dorm housemother periodically conducted surprise room inspections, which became our undoing. She came to our room one evening to find our windows open, our shades up, and a formaldehyde odor coming from under our beds. We were dissecting cats for comparative anatomy class. It was strictly forbidden to remove the cats from the laboratory, but we were behind schedule with the deadline approaching, so we sneaked our cats out and worked on them in our dorm room at night, keeping them under our beds. When the housemother found them, she was horrified. Then she looked in our bathroom and discovered a mouse swimming in a pitcher of lemonade. She turned red in the face and gave us a long lecture, "What if you got sick and a doctor had to be called. Wouldn't you be terribly embarrassed for the doctor to discover dead cats under the bed and a mouse swimming in lemonade in the bathroom?" For this infraction, we were sent for punishment to Dean Shelburne, a chore that proved a bit difficult for her. Her standard punishment was to "campus" the offending student. To be campused meant the student could not leave the campus and was limited to class, labs, or the library. Since that was all we did anyway, the Dean just gave us a stern lecture on keeping our room in better shape.

Another exciting event at TCU that year was when Miss Sherley, the rather stern English professor, was walking across campus and spied a coed sliding down a sheet hanging from a boy's third-floor dorm window. It was strictly forbidden at that time for a girl to be in a boy's room, and vice-versa. It seems the boy had looked out the window and seen his father coming up the front sidewalk, so he had his girlfriend slide out the back window on a sheet. Nowadays, the girl would probably have stayed put. Back then it caused an uproar.

Summer Jobs

During the summers of our college years we applied all over for summer jobs. Between our sophomore and junior years we got jobs at a Girl Scout camp near Bartlesville, Oklahoma. Rogene was responsible for leading a group of girls at the main camp. Roberta was put in charge of a wilderness camp group. The wilderness girls lived in tents, built their own latrines, and cooked food on a campfire. Two incidents clouded the serenity of that summer. First, a bank robber held up a bank in Bartlesville and was thought to be hiding in the woods near the camp. The camp director brought each of us a loaded gun and asked us to put it under our pillows to be used in case the bank robber showed up. We had never touched a gun before, so it was indeed fortunate that the robber was soon caught and the guns retrieved before we killed someone.

A second incident there involved an encounter with a copperhead snake. Late one night after all were in their tents, a girl came to Roberta's tent to say there was a big snake wrapped around her duffle bag under her cot. Roberta got her flashlight and went with the girl. A crowd of girls had gathered outside the tent. Roberta said, "Stay calm." Inside the tent the flashlight revealed a very large copperhead wrapped around the duffle bag. Roberta asked for a large stick, and someone handed her a tree branch. She aimed the stick at the snake's head but ended up catching it by the tail. Once more she cautioned the girls, "Stay calm." The snake tried to get away. Its head ended up outside under the tent flap. Roberta told one of the girls to hold the stick down tightly while she took the flashlight outside to look for the head. Armed with another stick Roberta went out. Just as she spotted the head outside the tent flap, the snake got loose and took off. Roberta went screaming into the night. So much for staying calm.

Another summer we got jobs at a private camp in the suburbs of Philadelphia, Pennsylvania. A rich lady had left money to establish a camp that brought together slum girls and girls from upper-class homes. Her idea was that they would learn from each other. And learn they did! We were put in charge of a barracks full of teenagers. We were not much older than the campers. One day there was a joint party with the camp for mentally challenged boys across the road. We spent much of the night retrieving our campers from their various rendezvous with the boys under trees in the adjacent forest.

The lady who donated the money for the camp had written in the conditions that devotions should be led by the camp director every night. The camp director could read, "God is love" and make it sound like a threat. The sad part was that the camp drama counselor had a beautiful reading voice. It would have been so much better for her to read the scriptures. We twins did enjoy, however, getting to go into Philadelphia to see the sights on our days off.

There was a lovely Quaker family who lived across the road from the camp. They paid us to teach their daughter Betsy to swim and invited us for family meals. They served salt from a salt cellar which Neany mistook for a sugar bowl and thereby ruined her ice tea. They prided themselves on always serving corn-on-the-cob within an hour of it being picked. Yummy! They took us to a Quaker service held in a Meeting House. Men and women sat on opposite sides. Announcements were made and then everyone sat quietly. Every now and then someone would stand up and say something they thought needed to be said, or they would tell about something they had experienced or heard about. For us, the experience was enlightening.

Final Years at TCU

During our junior year at TCU the administration decided that enrollment could be increased by bringing sororities and fraternities to TCU. Many students protested, saying they had come to TCU precisely because there were no sororities and fraternities. It was decided to hold an election so that students could vote yea or nay, with much campaigning on both sides. Heading up the antifraternity group was David Allred, son of former Texas Governor James Allred, later elected to the office of Texas State Representative. David was a junior at TCU, as were we. The idea was soundly defeated, whereupon the administration announced that the minority of students who had voted for the idea should have their voices heard. Those who didn't want to join a sorority or fraternity did not have to, but those who wanted fraternities and sororities should have that opportunity. In other words, the election was just for show. In protest, we moved out of the dorm our senior year and rented a room off campus.

A Tense Easter Vacation

In our senior year at TCU, our beloved German teacher, the one whose yodel produced hilarity, encouraged both of us to apply for Fulbright scholarships to Germany. What a thrill! She and many others warned us not to expect that we would both win scholarships. The most we could hope for was that one of us might make it. We worked hard at filling out the applications in the fall. Then we waited. Just before leaving school for the Easter vacation, Roberta received notification that she had received a Fulbright Scholarship to go to Heidelberg the next year. Hurrah! But Rogene did not get such a letter. It was a long Easter vacation for her. Upon returning to school, Rogene discovered her first piece of mail was a notification that she had received a Fulbright Scholarship to go to Munich. The sun was shining again. The twins would be together for another big adventure.

We graduated from TCU the spring of 1955 with double majors in chemistry and biology and double minors in math and German. We set up a picnic in Forest Park for our parents and any other relatives who showed up. It was the end of an important era in our lives. We had grown in important ways since leaving Breckenridge.

We came to TCU green as gourds, not having a clue as to what we wanted to do. TCU set us on a path that led to a life of excitement, opportunity, and adventure. Our education at TCU and the Fulbright Scholarships we obtained there formed a platform from which we were launched into a world of experiences and challenges that led to our greater understanding and awareness of the world and its cultures. TCU was the doorway through which we passed, indeed were propelled, into the wider world, saving us from the provincial mindset that might otherwise have been our fate.

Teaching Mother to Drive

That summer, in addition to preparing to go to Germany, we decided to teach our mother to drive. We had often taken her grocery shopping when we came home on weekends. Otherwise she had to call a taxi, because Daddy was too busy at his office to take her. Daddy did not totally approve of our plan. He feared Mother would have an accident and kill herself or others, but we were determined. After much practice Mother was ready to take her driving test. The patrolman in charge of issuing drivers' licenses came to Breckenridge only once a month, so in August we took Mother downtown. She did well except for running a stop sign. The patrolman said she should come back in September, but by then we were gone, and Daddy wasn't about to take her. Maybe that was for the best. Who knows?

3

THE EUROPEAN ADVENTURE

We were small-town Texas girls with tons of curiosity and energy, but now we knew of a world beyond our own that we wanted to explore. Our European adventure was the next step in a series of explorations that continue today, expanding like rings in a pond. Sometimes hapless, we nevertheless combined our mother's zest with our father's determination and our own relentless frontier spirit, tackling Europe as if it were a giant puzzle with thousands of pieces that sometimes covered us up entirely. Always, we kept going.

Fulbright Year

That fall we flew to New York City to board the ship MS *Italia* that sailed to Germany. That was before the invention of stabilizers on ships, so we got used to lots of rolling. The tabletops in the dining room had metal bars along the edges to catch sliding dishes. Our room was at the very bottom of the ship. The stairs leading to it were extremely steep. We wrote our parents that every time we climbed the stairs to get to the main deck, our ears popped from the change in altitude, a slight exaggeration.

The crew was mostly German with a few Italians. The ship sailed under the flag of Panama and was owned by a Greek. The other people on the ship were mostly Fulbright students and Germans. There were a few American wives going to visit their husbands stationed in Germany. The waiter at our table was German and helped us in our efforts to improve our language skills. There were also some language classes organized on the boat.

A week later the boat docked at Cuxhaven, a beautiful, well-landscaped port that contrasted with the dingy one in New York City from which we had sailed. A train took us to Bad Honnef, a pretty little resort town near Bonn, the postwar capital of West Germany. Lovely flowers abounded. We spent several days there for orientation and classes in the German language and local customs. We were met by a group of German students and assigned hotels that charged five dollars a night, three meals included. The German student who was supposed to perfect our German was frustrated because of our Texas drawl. He pretty much gave up.

Next day we walked to the home of Konrad Adenauer, commonly called "Der Alte" (the old one), who was chancellor of post-World War II Germany. He met us in his garden, where we presented him with a bouquet of flowers and had our pictures taken with him. We took a boat trip down the Rhine that afternoon. Coming from West Texas, we were amazed that in this area the towns were so close together that one could easily walk from one to another.

We toured Beethoven's house in Bonn and visited the Bundeshaus where the postwar government met. When the lower house voted there, they did it by a show of hands. If it wasn't obvious who won, they left the room and returned by two doors, one for ayes and one for nays, being counted as they walked through.

Roberta met Dr. Ruth, a professor from Heidelberg, and his assistant Wolfgang Schindler, a destitute refugee student from East Germany, now living in Heidelberg. Wolfgang explained the proper way to visit a German home. One should buy a few flowers—not roses, too romantic. Maybe carnations, not red, not white, maybe pinkish. Go to the door and knock, then quickly remove the paper covering the flowers before the door opens. For Germans there seems to be a right way to do everything.

We were taught the proper table manners for Germany. Both hands should always be on the table. If you had one hand in your lap, you might be hiding a weapon. The fork is always in the left hand. Roberta remembers later over-hearing a small child in a cafe commenting to his mother as he watched Roberta eat, "Look, Mom, that lady is playing with her knife and fork."

Breakfast is bread, jam, and coffee. Day-old bread/rolls are considered better than fresh, so if you ask for fresh bread at the bakery you will be given a discount. Germans are big on drinking wine—*in vino veritas* (in wine there is truth), they say. We were taken on a tour of the wine country and stopped in Boopart for a wine festival. Since most visitors can't afford more than one glass of wine, they make it last by nursing it for several hours while chatting with a companion in a restaurant.

Roberta
In Heidelberg

Wolfgang said he would go with those of us headed to Heidelberg, take us on a tour of the city, help us register at the University, bring us to the family we would live with the first month in conjunction with the Experiment in International Living, and find us a place to stay the rest of the year.

Wolfgang was very poor. He lived on a monthly stipend of a hundred Deutsche Mark (twenty-five dollars). I gave him fifty DM a month anonymously from my stipend through Dr. Ruth to help him out. Later in the year when I needed more money to travel during spring break, I stopped these donations and felt guilty about it.

Dr. Ruth had arranged for picnics, hikes, operas, teas, visits to factories, and so forth for us when we got to Heidelberg. He had negotiated with a chemistry professor to get me lab space, which was hard to come by. I later relinquished it to a German student who needed it more than I.

I found the German tertiary educational system to be quite different from what I had known in the US. Students there don't "take" a course but rather would "hear" a lecturer. There are no exams until after about two years. When a student has heard enough lectures to feel he is ready for exams, he signs up for them. It is considered very poor for a student to hear only one lecturer on the topic in which he wants to get a degree. If he wants to get a degree in organic chemistry, for instance, he should hear the lectures of organic chemists at several universities before taking his exams. I was told that it was understood that American universities would not give credit for the courses I was taking unless I took an exam. Therefore, they were willing to make a special exam just for me to certify to the university back home that I had taken the course and succeeded. I decided not to do that because (a) the language barrier meant I would have to spend a lot of time with my nose in a book and so lose out on experiencing life in Germany, and (b) I wasn't working toward a degree back home and didn't need the credit. The Fulbright Commission emphasized that we should socialize with the German people and promote good relations with them rather than spend all our time studying.

In Heidelberg I was assigned to the Weber family, refugees from Dresden, which was eighty percent destroyed during one night of bombing in World War II. The Webers lived on the top floor of a home high above the Neckar River on Albrecht-Ueberle Strasse, where Goethe is supposed to have strolled. Dr. Weber was a lawyer with an office in Mannheim. He was proud of a deep scar across his face, the result of a student duel when he was in the university. Frau Emmy Weber was the German president of the German American Women's Club of Heidelberg. She was always smiling, very charming. Their son, Hans Christian, was twenty years old and had just returned from a tour of Egypt and Greece.

The Weber family invited Herr and Frau Schultz over to meet me that first night. They, too, were refugees from Dresden. Herr Schultz had been an officer in the German army and was in an American prison camp when he heard that Dresden had been wiped out by an Allied bombing raid. Of course he was upset because he had no idea what had happened to his wife and baby boy. Eventually he found out that the baby boy had died of starvation. His wife had walked around the countryside pleading for milk for the baby, but people hoarded what they had for fear of needing it themselves. Heartbreaking.

The Webers had bought a bottle of gin to celebrate the occasion of my arrival. I had never had anything alcoholic in my life, so it was an awkward situation. They had obviously splurged to make my first night special. I tried to sip a little.

The next day I walked with Dr. Weber to a café where I had a delicious cup of hot chocolate with a mountain of whipped cream on top. In Germany if you order a dessert they will ask *"mit oder ohne?"* (with or without?), meaning whipped cream.

There was no way to take a bath other than a sponge bath at the sink in the Weber's apartment, so I decided to go to the public baths where one could shower for very little money. Each person was given a stall with a small changing area. The sexes were not separated, so once I found myself showering next to a baritone singing opera arias. Not bad!

The newest thing in Heidelberg that year was a small grocery store patterned after the American supermarket where you take a cart, push it down aisles of products, pick out what you want, and pay at the cash register. At other grocery stores in Heidelberg, you open the door and call out *"Guten Tag"* (Good Day) even if no one is in sight. It was considered very rude to do otherwise. When a clerk appears you say what groceries you want, and that person will fetch them and present you with the bill. Dr. Weber said he didn't approve of the supermarket because it would encourage a person to buy things not really needed or not planned on.

The good manners requirement that you must say *"Guten Tag"* upon entering any establishment caught Rogene and me off guard later that year when we walked into a youth hostel and waited patiently while the hostel host talked to a group of boy scouts. The host explained the rules and added that the scouts should be polite, not like these rude girls who had just walked in without saying, *"Guten Tag."* We thought we were being polite not to interrupt. A case of culture shock!

Frau Weber was distressed to see me drink a glass of cold water. She cautioned me that water is bad for the stomach. Cold water even worse. When I told her I drank lots of cold water in Texas, she told me, "You will suffer for it when you are older."

I took lots of nice hikes through the forests around Heidelberg, both with the Webers and with German students. Every Sunday the Webers dressed up in their Sunday best to walk for hours through the forest. They said each Sunday, "This might be the last pretty Sunday before winter, so we must take advantage of it." These hikes through the forest opened a new world for me. Even today the crunch of leaves underfoot is music to my ears, and breathing the fresh, open air brings a smile to my face.

I was told that at the end of the war, when food was scarce, people lived on mushroom soup made from mushrooms found in the forest. Frau Weber made some of this soup after she had gathered mushrooms on one of our walks. It was delicious. On their walks with me, we stopped for refreshments at various cafes along the forest paths. They often asked if I was tired and wanted to go into a town and catch a bus back to Heidelberg. I wanted to say yes but didn't dare. I was supposed to be a "tough Texan," after all. I did not want to appear weak.

At the end of World War II Germany had been divided into four zones, one for each of the Allied Powers— the US, France, Great Britain, and Russia. By the time I arrived, the US, French, and British zones had been recombined to form the Federal Republic of Germany, commonly referred to as West Germany. Only the Russian Zone, known as East Germany, remained separate. One thing that seemed startling to me was the animosity of the West Germans toward the East Germans who were fleeing the Russian Zone in droves. This flight made for a terrible housing shortage, and the West Germans didn't like it a bit. West Germans were building houses like crazy, but it was not enough. The wealthier Germans in Heidelberg looked with envy at their former large homes that had been requisitioned by the American forces for their officers' living quarters. Anyone with extra rooms was required to rent them out. That is why the Webers lived on the second floor of the house they were in.

All the Fulbright students in Heidelberg had a group discussion on "Sin, Guilt, and Forgiveness," in which the treatment of the Jews by the Nazis was discussed. Dr. Ruth seemed to feel a lot of guilt about their treatment, but the Webers said they had no idea what was going on, so could feel no guilt. They did mention that they didn't really care for Jews, an interesting attitude considering that they were quite enamored of the handsome guitar-playing Fulbright boy in Heidelberg and lamented the fact they had not been chosen to be his "family." He was Jewish, but they didn't know that.

Right after the war, American Occupation forces did not allow Germans to put up gravestones or memorials for their dead, but now in 1955 they relented. They also did not allow Wagnerian operas to be performed because it was Hitler's favorite music. Now they relented on that, too, and the Webers took me to *The Flying Dutchman*. Opera is very popular in Germany, and everyone goes. The state subsidizes the ticket price, so even the poor can afford to go. The Germans all seem to love classical music, even the teenagers. Not like West Texas.

After living with the Webers for one month under the Experiment in International Living, I found a room with kitchen privileges in a garret on Kornmarkt Square just below Heidelberg Castle. The room was adjacent to my landlady's room. The heat would come on only if you put coins in a meter. These coins had to be purchased at the corner grocery store. It was an endurance test to see who would give in and go buy the coins. The landlady rightly believed that because I was a "rich" American girl, I would suffer the cold more acutely and give in first. This was true most of the time. Only when I was away for a weekend or longer did she have to pay.

When the Neckar Froze

During that winter the Neckar River froze over, a very unusual event with disastrous consequences. The town was heated by coal that came up the Neckar on barges. No barges could come up the frozen Neckar, therefore no heat. The only place in town that had heat was the US Information Library, which had an emergency generator. This library was usually sparsely populated, but suddenly it seemed the whole town needed information about America.

At that time and maybe even today Germans did not keep their homes or classrooms as warm in winter as I was used to. When I attended university classes I wore a heavy winter coat while the German students wore heavy sweaters. Then came the day when a trainload of German prisoners of war, just released from Russian Siberian POW camps, arrived in Heidelberg. The whole town went to the train station to meet them. Many of the returning prisoners immediately enrolled in university classes. Coming from Siberia, they found the lecture halls too warm and wore short-sleeve shirts to class. Apparently the body can adjust to a wide range of temperatures.

I heard Dr. Staudinger of Nobel Prize fame lecture on Biochemistry of the Hormones. I had to get to his lectures early to get a seat. In Germany, when a professor walks into the lecture hall, the students knock on the desk to welcome him. If he says something they agree with or does a chemical demonstration that turns out as he predicted, they knock on the desks. If they disagree, or a demonstration fails, or if he talks overtime, they hiss and shuffle their feet or knock under the desks.

Refugee Circle

I joined two circles of the Christian Youth Group—the Refugee Circle and the Sick Student Circle. The Sick Student Circle visited sick students. They met in my room. I had some instant coffee from the US and put the jar out for everyone to help themselves. Real coffee was very rare in Germany at that time. Most people used fake coffee made of chicory. The circle members overindulged and told me the next day, "That was powerful coffee! We didn't sleep at all last night." Later on, the group leader dropped by and said he thought I needed more heat, so he brought a large electric heater from his home for me to use, along with a tapestry to hang on the wall. It was a nice gesture, but he didn't realize the heater meant I had to buy more coins for the electric meter. I taught this group some Texas folk dances. They loved that.

The Refugee Circle went out to Rot Lager, a refugee camp near Heidelberg for East Germans fleeing Communist-controlled East Germany. We played and sang with the children there. We students rode a commuter train to get there because the Lutheran pastor who sponsored the group did not want to take us in his Mercedes. He did make an exception one day when it was pouring rain, and another day he had us over for tea at his home. He preached a caring, comforting sermon at Rot Lager, telling the people there they must not think of themselves as unworthy but to remember that God loves them and they were needed to help rebuild Germany.

The refugees at Rot Lager lived in cubicles in barracks with only a sheet hung up to separate them from the next family. The outdoor latrine was filthy. These people had been successful professionals before the war. Some sought me out to ask if I knew anyone to sponsor them to come to the US. I felt very sorry for them.

A very nice German student named Rolf Caspar made friends with the Fulbright students in Heidelberg. He was the student body president and was studying biology after having been imprisoned by the Russians at age fifteen and sentenced to ten years hard labor. He had been released just nine months before.

Frau Mordecai

Frau Mordecai invited all the Fulbrights in the Heidelberg area, along with Wolfgang, to a tea at her house. She told us what it was like at the end of World War II. The first soldiers to come to her house were Americans and very nice. Then later more Americans came, and they were not so nice, looting houses of watches, jewelry, and gold crosses. Frau Mordecai said two French prisoners of war were living at her family's house. They helped with the farming. These French soldiers went out to meet the Americans and told them the Mordecais had been very good to them so to treat them nicely. These Americans took nothing and even gave them food. Sometime later Americans who had been coming to see Frau Mordecai's daughter came to tell them to leave because the Russians were coming, but they had nowhere to go. Five times during that night there was banging on the door. Each time Frau Mordecai went to the door and pretended to be crazy and scared the Russian soldiers away.

All the Germans seemed to feel very lucky to be occupied by American forces rather than Russian. They said the Russians were cruel, dumb oafs who stole everything. The comment was made that they were too dumb to know what to steal. They stole copies of paintings as zealously as the real thing. Frau Mordecai said some of the uneducated Russians were unbelievably crude and backward. Some had never seen indoor plumbing or a telephone. They ripped the pipes and phones from the wall to take back to Russia, so they could have running water and phones in their houses, too. They stole tapestries, silver, and china, piling them all into open train cars. They accused the Mordecais of being capitalists and therefore undeserving. Frau Mordecai was sitting in her yard one day when a Russian soldier came up with his laundry, telling her to wash it. She told him there was a woman down the road who was poor and would like to have the business. The soldier said, "No, she is not a capitalist. You are. You should do my laundry!"

Wolfgang said an American soldier had taken his father's watch, saying, "You're a Nazi. You don't need a watch." Then he rolled up his sleeve to show he had six watches already. The soldiers liked to play with Wolfgang's three-year-old brother and gave him food. The rest of the family grew very thin while his baby brother was a butterball. Then the Americans left, and the Russians arrived. One asked Wolfgang to help him buy gloves. He wanted three, one for each hand and one to hold in his left hand. Another Russian was a university student and very nice.

More evidence of war was all the children obviously of African American heritage. The Germans said this would give them an advantage in the next Olympic Games.

The Protestant church I attended was government supported, as were all the churches in Germany. Everyone paid a church tax unless they were willing to sign a paper saying they were atheists. The offering was used to help the poor, and most people put 10 (2.5c) pfennig coins in the offering plate.

At Christmas time the trees were decorated with white only. White lights and white ornaments. There were large Christmas trees in every square in Heidelberg. One enchanted evening the students gathered at the castle where we were given lighted torches to march around the castle singing German Christmas carols.

Saint Nicholas came on December 6, bringing sticks to bad children and cookies and fruit to the good. In some places it is "Black Peter" who comes with St. Nicholas to bring lumps of coal to bad children. Advent wreaths with four candles were in almost every home. One candle was lighted each week until Christmas, signifying the coming light of Christ. On Christmas Day the Christ Child came to leave presents.

Chimney sweeps wore black tuxedos and top hats and carried long, large bottlebrush-type instruments to clean chimneys. Touching a chimney sweep was considered good luck.

As Christmas approached, the students at Heidelberg University grew restless. If a professor mentioned he might cancel some of his lectures near the holiday, there was loud knocking on the desks to show approval. If the professor mentioned he expected the students to attend the final lecture, there was hissing and the sliding of shoes across the floor under the desks.

Rogene
In Munich

The Fulbright program had arranged for each student to stay one month with a family before finding accommodations in our assigned university city. It turned out that families varied greatly in their capacity or desire to educate the students in the German way of life. I would say that my family was about in the middle in that range. They were struggling like many middle-class Germans to recover from the war, and money was scarce. So they had taken me in for the money they were paid by the Fulbright program. The husband kept books for a furniture store; he owned the building where they lived and was considered rather well off for that reason. But the family lived on the fourth floor because it could get more money by renting the lower floors to others. There was no elevator, and the wife had to walk down many steps to the basement to get coal to burn in the coal oven used to heat the rooms and the single water heater. There were two teenaged boys, but they did not fetch the coal. Thus it was no wonder that the family bathed in the tub only once a week, on Saturday. First, the coal was fetched from the basement by the mother, and the water heater in the tub room was fired up. When the water was hot, the tub was filled, and father took the first bath; then came the mother, who also washed the four-year-old boy, who was also part of the family. Next came the two teenage boys. By now the warm tub of water was well used. I was offered to take a bath at the end of this line, but I chose to make use of the public bath down the street. When the teenagers had the money, they also went to the public bath.

There was no refrigerator, only a small room with a window to the outside that was always open. In the winter, this was a perfectly good arrangement. In summer, you could not keep much that required consistent cold. My room had a beautiful ceramic coal oven that was heated for me every night around 5:00 p.m. The room was not heated during the rest of the day, but I was usually in class anyway. I learned that the Germans dressed in layers to stave off the cold. A man dressed in what outwardly looked to be slacks and a jacket had many layers of clothes under that outer clothing.

The little four-year-old made friends with me, and I soon realized I was having a bad influence on him. He was not allowed to drink water, and I was always drinking water. He would imitate me and start to drink water. The family fussed at him over this. Water was not good for the stomach! He could sip beer but not water. So I tried not to drink water in front of him.

One of the teenagers told me how he used to hunt for meat for the family. He tried to catch stray cats, because most of the dogs had already been eaten. This story reminded me of their suffering not so long ago.

The mother noticed my sheer stockings that I had washed and hung in my room. She was alarmed and explained to me that it was too cold in Munich for such sheer stockings. She told me to go out and buy heavier hose.

The family did not go to church. I could not tell you if they were Catholic or Protestant. As Roberta has said, the churches in Germany were supported by the federal government. Citizens had to state their religion on their tax registration form so that the proper religious group could receive those funds. I was told that very few people declared that they were agnostic, even if they wished to avoid the tax, because being agnostic was frowned upon. But my family did not go to any church. Most of the Bavarian people were Catholic, so I had to search the neighborhood for a Protestant church. I found one close by and attended it regularly. The only heat in the church was warm water run through pipes along the floor between each pew, so worshippers had to wear heavy coats in winter. After several weeks, I did not bother to jump up early on Sunday to dress, but threw my floor-length heavy coat on over my pajamas to attend church.

Because the church got most of its money from the government, it did not collect much when the offering plate was passed around. In fact, if any bills were given, as opposed to coins, the pastor would announce the fact from the pulpit. He would say something like, "We are grateful for those who contributed five one-mark notes and one ten-mark note," or whatever happened to have been given. Once the pastor preached on a sad tragedy that had occurred during the week. Some older boys had pushed a young girl into the Isar River, and she drowned. The pastor pointed out that we have to accept such tragedies, and we could expect happiness only in heaven. I thought that attitude was quite fatalistic and perhaps the result of the suffering the people had just gone through.

In October, the family took me to the famous Oktoberfest. We went into a huge tent filled to overflowing with people drinking liters of beer. Needless to say, many were drunk and singing loudly. This was quite a sight for a West Texas girl who came from a teetotaler family. Rather than insult my hosts, I drank some of the beer but mainly just sat and observed all that was going on around me. The accordion music was great, accompanied by lots of dancing. The costumes were enchanting, with the men in lederhosen and the women in dirndls.

After one month, classes at the university started. Most Fulbright students moved away from their families and into their own apartments. I was fortunate, I think, in that my family wanted me to stay because they needed the rent money. I was glad to do so. The German university system was quite different from the one in the US. The purpose in going to class was to prepare for the major exam, the Abitur, that came after two years and determined whether a student could continue to get a university degree or whether a student had to drop out. So if a lecturer was not providing a student the information needed to pass an exam, a student stopped coming to that class. There were no exams in the class—just the major exam after two years.

I had one chemistry professor who had been deafened by a chemical explosion in his lab. The students did not like him because he did not respond to their signals of dislike, such as shuffling the feet, as Roberta has noted. But this professor could not hear the shuffling and made no response. So, gradually, the size of the class dwindled until I was the only one sitting there. The professor came in, looked me in the eye, and said in German, "*Fraulein*, this will be the last lecture."

Then he proceeded to give an hour talk exactly as if he had a full room of students.

In another chemistry class the teacher was a highly respected full professor. By tradition he was allowed an *akademischer Viertle,* that is, he could arrive as much as fifteen minutes late, and the students would wait for him. Lower-ranking teachers were not given this privilege, so the students would leave if those teachers were late. This professor also had a young assistant who washed off the blackboards for him. In the cold classrooms this young man would dip his raw, reddened hands into a bucket of water and carefully wash each board. I felt sorry for him.

A third professor I remember was giving lectures on Faust. I signed up for this course because I wanted to hear the German slant on Faust. The class was in the late afternoon, when the skies were turning dark on those winter days. The lecturer was elderly and must have already taught the class for many years. He would walk into the dark room with a fist full of papers yellowed by age. He turned on a desk lamp on the podium and began to read word for word from the yellowed sheets. The lamp gave an eerie glow to his face. As I listened, I invariably dozed off. So much for Faust!

There was a famous atrium at the University of Munich where the *Geschwester Scholl* (a brother and sister named Hans and Sophie Scholl) had staged a protest against the policies of the Nazi government and were executed for their actions. I participated in a torchlight parade honoring them.

During my year in Munich I was offered the opportunity not only to hear lectures, but also to take laboratory sessions. Here again, there was a major difference in these courses from those in US universities. Because of the recent war, laboratory space in Germany was scarce, so a student had to make A grades to take the laboratory class concurrently with the lecture. Also, each student had to personally buy all the necessary laboratory equipment, right down to the weights used on the analytical balance. At the end of the term the student could sell this equipment to new students, if the student chose to. Under the circumstances, if I accepted the lab assignment, I would be preventing a German student from getting a place. I decided that I should not do that because there was no scarcity of lab space for my studies when I returned home.

For entertainment, we students often walked a few blocks from the university to an area called Schwabing. There were nightclubs there, where for one mark (a quarter), you could sit at a table and nurse a glass of wine all night while chatting with friends. For students, it was economical. In restaurants in the neighborhood, rolls were served with all meals, but you had to pay for each roll you ate. The custom was to bring a large platter of rolls to your table, and when it came time to pay, you told the waiter how many rolls you had eaten. It was sort of an honor system. Adults eating in the same restaurant were almost always suspicious of students' honesty in this matter, so one had to get used to being challenged, not by the waiter, but by others eating at the same table.

As Christmas time approached, my German family introduced me to what was a new custom to me. On the sixth of December, Father Nicholas came and brought gifts for good children. A large evergreen tree was brought into the living room and decorated with white candles out of sight of the four-year-old boy. In the evening, the candles were lit, making a spectacular show of lights. Presents for the boy were laid around the tree. Then the boy was brought into the room, and I have never seen a boy show more happiness and delight. It was a happy time and fully separated from the celebrations on December 25, when the Christ Child brought gifts for the family.

Christmas Break

For Christmas Roberta went to Munich, and from there she and Rogene went by train to St. Veit, Austria, to ski. We decided to go with a student group because students pay halfprice for the train. Neither one of us knew how to ski, but the flyer said beginners were welcome. We nearly missed the train. We got to the station early and got aboard an empty-looking car. Later a conductor stuck his head in and said this car was staying in Munich, and we should transfer to another car. We grabbed our luggage and jumped off the train only to see the front of the train moving slowly out of the station. We ran after it as another conductor yelled, "Are you running for your life or that train?" We said the train, and he told us just to wait; it would come back on another track. We did and it did, so we made it.

Austria

We were met at the train station in Austria by a large, horse-drawn sled. We loaded our luggage onto it and hopped aboard. We were taken up a mountain to a spacious hostelry where there was a roaring fire in an immense downstairs dining room. The upstairs was a vast unheated attic lined with cots topped by feather beds. It was so cold you didn't want to go up there until you were ready to hop under that big featherbed to sleep. In the morning some European girls took sponge baths at the sink with the windows wide open. We did not even consider partaking in this morning ritual. It seemed to us to be a self-inflicted torture by ice.

There were no cars in the village. Everybody used sleds or skis to get around. You'd see mother, grandmother, and children all piled on one sled to come down the mountain to the village. The village school was surrounded by skis, long and short, propped against the outside walls. The village carpenter rented skis. His workshop and the stable for his cows were on the first floor of his home. His family lived on the second floor, which was partially warmed by the animals beneath. The stable was perfectly clean, no odors.

We wore our TCU sweatshirts, and that fascinated the other students, who asked if the other universities in Texas were not Christian. We learned the rudiments of skiing pretty quickly, but not without a lot of falls. The instructors dashed over to help us get untangled whenever we ended up in a pile of skis, arms, and legs going in all directions. They often thought surely we had broken a leg, but we never did.

They said "Die Maedchen aus Texas haben gummi Beine." (Those girls from Texas have rubber legs.)

When school let out, children who looked to be as young as four years old would come over to watch us and literally ski circles around us. Some of the children took us twins on a sled ride that was scary, to say the least, mainly because we were too inexperienced to know we had to lean into the mountain around the curves. When skiing was over for the day, the hostelry had amazing steaming-hot dumpling soup ready for us to eat. I don't know if we were just hungry, but those were the best knoedel (dumplings) we had ever eaten.

The Race

One day while we were in the mountains, a race was set up for all the students. The boys had to draw names of girls to see who would be their partners. The idea was to ski down a marked trail to a hut, circle the hut, and cross the finish line together with your partner. Roberta could tell by the look of horror on the Dutch boy's face when he drew her name that he was serious about winning. She tried her best, but when the hut came in view she was going too fast to stop and whizzed right past it. She was headed for a creek and had to sit down to avoid going into it. She staggered back up to the hut. Fulbright students are supposed to foster good feelings with foreign students they meet, but she generated only disgust in that boy from Holland.

Christmas Eve

Christmas Eve was very special. Toward midnight we saw streams of light coming down the mountain as the skiers and sledders carried torches to make their way down the mountain to go to Midnight Mass at the little church on the hill. All the lights came together at the bottom of the mountain, then formed a much broader column going up the little hill to the brightly lit church. It was a beautiful sight, calm and peaceful, making us think of the meaning of Christmas, the coming of the Christ Child to bring light and hope and peace into a darkened world.

When it was time to return to our university studies, Epiphany was near, and school children from the area came into the dining room dressed as the three kings. They sang and collected coins at each table.

Later, back in Heidelberg, Roberta was invited to have tea with Mrs. Conant, wife of the US ambassador to Germany, who was very charming. *Faschings* (Mardi Gras) brought many invitations to balls. Roberta went to three, one given by the preclinical medical students, one by the German American Women's Club, and one by the English Seminar. Somewhat later in spring Roberta went to the Theologian Ball with a German student friend Thomas Dell. The ball was lovely, held in the Schwetzingen Palace, which looks like a chateau at Versailles with beautiful gardens filled with flowers and fountains. About midway through the ball all the couples promenaded through the gardens, the girls carrying brightly colored lanterns. Gorgeous! Then they sat in the gardens while a group of musicians played and a professor gave a short talk, after which they promenaded back into the ballroom and finished the dancing at 3:00 a.m. It was 5:00 a.m. before Roberta got back to Heidelberg. Her landlady gave her quite a look.

Easter in Berlin

All Fulbright students were invited to Berlin at Easter. Although located within the Russian Zone, under the four-power agreement, Berlin was an open city. It was the only place where one could freely pass from East to West, that is, you could go freely from the East sector of Berlin into the West sector of Berlin and vice versa. Only when you wanted to go into the East Zone, that is, outside the city limits of Berlin, did you have to get a special visa.

We met in Frankfurt and left for Berlin by military train. The trains ran only at night, and we were told to keep the shades drawn. We slipped a copy of the *Breckenridge American* newspaper from home out the window as we crossed through the East (Russian) Zone. That was our little effort to publicize democracy. Probably a German family used it for toilet paper. We were assigned rooms by the Free University in Berlin. We and two other girls stayed with an elderly lady who was very gracious and helpful. She told us what we should see and also what proper young ladies should not see.

Texas Willie

We went on a bus tour of the city and saw the Brandenburg Gate that separated the British and Russian sectors. We picked up Herr Kressman, the mayor of the British sector. He was called Texas Willie because he had visited Houston and been made an honorary citizen. He explained why there were so many ruins left in his sector. The Russians would not allow them to move trash through the Russian sector. Emergency exits had been built for people who lived in houses on the edge of the British sector whose front door opened onto the Russian Zone, so they could pass in and out of their homes without going into the Russian Zone.

We went to a nightclub with telephones and message-senders on each table, so one could communicate with people anywhere in the nightclub. This was long before the invention of cell phones.

Berlin Refugee Camp

The next day we went to visit the refugee camp in Berlin. Very depressing! We walked in the front door to see a large sign that read, "Beware of your purse and belongings. Thieves live here." The refugees were separated into two groups—the recognized and the unrecognized. The recognized are those who came out of necessity—to save their lives or because their means of livelihood had been taken from them. The recognized also included any youth up to the age of twenty-five. If a government committee decided you fell in this category, you became citizens of West Germany and were flown out of

Berlin to the West as soon as possible. The others—the unrecognized—were held in this camp, men separated from women. They were given 1.5 marks (1 mark=25c) spending money a week and not allowed to seek work. The government gave the camp 2.5 marks a day for each refugee. All refugees, no matter their history, had to be accepted, so there were problems with thieves who stole in the West Zone and went back to the East Zone to sell their loot.

We went to a coffee and heard several speakers—the rector and a student of the Free University, the rector of the Technical University, and a member of the Fulbright Commission. We went to see Peer Gynt at the Schiller Theater.

A Visit to the East Sector of Berlin

We were told we could visit the East sector of Berlin, but we were to go in groups of four to six, and we had to have a German guide. We went with Ron from Heidelberg and his soldier friend and two Germans, one from the West sector and one from the East. The boy from the East sector was studying history and philosophy at Humboldt University. He defended everything the Russians did and took us to a showcase apartment to show how well East Germans lived. The people there said they could not vote now, but as soon as the government had taught everyone how to vote correctly, they were sure they would get to vote.

A new law had just been passed that stated foreigners could not buy anything in the East sector unless they had a receipt showing they had exchanged West German marks for East German marks in the East sector, where the exchange rate was one-to-one. We ignored this requirement, because in the West sector the ratio was one-to-four. Nobody asked us for a receipt. In a bookstore we ran into US Ambassador James Conant and his wife.

The boy from the East sector showed us Stalin Allee, the only street in the East sector that had been decently rebuilt. Most streets there were practically empty, in contrast to West Berlin. Most stores were marked as government owned. Propaganda posters were every-where. On the schoolhouse was a sign that read, "We children are loyal to our friends of the Soviet Union." That Sunday it was an-nounced that the people of the East sector could no longer repeat the Apostles' Creed in church. Sunday afternoon we went by ourselves into the East sector to the National Gallery to see a group of paintings from Dresden—Raphael, Rubens, Van Dyke. It was scary getting on the elevated train to go back to the West sector. If you got on the ex-press train, it would take you right through the West sector into the East Zone. We were told a Fulbright student had inadvertently done this a year earlier, and it took twenty-four hours to get him out of there. We managed to get on the right train.

Passport Crisis

A crisis of momentous proportions developed when we started to leave Berlin and go back to Frankfurt, where we planned to get a train to Munich, repack, then go on to Genoa where we would get a boat to Egypt to spend the rest of our spring vacation with a group of other university students. To get back on the military train we had to show our passports, our travel orders, and the Russian translation of our travel orders. Neany had these in hand and laid them, along with a book, on the shelf above our heads on the train. She forgot them when we arrived in Frankfurt. Roberta noticed and picked them up but missed the passport, which was on the bottom. We discovered this loss not long after the train to Munich left the station. Panic! US pass-ports were very valuable. If the wrong person found it, it could be sold for several hundred dollars.

Rogene got off the train at Heidelberg, and Roberta went on to Munich to repack our luggage and go to Genoa, where she hoped to meet Rogene again.

Poor Rogene! She went to the Army Railroad Transportation Of-fice in Heidelberg. They called Frankfurt and asked them to look. They did but couldn't find her passport. Neany took the noon train back to Frankfurt. The train car in question was still in the Frankfurt station being repaired. They didn't want to let her go look for the passport because they had a surprise inspection going on. They said they would look later, but she pleaded since she knew she'd miss the boat in Genoa if she didn't find it quickly. Finally, they escorted her to the car and— lo and behold— it was right where she'd left it. She got the 4:00 p.m. train to Genoa and arrived before Roberta. Our mother later said she sensed something was terribly wrong at the time of this crisis.

After Berlin, an Easter Trip to Egypt

Our trip from Genoa to Egypt was on a Turkish freighter that had no dining room for guests, so Neany had stashed a lot of canned goods in her Munich apartment for us to take along. Roberta had to pick up all this and haul it to the boat in Genoa. She complained bitterly about the weight of the food. "Surely," she said, "you could have found something lighter."

We traveled on the boat in a dormitory-style room with other women who were also traveling steerage. In our room were thirteen girls, including two French nuns, an Italian woman and her two children, two German girls, two French girls, and two other American girls. The woman with the small children occupied the bunks near us. She had a huge sack of hard-boiled eggs, which she fed the children for the whole trip. Not a bad solution for their nutritional needs.

There was a Turkish guy on the boat who slept on the deck with his harem. He had a large knife strapped to his leg to defend his ladies. We kept our distance. The ship stopped in Naples, where we took a tour of the city.

The trip took three days. We docked at Alexandria, Egypt, to another world. Streets were bustling with people and horse-drawn carts. The harbor was filled with small sailboats filled with waving people coming out to greet our boat. We were met by the family of an Egyptian student studying in Heidelberg. He had offered to show us around Egypt in return for the price of his ticket. His family reported that his mother had died, and we told him he did not have to fulfill his end of the bargain. He said no. His mother was now happy in Paradise. We would visit her grave and go on.

We sailed down the Nile, visited the pyramids, explored the ruins of the temple of Luxor, took a ride on a camel, and admired the gold-headed statue of King Tut. The sight of sailboats on the Nile in the evening dusk was memorably beautiful.

Dinner in an Egyptian Home

When we returned to Alexandria, the Egyptian boy's family had us over for dinner. For the meal we all sat at a long table and were served heaping plates of all sorts of food we didn't recognize. There were lentils, lots of rice, and bits of lamb and vegetables. Here is where the differences in culture nearly did us in. We tried to "clean our plates" as we had been taught as children, thinking we were showing how much we liked the food. Unknown to us, the Egyptian custom is to never let a guest's plate go empty. To empty one's plate is a type of insult, indicating you have not been fed enough. A servant kept putting more food on our plates. We kept trying to eat it. The next day we were very sick. I think they must have served us garbage in an attempt to keep our plates full.

The second cultural conflict was that, in this family, only the men ate at the table. The women ate in the kitchen. So we were considered odd not only because we cleaned our plates but also because we traveled and ate with men. After the meal we visited a racetrack with a type of clubhouse left over from the British regime. The family men seemed very proud of having taken over the place and being able to enjoy it as a local clubhouse. In the discussions (all men), it became obvious that Germans were held in high esteem, the British were considered devils, and they were not too sure about Americans. Perhaps because Americans were among their guests, they did not express antagonism toward the US, but we sensed that they rather wished Germany had won in World War II.

The next day we left the group, taking a boat to Athens, where we stayed in a small hotel and ate at the YMCA. We were so sick we thought we'd die. When we did go out it was hard to find our way around because the street signs were all in Greek, and we were not familiar with the Greek alphabet.

Cyprus Uprising

The boat that brought us from Egypt to Greece was very nice. A Greek bishop was on board. He was coming because of the uprisings in connection with Cyprus. Cyprus wanted its independence, free of British control.

The people were angry at the British, so we tried to act as if we were Germans. We went to see the Acropolis. Very cold and windy. We saw Mars Hill, where Paul made his speech to the Athenians. Next day we took a bus to Daphni to see a "lovely Byzantine Church," a phrase we heard often at the tourist bureau. We took a bus to the coast to see some temples and looked at the animals along the rocky coastline.

Next day we started out walking to a museum, but the road was blocked by a funeral procession for the Archbishop of the Greek Orthodox Church. While we waited we talked to some Greek students, who said that the week before there had been a big demonstration against the British over Cyprus. One said that he thought Americans were imperialists because of the policies of John Foster Dulles and because we didn't support Greece in the UN. The procession was very impressive with priests, soldiers, sailors, heads of state, and the king himself. We passed by the British Embassy, surrounded by soldiers and barbed wire.

Orient Express

We took the Orient Express train to Belgrade and rode in a compartment with several Greek men. They thought we were German, but we told them we were Americans. Their faces fell and one said, "If you don't give us more dollars, we'll become Communists." Another man said he was on his way to study in Germany. He explained that the Greek people used to like America very much but were disappointed that the US had not taken a stand against British colonialism. He said the Greeks had fought for freedom in World War II and against Communism, so now they expected the US to be on the side of Greece in freeing their people on Cyprus. One of the other men gave us the name and address of his sister in Belgrade, along with a note telling his sister to show us Belgrade and let us stay at her house.

Later most of the Greeks got off the train. An Italian and some shepherds from the Macedonian region of Yugoslavia boarded the train and came into our compartment. The shepherds were quite merry and sang beautiful folk songs. Around suppertime they pulled out a sack and brought forth a whole roasted chicken and several loaves of bread. The Italian opened a bottle of wine. They were concerned that we had nothing to eat, so they passed chunks of bread to us and also the bottle of wine. It seemed almost as if we were having communion. The shepherds pulled off a chicken leg and gave it to Neany and a hunk of breast meat for Buzzy. They gave us each some cheese. It was a delightful time of camaraderie between people of disparate ages and cultures.

Belgrade was cold and rainy when the train arrived that night. We went across the street from the train station to a hotel. We were told the hotels were all full. This fact seemed strange since there were no cars anywhere and no people. A man appeared and said he'd take us to a travel bureau that could get us a private room. We went and they did. The next day we looked up the Greek man's sister, who took us around Belgrade. We got tickets for the opera Carmen, which turned out to be a good production.

There were signs of poverty everywhere, and the shops were practically empty. We decided to leave a day earlier than planned. The lady where we were staying nearly came unhinged when we said we'd be leaving. She said she'd be in real trouble with the police if we didn't go to some registration office and explain why we were leaving. She said it wasn't far and she'd walk with us. It was far, and we were carrying our luggage. Then she didn't want us to take a taxi to the train station. "Not far!" she said. It was far! We made it and went to the American Embassy across the street to eat a second breakfast before getting on the train to Frankfurt. On the train a Yugoslavian man was very surprised that in the US we didn't need to carry an ID or register with the police when we stayed in a city. "It must be nice to live in a democracy," he said.

We got to Frankfurt the next afternoon and joined a student group going to Spain. You might wonder why we frantically traveled around Europe so much. We honestly felt this might be our only chance to see these countries. We didn't want to waste a single day of university vacation time. We even considered buying a used moped to tour Europe. At one point we hitchhiked and got a ride with a trucker who said he thought all Americans had cars. Once when we tried to hitch a ride, a German policeman picked us up and deposited us at a bus terminal. Ah! The craziness of youth! Traveling with student groups proved to be the better alternative, both practical and cheap.

Little did Roberta know that she would eventually marry a man who loved to travel and who would take her all around the world. Nor did Rogene know she would become an internationally respected inhalation toxicologist, working with the World Health Organization, the National Institute of Health, the National Academies of Science, and the Environmental Protection Agency, and being consulted and called on to speak at conferences around the world.

Spain

We arrived in Barcelona and learned that in Spain, all buildings were locked after 8:00 p.m. The only people with keys were watchmen, who bought their positions from the government and were stationed every few blocks. If you came home after 8:00 p.m. you had to clap your hands until a watchman appeared to open the door. We arrived at 11:00 p.m. and were told to go to our assigned lodgings, drop our bags, and go to a certain restaurant. A boy went with three of us assigned to the same spot. He clapped, and a man appeared and unlocked the door. We left our luggage and tried to leave, but the door had been relocked. No amount of clapping brought our release, and we were very hungry. Dr. Schmidt, the leader of this student group, brought us sandwiches about 2:00 a.m. Those watchmen were really powerful. No boy would be able to smuggle his girlfriend into the building. Maybe we were supposed to bribe him with a tip. Who knows?

In Spain, breakfast was served between nine and eleven in the morning. Lunch was from 2:00 to 4:00 p.m., and dinner 9:00 to 11:00 p.m. The next day we saw the sights of Barcelona, the cathedral, the Columbus statue, a reconstruction of the "Santa Maria," and many beautifully landscaped parks with governesses wheeling their charges around in baby carriages.

The Spanish scenery is fascinating. As we drove through the countryside, we saw fields of olive, orange, and lemon trees, women washing their laundry on river banks and spreading it on grass to dry, people living in caves and others in mansions, brightly dressed donkeys hauling pots of dirt or people, open-air markets where beautiful fabric sold for a nickel a yard. We visited the elegant Alhambra, the palace and fortress built for the last Muslim emir in Spain. That same night we watched some very exciting gypsy dances.

Tangiers

In the morning we went to Algeciras, where we got the boat for Tangiers. It took just two hours to get to this completely new world. The city, as with cities in Egypt, is divided into a European quarter and an Arabic quarter. We bravely stayed in a hotel in the Arabic quarter, which had the advantage of a big balcony from which we could take pictures of the Arabs who otherwise would not let us take their pictures. The Arabs here dressed differently from those in Egypt. The men wore long robes with hoods that looked like feed sacks. They looked like crude monks. They wore leather pointed shoes similar to our house shoes. The women wore what looked like a sheet with an embroidered veil over their faces. They walked behind their husbands. Several women trailed behind one man, their common husband, who might be in European garb.

Independence for Spanish Morocco

The market was colorful with all sorts of flowers and varicolored spices, but it was a solid mass of milling people with plenty of thieves. One woman in our group had her pocket picked. We had planned to leave the next day for Tetouan, where we were to stay in the best hotel in Spanish Morocco, but then our leader discovered that Spain had just given Spanish Morocco independence, and the Sultan of Morocco would be coming to Tetouan and staying in that hotel. Our reservations were canceled, so we stayed in Tangiers another day. There was much celebrating in the streets, chanting and singing and such. Next day we set out in fear and trembling for a day trip to Tetouan. Trucks and buses filled with Arabs and decorated with streamers and pictures of the sultan were leaving Tangiers to go to Tetouan to see the sultan, who had not visited Tetouan in that century.

There was a French girl in our group. A French soldier in Tangiers told her she must not go to Tetouan because of the antagonism felt toward the French for colonizing Morocco, so she and a few others of our group stayed in Tangiers.

In Tetouan we got off the bus and huddled together until our leader asked a policeman if there was any danger. "Not at all," said the policeman, so off we went. The Arabic quarter was deserted, as everyone was downtown to see the sultan. A crowd collected along one street, where we saw boy scouts and some disorganized soldiers marching along. After that came a colorful regiment on horseback and one on foot with beautiful costumes and long spears. Then came the sultan riding in an open car.

We went to the hotel for lunch and left to go back to Tangiers just as the sultan was about to arrive at the hotel. The next day we took a boat back to Spain.

Back in Spain and Madrid we enjoyed El Greco paintings at the world-famous Prado Museum, the ruins of an old Roman city showing the combining of Roman and Spanish art, and the home of Saurian with his very realistic paintings—a break from all the religious art. We went to an opera that started at 10:30 p.m., in contrast to Germany, where all public performances were required to be over by 10:00 p.m.

We came back to Germany through France and stopped for lunch in Bordeaux, where we got lost getting back to the bus. It was frustrating not to speak the language. We knew the bus was parked by a river, so we finally pantomimed that and found our way back. We were twenty minutes late, but they had not left us. Whew! French cooking was great, especially the white beans and roasted chicken.

Venice

When we got to Heidelberg we still had vacation days left before university classes began anew, so we spent the night and took off for Italy. Our first stop was Venice, which was warm and sunny. The people were friendly and we loved it. We stayed in the youth hostel there, Casa San Georgio, on an island out from the main city. It was primitive but cheap and full of interesting people. In Venice we met Lee Preston Jr., who was stationed in Europe and whose mother was a friend of Aunt Bob, and his friend Whit. He had been sent on a mission to "rescue" us. Who knows what Aunt Bob had in mind! He said he knew how conservative Fulbright students were and thought we should eat one really good meal, not just spaghetti all the time. He took us to lunch and dinner but did not offer to pay, so after that we didn't have enough money to eat even spaghetti. Back to cheese and crackers. Some rescue!

We visited the Lido and then had coffee at an open-air cafe on the Piazza San Marco in front of the cathedral. Sitting in the sun watching the flags, the pigeons, and the people was enchanting. We visited the beautiful cathedral there and the Doges Palace and went on the obligatory gondola ride.

Florence and Rome

In Florence we stayed in a youth hostel that had once been a private villa. It was on a hill on the outskirts, so we had a beautiful view of the whole city. We saw a host of artistic masterpieces there—works by Raphael, Rubens, Michelangelo, Van Dyke, and many others. We visited the galleries at the Uffizi and the Pitti Palace, where we saw Raphael's Madonna and Child painted on the round end of a keg. We had studied that in grade school. The best was Michelangelo's statue of David!

We left Florence for Rome. Unfortunately, we left our umbrella on the bus, and it started raining. We had to walk around in the rain looking for a place to stay. A kind older nun came to our rescue and phoned around to find us a place, then sent a man with an umbrella to show us the way. We saw the sights of Rome, then headed back to Munich and Heidelberg and classes. We traveled by train through Brenner Pass in snow.

Protest in Heidelberg

Many of the professors did not return from their vacations in time for the beginning of classes. The students organized a protest, and Roberta went along as they marched silently through the streets of Heidelberg bearing signs that said something like, "We are here to learn. Where are our professors?" Can you imagine that happening in the US? Roberta knew that attending classes was purely optional for university students in Germany, but she hadn't realized that the professors could also decide to be tardy or even absent.

Paris

At the end of May there was another break in classes at the universities. We twins took off for Paris. We stayed in some sort of home for wandering students in the marketing section of Paris. We paid fifteen dollars for six days, including round trip transportation from Bonn, private room, hot water, showers, breakfast, and supper. What a deal! We fell in love with Paris. This area really came to life after midnight. Lots of loading and unloading of merchandise. People going home from the opera or theater stopped by small cafés to have a bowl of onion soup—and what wonderful onion soup it was! In the few days we were there we learned to use the subway, went to the opera and a ballet, saw the Eiffel Tower, the Arc de Triomphe, the Louvre, Notre Dame Cathedral, Sorbonne University, the Church of the Sacred Heart, and Moulin Rouge. One afternoon we took a train to Versailles to see the chateau and gardens there. On our last day we went to a show on the Champs-Elysées and afterward had onion soup at "The Feet of the Pig" café.

Holland and Belgium

We took a train to Cologne, Germany, where we found the youth hostel full, so we slept in an old air-raid bunker for fifty cents. We left the next morning for Holland, which impressed us as a pleasant and prosperous country. Everyone seems to ride bicycles there, and bikes have the same privileges as cars. We saw many dignified older men and women riding bikes. We saw Haarlem where the Dutch were "taking" land from the sea. We loved the Dutch breakfasts of ham, cheese, bread, butter, and jelly, a feast compared to the German coffee and roll.

In Belgium we saw Van Eyck's altar piece *The Mystic Lamb*. The colors are beautiful, and each person seems a portrait. We found Bruges to be a fascinating little medieval town. Every turn of a corner brought another pretty scene. Ladies sat in their doorways making lace in the sun alongside chocolate shops and cozy outdoor cafés. We saw a statue of the Madonna by Michelangelo in the cathedral of Notre Dame there. We went to Brussels, where we saw works by Rubens, Van Dyke, Rembrandt, and Brueghel, plus sculpture by Rousseau. Then we headed back to our universities.

Roberta

Back in Heidelberg

There was another protest demonstration by the students at the university in Heidelberg that spring. They protested crowded classrooms, too few professors, high rent for student rooms, and poor food in the student cafeteria. About a thousand students, including me, marched through the streets in protest. Rolf Caspar, student body president and a friend, made a speech and read a petition. The rector made a speech supporting the petition. It was mainly directed toward the Education Commission in Stuttgart, whose job it was to appoint professors. A picture and write-up appeared in the Communist newspaper. I was surprised at how orderly and quiet the whole protest was. Hardly a sound was heard from the crowd during the speeches.

Egon Schuler was a teacher of the deaf. He liked Americans and wanted to get to know the Fulbrighters better and to show us the good side of Germany. He suggested hikes for those of us who so desired, served as a guide, and brought along his guitar for group singing. He looked very fetching in his lederhosen. One time we hiked to the little town of Waldhilsbach, where the townspeople were having some sort of celebration with picturesque music, singing, dancing, and beer drinking. Another time I went hiking with Egon and his deaf students. They were sweet and kept bringing me blueberries and strawberries from the fields.

Neany came one weekend to see the Heidelberg *Schloss Erleuchtung*, fireworks at the castle, meant to imitate what happened years ago when the castle was under siege. The fireworks really made it sound and look like a battle was taking place, complete with moaning sounds from what might have been the injured and dying.

The Thursday before I was to leave for home on Tuesday a party was held in my room. Fulbrighters Janet, Louis, Gwen, and Jim, plus Germans Egon and Rolf were there. Louis painted a picture of our room, and since someone had sent Jim a can of maple syrup, we had pancakes and popcorn. On Friday night the Caspars, Rolf's parents, gave the Fulbrighters a farewell party.

Then on Saturday and Sunday a group of us went on a two-day hike and had a wonderful time. Fulbrighters Gwen, Louis, Janet, Jim, Dorothy, and I plus Germans Egon and Jupp took the streetcar to Neckarsteinbach where we picked up Brigitte and a guitar for Egon and started out over a mountain. The weather was perfect and the scenery beautiful. About 2:00 p.m. we came upon an inn on the mountainside, had lunch, and sat around singing. Just below us on the mountainside were a peasant woman and her two children raking the hay into bundles. The red-haired little boy was about ten and wore lederhosen. The little girl with long blond braids looked about eight. A storm was blowing up with high winds. The dark clouds, the dark green forest and meadows, the yellow hay, and the picturesque peasants created a breathtaking picture.

In the afternoon we came to a castle overlooking the Neckar. We got lost, and Egon had to run back to find the trail. When it got dark, we were nowhere near the youth hostel we meant to stay in, so we went into a little village and asked where we could stay. We were told all the inns were full, but a man with a truck said he would take us up the mountain to a hikers' hut. It was an hour's drive and the hut turned out to be full. Then the truck driver took us to a farmer he knew and, after eating at an inn nearby, we slept in his barn. Egon pitched hay over us to keep us warm. A band in the village played till 4:00 a.m. We ate breakfast and hiked on to another town for lunch.

Someone spied a bus going to Heidelberg, and most of the Americans hopped aboard. Dorothy and I and the three Germans continued on. We stopped by a little church Egon had attended as a boy. We sat under a tree and sang. We got back to Brigitte's about six in the evening. She had coffee and cake for us. I went home and collapsed. I had never been so tired in my life.

Monday Egon and Brigitte had me over for supper, and Brigitte made spazelle noodles by hand. Yummy! After a cruise on the Neckar, there was a sad parting. Next morning I made the train for Munich in the nick of time. Thomas gave me a box of candy and Egon a book of German folk songs. A fantastic farewell to Heidelberg. One of the songs we sang was *"Ich hab' mein Herz in Heidelberg verloren,"* "I lost my heart in Heidelberg." True enough! Over fifty years later I met a woman who said she grew up in Heidelberg during World War II. I began to sing that song, and she joined right in.

When Rogene got back to Munich after all our travels, she discovered that a Swedish student who wanted to learn German had moved in with the family with whom she was staying. A French student was expected within the next week. So her place was becoming quite international. She had time for many good outings with an American student named Dick. On three unusually warm days they went swimming and to the theater. There were also sailing events and a visit to see the Landshuter Fursten Hochzert of 1472. This was a very colorful reenactment of the marriage of a prince in Landshut in 1472. For a final treat, Rogene and Dick joined in as the International Students Club celebrated its thirtieth anniversary with a tour of several factories and breweries and a surprise thirty-minute flight over the city of Munich. They enjoyed an in-flight serving of cake and coffee. Then began the painful task of repacking for the trip home.

On to Southampton to Catch the Boat Home

In Munich, Roberta met Dick, Rogene's friend with whom Rogene seemed smitten. We twins left Munich the next day for Passau, where we took the boat to Vienna on the beautiful Danube River. It didn't look blue to us. We found Vienna to be a beautiful city and the people very friendly and helpful. We ate a picnic supper in a park and heard a Strauss concert played by the Vienna Philharmonic Orchestra. Afterward the city illuminated the Rat House (Court House). Very pretty. On Sunday we visited an American church where the pastor was a Czech who had married an American, now deceased, so he preached in three languages—Czech, German, and English. He took us to dinner afterward.

That afternoon we visited the palace and gardens of Schoenbrunn, where Maria Theresa and Franz Josef had lived. That night we took the train to Aachen to catch the student train to London. The ship from Ostende to Dover was so crowded we had the choice either of freezing as we sat in chairs on deck or dying of fatigue standing up inside. It was early morning before we got through customs and arrived in London.

London

We went to a ballet, to the Old Vic Theater, the Wax Museum, Westminster Abbey, Parliament, the Changing of the Guard at Buckingham Palace, the British Museum, and London Bridge. We saw Anthony Eden leaving Number 10 Downing Street. He and Dulles were conferring on the Suez Canal. We saw G. B. Shaw's *Caesar and Cleopatra* and took a bus to Oxford, where we heard a choir singing on the steps of Christ Church. We went to Stratford-upon-Avon and saw a great production of *The Merchant of Venice*. Then we went hiking in the beautiful scenery of the Lake Country.

Scotland

Next day we took a bus to Edinburgh where we had a lovely visit. The castle high on a hill gives a great view of the Firth of Forth. There is a memorial to all the Scots who died in the two world wars, right down to the horses, cows, and the rats sent down tunnels to check for poisonous gas. The Scottish word for island is *inch,* so their sailors say they are the best in the world because they can steer a boat through two inches. We saw many men in kilts.

We took a bus to Glasgow on Sunday. What a change. Cold, windy weather. Gray buildings. Few people about. We ended up in the public library and took a boat to Dublin the next day. A nice boat, but so many people were seasick we had to curl into balls on a deck chair and cover up with a coat to avoid being splashed on.

It was sunny in Dublin. The YMCA was full but sent us to a boarding school that took in tourists during school vacations—seventy cents for bed and breakfast. We took a tour of Liffy Valley and the Blessington Lakes. We saw lots of very pretty racehorse farms and the Aga Khan estate where he and Rita Hayworth honeymooned.

We left Dublin to go to Galway by bus and discovered bus fares in Ireland to be almost twice the price in England. Running short of money, we should have gone straight to the Southampton boat that would take us back to the US. But with bravado, we naïvely went on. To get to Galway we came through the most God-forsaken country you can imagine, mostly rocks and marshy peat bogs and whitewashed houses with thatched roofs. The women wore long black shawls over their heads and down to their hips. The very young and very old spoke Gaelic, and those in between a mixture of Gaelic and English. The hotel had no electricity, and the staff there were surprised that we said we'd stay two nights. They said no one ever stayed two nights. For water we had to walk a quarter mile to a stream. We walked to the nearest store and got bread, jelly, beans, and potatoes, then stopped at a farm and bought ten eggs.

Panic: Would We Miss the Boat Home?

Saturday morning we left Galway on the train to Limerick and got there at 2:30 p.m. We needed to be in Southampton the following afternoon to catch the boat home. We asked for straight-through tickets to London going via Rosslaire and Fishgard harbor. The man explained that we needed reservations. It was a bank holiday, and they were sold out. We were exhausted and hungry with very little money left. We were looking forward to the three meals a day that would be available on the boat home, but first we had to get to the boat. Scary! Neany started calling all sorts of people and places to try to get help—to no avail. Then a voice (angel? operator?) broke in on the phone and said, "A boat train leaves for Dublin at 3:45 p.m. It'll take you right to the boat. You'll be in London by 9:00 a.m. tomorrow. Will that do? You must hurry to the platform and jump on the train. You can buy tickets from the conductor." We ran and just made it! What a relief! A miracle, indeed.

When we got home we discovered that Daddy had sent the local newspaper all our letters, and they had been published. We were pleased that Daddy had been so proud of his twins but also a little worried about what we might have inadvertently revealed. Daddy had his secretary type up our letters and gave us each a copy. That explains why we can still remember our year in such detail.

4

HIGHER LEVELS OF LEARNING

Graduate School

After our exciting stay in Europe it was time to return home. We had learned there was a big, wide world outside of Texas. We had enjoyed close friendships with people far outside our usual social circles, friendships that lasted even after our return. We learned how the West Texas small town way of living and thinking was not the only acceptable way of life. We had discovered females can and do make contributions to the world, and not just as home-makers. We had choices to make, heretofore not imagined.

Back we went to the University of Texas at Austin where we had Rosilie B. Hite Graduate Fellowships waiting for us. Roberta worked under Dr. Shive in the Biochemistry Institute doing research on the vitamin biotin. Dr. Joanne Ravel directed her research. Rogene worked under Dr. Eakin, also at the Biochemistry Institute. She studied the regenerative properties of the Planaria flatworm.

We remember with special fondness two of our chemistry professors. One was Dr. Lockte, who had an interesting way of testing. At the end of a lecture, he might surprise you with a test. When you came in for the next lecture, there would be a new seating assignment. The lecture hall had arena-like seats, with the front row at floor level and each subsequent row at a slightly higher level. Dr. Lockte sat you according to your score on the last test. The lowest scores were placed on the front, ground level, so he could concentrate on you. The higher you scored, the higher up you sat. We managed to remain elevated, but were attentive in class so we could remain so.

The other professor we remember was Dr. Williams, a well-known nutritionist who had grown up in India with missionary parents. He

115

insisted that he did not want us to memorize anything. He wanted us to know and understand the material so well that we did not need to memorize it. Just before the first exam, his assistant, Dr. Lorene Rogers, came in and saved the day for most of us. She said that she knew that Dr. Williams had said not to memorize anything. She explained that what he meant was that he expected us to know the material like the back of our hands. She suggested that we had better do some memory work. Sure enough, the first test was: "Name the essential amino acids, draw their structure, and describe their properties." We have always been grateful for the thoughtfulness of Dr. Rogers's advice. She eventually became president of the University of Texas.

It was in biochemistry class that Rogene and Roberta met their future husbands. The class was huge. We sat in numbered seats. The roll checker determined who was absent by writing down the numbers on the empty seats. On the classroom door was posted the list of students and what numbered seat they were to occupy. So when a handsome young man wearing no wedding band attracted Roberta's attention, she went to the seating chart and found his name listed as Eldon Sund. She thought that was surely a Chinese name and he didn't look Chinese, so she assumed Eldon Sund had paid someone to occupy his seat, a common practice.

We sat higher up in the lecture hall, where eventually Eldon and his friend Richard Henderson migrated to sit behind us. The professor asked after class if we were bothered by these two young men; we said no. Eldon and Richard were both veterans of the Korean conflict, studying under the GI Bill. Eldon had been a navigator in the air force, and Richard had been in the Army Medical Corps. They asked if we would go with them to a ball game, and we agreed. When our dates arrived at the home where we had rented a room, we were pleasantly surprised to see they had driven an exciting car, a baby-blue Cadillac convertible. When Eldon opened the door, Roberta let Rogene get in first, so Rogene was sitting in the back seat with Richard. Then

Roberta got in the front seat with Eldon, obviously the owner of the neat car. The rest is history, as they say. We each ended up marrying the man we sat by on that first date. Much later Eldon and Richard confessed that they knew we had activity tickets and would therefore be cheap dates for all university activities. How frugal!

This is the point at which we twins went our separate ways, so each will tell the rest of her own story. Some people thought we might have problems separating from each other, but such was not the case. We were happy in our new lives with our spouses.

The twins' double wedding.

5

ROBERTA

ROBERTA AND ELDON MARRY

Eldon was indeed frugal with his money. Most of our dates were to the free movies or performances on campus. By Thanksgiving we were engaged to be married the following May. Eldon came home with me for Thanksgiving dinner in Breckenridge, causing all sorts of excitement among my parents and siblings and their families. My young niece, Miss Becky, followed us around saying, "I never saw anyone 'in love' before."

During Christmas vacation Eldon drove to North Dakota to his parents' farm to tell them he was engaged. When he tried to call me on New Year's Eve, I didn't hear the phone ring because my nine-month-old nephew, Jim Carey, was sleeping draped across my head. My sisters had gone out partying, and I was left to babysit. Eldon said his parents looked at him knowingly and seemed to believe his fiancée was out on the town.

Rogene and Richard Henderson decided to get married with us in a double ceremony. We married in Breckenridge at the First Christian Church on May 30, 1957. The church has two major aisles, which worked out well for two brides to come down the aisles to meet Daddy at the front of the church.

After a New Orleans honeymoon, Eldon and I got back to the university in time for summer classes. Eldon, Richard, and Rogene all got their PhDs. I chose motherhood and settled with a master's. I quickly got pregnant, and we were blessed on March 6, 1958, with an adorable red-headed, blue-eyed little girl. We named her Sharon Ellen. I had told Eldon that when I went into labor I would call him at his lab and sing, "This is the day they give babies away at the county fair!" Alas, when I went to Doctor Blewett for a check-up, he said my blood pressure was way too high. I had pre-eclampsia, a condition that can be fatal to both mother and fetus. I was told to go immediately to St. David's hospital for a C-section, so I made a tearful phone call rather than a singing one. Dr. Blewett's comment was, "I am so pleased to have come out of this with a live mother and a live baby." I had not realized just how serious the situation had been. The nurse came in to talk to me about breastfeeding, and Dr. Blewett said, "Absolutely not!" Another plan foiled. I learned that life does not always go the way you plan!

Sharon was beautiful and very bright. She wanted to be held, and cried when I put her in the crib. Eldon and I had many arguments as to whether it was best to let her cry or to pick her up. She loved to go for walks in her stroller. No matter what subterfuge I tried, when I turned to go back toward home, she knew and objected vigorously. When Sharon was a year old we went out to eat at a restaurant, a very rare occasion since we were living on a student stipend and Eldon's Air Force Reserve pay. As Sharon sat in a high chair, we gave her a cracker to munch. She crumbled it up, dropping some on the floor. A waiter dashed over and swept up the crumbs. That amused Sharon. She chuckled and kept throwing crumbs on the floor and looking at the waiter to see if he would come again. He did. After several repeats we took the crackers away, much to baby Sharon's distress.

Eldon got a job offer from DuPont in Wilmington, Delaware. He wanted to teach, but the industrial research salaries beckoned. By then we were expecting our second child.

Confusion at the Elevator

Rogene had her first child, a boy, about nine months after Sharon was born. I had passed my maternity clothes on to her, so now she passed them back to me. All this was confusing to Dr. Koike, a Japanese scientist who worked on the second floor of the Biochem Institute.

Sharon, 1963

Elizabeth, 1964

He was rather shy and almost never spoke to anyone. Rogene worked for Dr. Eakin on the first floor of the institute, and I worked for Dr. Shive on the second floor. One day as I was waiting at the second floor elevator, very pregnant with my second child, Dr. Koike came up to me and said, "Excuse me. I hope you do not find me rude, but it seems to me that you have been pregnant for three years. When is that baby ever going to come?"

Elizabeth was born November 16, 1959, at St. David's Hospital in Austin by C-section. As soon as I could travel, Eldon drove us to Breckenridge to stay with my parents while he drove on to Wilmington to find a home for us there. Elizabeth was beautiful, with brown hair and big brown eyes and a very calm disposition, always smiling.

New Castle, Delaware

We lived in an apartment in New Castle, Delaware, near the Delaware Memorial Bridge, which Eldon crossed every workday to get to the DuPont Chambers Works. At the neighborhood grocery store Sharon amused the clerk by singing "Jingum Bells" in a loud voice as she sat in the grocery cart. I was amazed at how different the items in the grocery store were from what we had in Texas. Something called scrapple looked inedible to me. And they pronounced pecans with the accent on the first syllable and the *a* as a hard *a*.

Lost Baby

We had no washing machine in the apartment, so I had to drive to a laundromat. Two babies meant a lot of washing, although I did get a diaper service. I used only cloth diapers, because Sharon had very sensitive skin. One day I drove to the laundromat with Sharon in the back seat and baby Elizabeth wrapped in blankets in the front seat. Children's car seats had not yet been invented. When we got to the laundromat, I carried the dirty clothes inside with Sharon holding on to my skirt. I returned to pick up baby Elizabeth, but to my horror, the bundle of blankets was empty. I panicked! Where was my baby Elizabeth? Moments later I found her sleeping soundly in the space between the front seat and the car door. She must have slid out of the blanket as I turned a curve. Was I ever glad to find her!

Newark, Delaware

Right away we started looking for a house to buy. We found the house we wanted in Newark, Delaware, a university town with beautiful housing developments. We contracted to build a house in Nottingham Green through the affable agent Mr. Rinard and his able assistant Mrs. Machuga. The house was two stories with four bedrooms and a bath upstairs and a living room, dining room, kitchen, den, powder room, laundry, and garage downstairs. We didn't have much furniture, just one bedroom suite, a crib, and a kitchenette set. Sharon had to sleep in a playpen until we could buy her a bedroom suite. Going to auctions and looking for bargains, we eventually got the house furnished. The living room was the last to get furnished, so we used it as a playroom. To my dismay I walked into the living room one day to find Sharon drawing pictures on the walls with her crayons. I have to laugh about it now, but it seemed tragic at the time. The house had a full basement, which was also a nice play area. The children would eventually ride their tricycles there when it rained. Years later we learned that Sharon developed a fear of the crawl space that branched off the basement under the playroom. She had nightmares about it, but we were clueless. When the children watched Captain Kangaroo on television, Sharon always left the room when the dancing bear came on. I thought it was because that was just too silly for our intelligent Sharon but later realized she was frightened. I made the mistake of thinking my children would have the same fearlessly adventurous spirit I had as a child. Sharon turned out to be easily frightened, suffering from terrors unknown to me.

Soon after we moved in, I had put the girls to bed and gone upstairs to go to bed myself. I was shocked to find Eldon lying perfectly still, face down on the floor next to the bed. I screamed! I thought he was dead—had had a heart attack or something. It turned out that he was listening to the crunching of borers that lived in the flooring. The builder had to replace a good bit of the lumber used in the bedroom flooring.

We had nice neighbors. Shortly after our arrival, Marion Lynch came running up to me as I stood in the front yard, introducing herself. She exclaimed, "I'm so excited. I just saw a Rufous-sided Towhee." I confessed I didn't know what a Rufous-sided Towhee was and hoped it wasn't some dangerous animal. She laughed and said it was a bird about the size of a robin. Thus Marion introduced me to the world of bird watching and on to squirrel watching, rabbit watching, and whatever-inhabited-our-backyard watching—a great gift for which I am grateful. What a boost it is to see the first goldfinches at my bird feeder in late winter—a sure sign that spring is on its way.

We became good friends with Marion, a librarian at the University of Delaware, and her husband Jerry, who worked for DuPont. Jerry was a tall, husky guy and the seamstress in their house. He sewed just about all Marion's clothes, her dresses, swimsuits, winter coats, and even the drapes that hung at the windows. Marion was a diminutive young lady who loved to work in the garden. She was a birdwatcher and looked after the flower beds and landscaping. They had a son and a daughter, Michael and Jane, a little older than our children.

After a visit to Longwood Gardens in Pennsylvania to see the colorful fountain display, Jane told our children her father had explained to her how the fountains worked. "There are little men under the earth who toss buckets of water up into the air," she explained. Jerry was a teaser.

If I needed a babysitter in an emergency, Marion was always willing. Their neighborhood parties were a delight.

A turning point in my life came after we settled into our new home. I felt I should make use of my education and applied at the University of Delaware to work in the research labs there. A very helpful professor offered me a job. He had even found a woman to come to my home to look after Sharon and Elizabeth while I was at work. I was ready to accept when I realized I was pregnant again. Somehow I felt I shouldn't inflict a pregnant employee on this nice man. Also, I wanted to be home to see my children grow and develop, to hear their cute and clever sayings, to observe their personalities evolve. I turned down the job.

Mean Dog

Many people in the neighborhood worked at DuPont Chambers Works, so a carpool was formed. There was a mean dog in the neighborhood, causing men in the carpool to sprint to the car to avoid being bitten. One day when I had the girls out in the front yard for some fresh air, here came this dog. Baby Elizabeth was wrapped in blankets in a little wagon; the dog ran toward her. I ran to her screaming. The dog growled and snapped at me. I grabbed the baby and made it back into the house where Sharon had fled. I called the police, who came right over. The policeman came to the door and explained that the dog was harmless, just friendly. Then the dog attacked him! That was the last anyone saw of that dog. Several neighbors thanked me profusely.

Sore Toe

Our mailbox was located next to the front door. The mail came early in the day when I was usually still in my nightgown. I had worked out a method to get the mail without actually stepping on the front porch, which was cold to my bare feet. I would open the door and, holding onto the door jamb, swing around, grab the mail, and swing back, balancing on one foot. This worked fine until one November day. I had decorated the front porch with a pumpkin, and when I made my swing for the mail, my big toe careened into the pumpkin causing a painful injury. Lots of pumpkin ended up under my toenail. I cleaned it up as best I could, but infection set in. The toe swelled, but I limped on. When I went to the grocery store to buy the Thanksgiving turkey, I picked up a frozen, twenty-pound turkey. It slipped out of my hands and landed right on my sore toe. I screamed bloody murder. Everyone in the store looked at me and then turned away. When I went to the doctor, he laughed and laughed. He cleaned a lot more pumpkin out from under my toenail and said the toe was probably broken but there is nothing to do for a broken toe.

JFK Is Shot

Sharon went to kindergarten at St. Paul's Lutheran Church. I remember the day John F. Kennedy was shot. It was Sharon's turn to bring cookies to the kindergarten class that day. She and I had baked and decorated the cookies the night before. Sharon was very proud of those cookies. On the way to pick her up that day, I heard on the car radio that Kennedy had been shot. When I reached the kindergarten I found both Sharon and her teacher in tears, the teacher because Kennedy had been shot, and Sharon because her teacher had not passed out those cookies but instead fed them to the birds. She thought the children shouldn't be eating cookies when the President had been shot.

April Fool's!

I was big on having holiday traditions. I wanted the children to remember these when they were older. Sometimes I got carried away. One April Fool's Day I scared Sharon by saying the school bus had come early and was waiting for her. She came flying down the stairs, and I said "April Fool's." She was a very conscientious first grader and did not appreciate the humor at all. That same year I called Eldon at work and told him the pine tree had fallen onto the house and made a hole in the ceiling; pause: "April Fool's!" He didn't appreciate that either, which ended my traditional April Fool's jokes.

Sharon enjoyed riding the school bus with her friend, Mark Padrotti, who lived up the street. She loved school, where all went well except for the one day that I got a phone call from the school nurse. Sharon had had an accident. My heart fell. I asked how badly she was hurt. The nurse said, "Oh, not that kind of accident. She just wet her pants, and we need for you to bring her fresh ones."

Elizabeth, the Soft-spoken Designer

The J. R. Downes Elementary school was soon built near us, so Sharon could walk to school her second year. She loved school and excelled in her studies. Sharon had always talked so softly we were worried until she went to school. She came home speaking very loudly, so no more worries. When Elizabeth started school, we expected the same would happen, but she continued being soft-spoken. Elizabeth loved playing with her dolls and built lovely little doll houses out of boxes, complete with furniture she designed herself. At the time I wished we could afford to buy her a doll house, but now I think it's nice she had the opportunity and determination to build her own.

Phillip Arrives

Phillip arrived on March 2nd, 1961. Dr. Blewett had delivered Sharon and Elizabeth in Austin by C-section. I asked him to recommend an obstetrician in the Wilmington, Delaware, area and he did. By the time Phillip was on the way, I thought it would be so much easier to see an obstetrician in Newark where we lived rather than drive into Wilmington. This doctor wanted to take Phillip at the end of February, whereas I thought the first of March would be better because then he'd be larger and healthier. Not a good idea. Pregnant women don't always think straight. I don't remember the doctor's name, but he didn't stitch me up after the Caesarian birth. He just put clamps on, which left a hideous scar.

Phillip, 1964

Phillip was a big baby all right, over nine pounds. He surprised us by how quickly he went from baby formula to whole milk. He grew fast and walked at an early age. He loved to use his toy screwdriver to work on screws around the house. One morning when I came into the kitchen and leaned against the stove, its entire front fell off. Phillip had unscrewed everything. He would also crawl around unscrewing screws that held the heater ducts to the wall.

On The Roof in Diapers

Phillip scared the daylights out of us one day. Eldon had put up a ladder to reach the second story roof of our house. Suddenly we saw Phillip in diapers at the top of the ladder. When we screamed for him to stop, he giggled and jumped onto the slanted roof. He was fearless and loved to be chased. I just knew he would slip and fall off the roof if we came up after him. Somehow Eldon managed to get him down. Phillip loved anything mechanical and said he wanted to be a mommy when he grew up because mommies got to use mixers. He never got to see what his daddy did at work. DuPont was very secretive and would not let family visit their employees' offices or labs.

Phillip loved to ride up and down the sidewalk in front of our house in his toy pedal car. One day the doorbell rang, and I found a very angry lady on my front porch. She said she couldn't drive down the street because this child was blocking the way. She pointed to Phillip, who was in the middle of the street in his pedal car. Phillip looked very stern and kept repeating, "My street!" How embarrassing! He was just two years old. We had a talk about staying out of the street and that the street belonged to everybody.

The University of Delaware had a very good preschool program that was hard to get into. The students were from two to five years old. After much effort, Sharon, Elizabeth, and Phillip were all accepted. They loved it. The carpool for that preschool provided some interesting conversations. One little girl bragged about some toy she had, and Phillip announced that he had something that girls didn't have, and he would show her. I put the quietus on that. Another little boy told his sister that he was going to bury her in the ground, and she would not come up until spring.

Sharon's Safety Poster

Sharon entered the DuPont Safety Poster Contest and won for her age group. We got to go to a ceremony to see her get the award. Her slogan was "Matches are for lots of things that older people do. So I tell my sister they're not for me or you." We bought her a new dress for the occasion and were very proud.

Our backyard became a gathering place for neighborhood children. Jane Lynch, the daughter of Marion and Jerry Lynch, often came over to play. Many times a flock of nine Catholic siblings would descend upon us. Their mother said that she had done her duty having all those kids, and the rest was up to God. Although their parents had plenty of money, there was not a single swing set, sandbox, playhouse, or toy in their yard, hence their migration into our yard.

Nancy was born September 12, 1962. Phillip had requested a baby brother, but that was not to be. This time I used the obstetrician recommended by Dr. Blewett, who did a splendid job. Since I had an epidural anesthetic I could hear what was going on. I heard the doctor and his assistants gasp when the incision was made. I thought something was horribly wrong. Then the doctor asked the nurse to go get any medical students hanging around to come see this rare phenomenon. I thought the baby had two heads or something. It turned out that the wall of the uterus was about two cells thick, and the baby could be clearly seen through the paper-thin uterine wall. If we had delayed the birth, it might have been fatal for the baby and me. Good thing I had also asked for a tubal ligation.

Naming Nancy

We discussed with her siblings what we should name our new daughter. If she had been a boy we were going to name him Andrew, but we hadn't really decided on a girl's name. Elizabeth said she

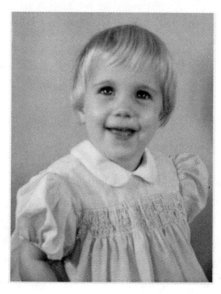

Nancy, 1964

wanted her to be named Susan. We finally decided on Nancy Annemarie, the Annemarie after the Danish princess. Because Eldon's father had been born in Denmark, he took great pride in anything Danish. I took a little longer recovering from this last C-section and so missed several Sundays at church. When I returned to church everyone wanted to know how little Susan was doing. It seems that Elizabeth had told anyone inquiring that the new baby was named Susan.

Snow Driving

Nancy returned to the hospital when she was eighteen months old. When I was baking cookies in the kitchen, Nancy had managed to reach up on tiptoes and get one off the counter. I said she wasn't to have one until she had eaten her supper, and she screamed her defiance. The screaming caused a nut fragment from the purloined cookie to lodge in her bronchial tube. She coughed and coughed but could not get it up. After several hours of her coughing I called the pediatrician, who asked me to take her to the hospital where they saw bubbles in her lung, so we spent the night there. A specialist was to insert a tube to suck it out in the morning, but fortunately it dissolved during the night. I was told not to let her have anything to eat or drink during the night. A nurse who came to check on her was drinking a coke. Nancy went into hysterics wanting that coke. I could have killed that nurse.

The next morning we woke up to heavy snow. Fortunately Marion Lynch was keeping the three older children. The doctor came and dismissed Nancy, who was very sleepy from the sedation they had given her. I carried her to the car and started down the road. Having grown up in Texas, I was not accustomed to driving in snow. I went very slowly. I was driving down a six-lane expressway with almost no fellow drivers. Very soon I could not see where the road was. I had to judge by the fence posts on either side. I was so scared. It is a wonder we did not end up in the ditch. There weren't even any tracks to follow and no cell phones to call for help. Oh, woe! It is a miracle we got home all right.

We met George and Estelle Null at St. Paul's Lutheran Church. He worked for DuPont, and she was a nurse at the University of Delaware. Their children were very close in age to ours, and they lived on a farm just over the state line in Pennsylvania. Our children loved to visit them at the farm. We would take turns having all the children at our house one weekend, and another time they would all stay at the Nulls. We traded having Thanksgiving dinners as well. Sharon played with Kathy, Elizabeth with Michael, and Phillip with Daniel. Samuel wasn't born until later, so our youngest child, Nancy, hung around with anyone who would accept her.

Phillip's Waterfall

Phillip showed evidence of engineering potential. I had lost sight of Phillip and Nancy one day and looked around the house for them, to no avail. Then I heard a splashing sound coming from the basement. I opened the basement door and discovered Nancy and Phillip sitting on the top basement stair, like a couple of tourists, admiring the waterfall coming through the window at the top of the basement. Phillip had knocked a hole in the window with his toy hammer and stuck the garden hose in it to create a waterfall. With a big smile he proudly proclaimed, "Look, Mom! I made a waterfall for Nancy."

Nottingham Green had a very nice swimming pool where I enjoyed taking the children. Since I had taught swimming for the Red Cross in my younger days, I thought I could teach my children as well. That worked out pretty well except for Phillip. He always wanted to do things for himself. I gave up and Phillip, who is a sinker, taught himself to swim. He swam about six inches below the surface of the water, coming up for air when needed.

We enjoyed going camping with the children, first in a borrowed tent and later in a tent trailer. Sharon and Phillip both loved to make a fire, and we toasted many a marshmallow to make "some mores." Elizabeth was a reluctant camper. She would look longingly at any motels we passed on the way to a campground and say, "That looks like a nice place to stay."

Sharon's Hamster

Sharon asked Santa for a hamster one Christmas. We placed one in a cage under the tree. It was happily going around on the exercise wheel when we went to bed. Next morning it was lying on its back with four feet in the air, looking very dead. I was horrified. How awful it would be if Sharon found that Santa had left her a dead hamster! I tried a hamster version of CPR, that is, I blew in its face and massaged its body. Amazingly, it worked!

It turned out to be a very clever hamster. It figured out how to open its cage door, fill its cheeks with food, and take up residence under the big bookcase in the playroom. When it ran out of food, it would run up the stairs during the night to Sharon's bedroom and run across her face until she woke up. She would put it back in its cage and refill its food container. Before long the story would repeat itself. It took us awhile to find his "home away from home" under the bookcase.

Farewall to DuPont

After seven years of industrial research, Eldon grew weary of working on projects assigned to him that he knew would not be successful. He had no say-so in which projects he was assigned, but his salary was determined by their success. He decided to find a teaching job after all, if I would agree to teach as well. Of course, I agreed.

Sharon was in third grade and Elizabeth in first at John R. Downes Elementary School. Both were doing very well in school. Sharon was a star runner on the track team.

Now we had to sell the house and move to wherever Eldon landed a job. Unfortunately, the economy was down, and it was hard for potential buyers to get a loan. Eldon had to move without us to Ada, Ohio, where he taught at Ohio Northern University. The children and I stayed in Delaware trying to sell the house.

Phillip's Boat

Phillip was just a little tyke but very determined. We would take walks that took us by a small creek. One day we were in a toy store where Phillip saw a little plastic boat with a paddle. He decided he needed that boat to go out on that creek. I told him no, but without his daddy there to reinforce me, it seemed to fall on deaf ears. Phillip used his favorite plea, "My needs it!" over and over. After much agitation every day, every hour, I decided to let him have it. Wow! He loved that boat and took Nancy and Elizabeth for many rides in it. The creek was very shallow, so the ride really wasn't dangerous.

Scary Midnight Rendezvous

At Christmas, Eldon got a ride to a stop on the Pennsylvania Turnpike, and I was to drive the station wagon with the four sleeping children up to meet him there in the middle of the night. The station wagon had been giving us problems and had to have oil put in frequently. I didn't think to take oil along and lived to regret it. Around midnight in the dark woods of Pennsylvania the car began to make noises that I knew meant it needed oil. It was very cold and snowy. If the car conked out in the middle of this forest, we would all freeze to death! There were no cell phones to rescue me then. How could I be so stupid as to forget to take an extra can of oil? I spotted a village down the road with one light on. I coasted down the hill to that light, which turned out to be in a bar. I got out and went in. All heads turned to look at me and then turned away. They were all black. I spoke loudly of my problem and explained I had four sleeping children in my car, and they would freeze to death if no one helped me. Silence. I contemplated bringing the children into the bar. Then one man came to me and said he would take me to the home of the town's car mechanic, but I would have to wake him myself as he would likely be shot if he did it. He drove me to this house and I knocked and yelled. A very grumpy man came and finally agreed to get me the oil so we could be on our way.

A very terrifying experience! The man who helped me was an angel. No doubt about it! We did get to the turnpike, where Eldon awaited us.

I kept thinking if I painted the rooms just right, the house would sell, so I did a lot of painting, and the children knew if I said a prospect was coming, they were to hastily put away their toys and clean up the playroom. After almost a year, the interest rates went down and the house sold immediately. This delay in selling the house was fortunate, in a way, because Eldon had decided Ohio Northern was not a good fit for him, and he had accepted an offer from Midwestern State University in Wichita Falls, Texas. We packed up our belongings and put them in the moving van for the trip to Texas. While the van made its way to Texas, we took off with our tent trailer to the Montreal World's Fair.

We camped near the fair, where Elizabeth came down with the mumps the first day. We had no home to go back to, so we loaded her up with aspirin and wheeled her in a stroller through the fair, poor thing. The moving company told us it'd be two weeks before they got our load to Texas, so we made a stop to visit Eldon's parents on the way. They had just moved to a farm in Wisconsin.

Back to Texas, Where I Become a Teacher

We arrived at my parents' home in Breckenridge, Texas, shortly before school was to start. We left the children with Mom and Dad and drove to Wichita Falls to buy a house. We found one rather quickly, at 4903 Marsha Lane. It wasn't exactly what I wanted, but it had the advantage of being within walking distance of a highly recommended elementary school and in bicycling distance of MSU, where Eldon would be working. We added a bedroom to the house later and prettied up the back yard with a fishpond and pine trees.

Claustrophobia

While we visited in Breckenridge, Daddy took us out to see the new Lake Hubbard, which had recently been formed by the damming of Hubbard Creek. He drove us there in one of his used cars, which he parked nose-in to the edge of the lake. When it was time to leave, he couldn't get the car to go in reverse. He told me that this had happened before and could be fixed by crawling under the car and reattaching a bolt that had come loose. Since the car was parked in a rut, it was decided that I was the only one skinny enough to crawl under it. This was the moment I discovered that I am extremely claustrophobic— maybe the result of beginning life in an overcrowded womb. Who knows! I had to fight panic, but I got it done.

Midwestern State University

We visited Midwestern State University and toured the newly built science building. The biology professor we met in the hall cautioned Eldon not to expect as much of the students at MSU as one might at eastern universities. He said they were just not as well prepared and not as capable. This observation insulted me, as I had grown up in the area, but I said nothing. After Eldon taught a rigorous organic chemistry course, the premed students at MSU were so well prepared they were eagerly accepted by the medical schools to which they applied. One student who went to Southwestern Medical School in Dallas, Texas, reported back that one of the professors there had remarked to an Ivy League graduate that Midwestern State University students could run circles around him.

No PE or *Weekly Reader*

We enrolled Sharon, Elizabeth, and Phillip in Fain Elementary School and Nancy in the Methodist preschool. Sharon was disappointed that there was no track team for her. Indeed, no PE whatsoever. The principal told me, "There is no need for exercise programs. Since the weather is consistently nice here, the students can exercise at home."

At Downes Elementary in Delaware, the children looked forward to the *Weekly Reader* and the little paperback books they could buy through that program. We were told it was not available at Fain. When I talked to the assistant superintendent in Wichita Falls about this, he told me they were afraid of what books might be bought. He said, "If it were up to me, the children would not be allowed to read any book but the Bible." Deeply religious as I was, I still cringed.

TCU to the Rescue

I enrolled in education classes at MSU, so I could get a teacher's certificate and help support the family. I had to get TCU to certify that I was qualified to teach science and math. I asked the MSU biology professor we had met that first day if he would certify me in science and showed him my transcripts from TCU and UT. He said no, I would have to take his biology course first. He must have been hard up for students.

After classes one day I stopped to pick up Nancy at her preschool. Her teacher told me they were being very careful not to give Nancy chocolate, since she had told them she was allergic to it. That was a surprise! It turned out there was a boy in her class who was allergic to chocolate, so every day he got a "special" drink when the others got chocolate milk, ditto on desserts. Nancy just wanted to be "special," too.

We joined the Fain Swimming Pool Association and spent many summer days there. The children could ride their bicycles to the pool. One day Nancy came home without her bike. We didn't discover this until the next day. When we asked Nancy about it, she explained that this boy she had a crush on had asked to walk her home, and she didn't want to admit to having a bike for transportation. Sadly, when we went to retrieve it, the bike was gone.

Practice Teaching

To obtain a teacher's certificate I had to "practice teach" the spring semester. I was assigned to the morning classes of a chemistry teacher at Wichita Falls High School, otherwise known as "Old High." The teacher looked on this as a great good fortune for her. She never entered the classroom while I was there but sat in a little room nearby in a recliner. She advised me, "If a student asks a question you can't answer, assign that student to investigate the answer and write a four-page theme on it. That will keep the students from asking questions."

Teaching German

The next year, 1969, much to my surprise, I was hired to teach German. I was to be a "traveling teacher." I taught classes at Hirschi

High School in the morning, then drove to Wichita Falls High in the afternoon. I was given an extra travel period to do this and so had four classes instead of the usual five—a nice situation, I thought. I could do all sorts of errands during the travel time.

There was quite a difference between the two schools. At Hirschi I was treated with respect and appreciation. The students came from essentially mid- to lower-income families. They were amazed that I would spend extra time with them for German Club without being paid extra.

It was the year of integration and therefore a little tense at times. One day a group of black students came to my classroom door and said they wanted to see a certain student. They were going to *"git"* him, they said, as they began to shove their way into the room. A black student in my class named Maynard Hawkins jumped up and came to stand by me. He told those guys in no uncertain terms that they were to back off and not return. The amazing thing to me was that Maynard, who spoke perfect "white" English, could switch into "black" English so smoothly. Maynard later joined the city police force and performed equally well with them. He was my hero.

At Wichita Falls High School I had mainly upper-income students. They were polite to me, but it was as if I were a servant. They let me know what was expected of me, particularly when it came to giving out grades.

Bus Driver's License

I wanted to take the students in my German classes to compete in the German Days Meet at Austin College, some ninety miles distant. When I put in my request for the school van to take us there, I was told to get my bus driver's license so I could drive the van myself. When I called the license bureau, I was told to come with a bus to be tested. I went to the bus barn where I was directed to a huge, long bus and told to take that. I had never driven a bus and was scared beyond words. It did have automatic shift and power brakes. I had to drive it down the expressway to get to the driver's license bureau. Somehow I made it and passed. Then I was allowed to drive my students in the much smaller van.

Soccer Coach

At the German Days Meet some of the football boys from Hirschi High School asked to enter the soccer tournament. They assured me they knew how to play soccer and only needed me to sign on as their coach. Big mistake! The referees were constantly blowing their whistles and screaming "off sides." I got a stern lecture and my team was disqualified.

We won some prizes. One student who didn't do well on written tests came home with a first-place blue ribbon for his pronunciation. Until then I hadn't realized his grandmother was German, and they conversed in German at home.

Snorkeling

Eldon and I decided to take a second honeymoon to the Virgin Islands and Puerto Rico. We enrolled Sharon, Phillip, and Elizabeth in a Concordia College Summer German Foreign Language Camp in Moorhead, Minnesota. Nancy was too young, so she stayed with Eldon's parents on their farm in Milltown, Wisconsin, while we went off to learn to snorkel at St. John's in the Virgin Islands. Snorkeling turned out to be a terrifying experience. After a brief introduction to snorkeling, we were taken out on a windy day and dropped into the ocean. The waves were so high that we couldn't see the boat that brought us out. I lost my lunch, that is, I fed the fish and thought I was going to die. A boat came up and someone yelled at me, asking if I knew where my husband was. Apparently they were watching me and lost him. Now I was really terrified! It turned out that Eldon had followed another group of snorkelers instead of our group. We survived to learn to snorkel in better weather.

A footnote to that snorkeling adventure was the horrible sunburn I acquired. I was nauseated and unable to sleep that night. It was almost certainly the cause of the melanoma that appeared on my left cheek months later.

Canoe Boundary Waters

Another summer we took all the children on a camping trip to the Canadian Canoe Boundary Waters. We rented two canoes and necessary equipment and camped on our own little island. We had been told that we needed to camp on this particular island because we wouldn't have to worry about bears there. It was lots of fun but also hard work when we paddled against the wind. We teased Eldon and Phillip when we saw them paddling as hard as they could but going backwards around a bend. Some Boy Scouts camped on an island near us, and we noticed they tied their canoes together and were pulled by a little motor on the back of the lead canoe. No fair!

Barbara Schuler, the daughter of Egon Schuler from Heidelberg, visited us one summer. We went to the Grand Canyon. The air conditioner in the car went out on the way home, causing us all to suffer except for Egon's daughter, who said Germans were too tough to be bothered by one-hundred-degree heat. Our daughter Sharon visited Egon's family in Germany one summer and had a good experience.

Fervent Effectual Prayer

Nancy was now in first grade at St. Paul's Lutheran School. With a September birthday, she was not eligible to go to public school. She was required to memorize a Bible verse every week, which was hard for her. Her best friend memorized easily, and Nancy wanted badly to do the same. One week the Bible verse was "The fervent effectual prayer of a righteous man availeth much." The whole family went around saying it for the entire week to try to help Nancy. Alas! It didn't work.

A doctor (she) and a dentist (he) lived across the street from us, and their son, Paul, loved to come over to play at our house. Sharon had a red-headed girlfriend, Sue Moss, who lived nearby. When we first walked around the neighborhood trying to determine which route would be best for the children to walk to school, we were stopped several times by people greeting Sharon and saying, "Hi, Sue—are these your relatives visiting?" We hadn't yet met Sue but knew she must look a lot like Sharon.

Visit to Emergency Room

The house we bought had a playhouse in the backyard, built on stilts made of oilfield pipes, sort of like a tree house without the tree. The children loved it and even spent the night up there at times. One day Phillip and Nancy played a trick on me. Phillip held Nancy by her legs out the playhouse window and then screamed that Nancy needed help. I ran to help and tripped over the tetherball pole, which was lying on its side. My chin landed on the wooden edge of the sand box located underneath the playhouse. When I got up I couldn't close my mouth, and blood was pouring down my front. Eldon was off running errands, and I couldn't speak. I got Sharon into the car with me and left Elizabeth to look after Nancy and Phillip. I drove to the emergency room where Sharon registered me. They and I thought my jaw was broken, but x-rays showed it wasn't. My lower teeth were embedded in the skin of my lower jaw, and there was a gash on the outside along my jaw. No plastic surgeon was available to do a pretty job, so the emergency-room doctor did his best to sew me up. He called Sharon in to watch him sew and even asked if she would like to take a stitch. Sharon grew faint, and they had to put her on a gurney next to me. I still have an odd-looking jaw.

Melanoma

After a few years of teaching I noticed a mole on my cheek. It looked funny, so at the urging of my parents, I went to the local skin specialist. He assured me it was nothing, but as time went by, it kept growing. When it started to bleed spontaneously, I went back to the doctor. He said it was nothing, but he would take it off and have it biopsied if it bothered me. The next Sunday night I got a call from the doctor who said the biopsy showed melanoma, and I should consult another doctor immediately. Eldon took me to M. D. Anderson Cancer Hospital in Houston.

We went on a Wednesday, which was Head and Neck Day at the Cancer Clinic. Walking through the front door was like entering another world. Little children dressed in white gowns making them look like angels pushed IV poles before them as they strolled through the lobby. Other patients circled about in wheelchairs. All had red lines drawn on hairless heads and faces. I went to the registration desk where they asked, "Name? Age? Insurance? Body to be sent where?"

"I'd like to keep it myself, thank you." I replied.

"Sorry, we have to ask."

Now I was feeling very scared. I definitely did not want to join this crowd of obviously very ill people with the ubiquitous red lines. Would I come out looking like them? Some spoke to each other in guttural gasps. Would I speak like that? What would my treatment do to my pocketbook? There must be horrendous charges. I was on the verge of fleeing when a voice called my name and I was sucked into the dark unknown behind a door.

A large chunk was taken out of my face. I was told not to let anyone repair that for two years to be sure the melanoma was all gone. Dr. Singleton saw me at a party about a year later. We knew each other because I was now teaching his brilliant son Scott chemistry at Wichita Falls High School. I had been assigned to teach chemistry when the former teacher retired. Dr. Singleton told me he could repair that hole in my face when the time came. And he did a great job with a series of small repairs until it was finished.

Here I must tell the rest of the story. When I went for my final check-up at M. D. Anderson, I told the surgeon about Dr. Singleton's offer. He said I should at least talk to their plastic surgeon, Dr. X. Dr. X seemed to think he was God. He told me that those doctors in Wichita Falls were not capable of doing a good job. He insisted that only he could do it right. This meant another sixteen-hour round trip to Houston by car, but we did it. When I registered at the hospital, I was sent to change into a gown and lie on a gurney along with a dozen others. Someone forgot to give me the sleepy shot, so I was perfectly awake when a young resident came in and announced that he had been out partying all night and to leave the door open to the bathroom as he might throw up at any moment. Then the nurse came by and said to another nurse that I would be operated on by some name I didn't know. I rose up and said no, I was Dr. X's patient. The nurse said that Dr. X never did simple things like this but always had his resident do them. "Then I'll go back to Wichita Falls," I said. I got up and headed for the dressing room to put on my clothes. I heard the nurse paging Dr. X, saying his patient was leaving. Dr. X agreed to do the job, but he was really angry. He fixed my face, but it looked like a tire patch and that's what Dr. Singleton repaired. Dr. X had the nerve to send me a letter some time later saying he was setting up a private practice and would love to have me as a patient. It was on gold-embossed stationery.

Teacher-in-Space Effort

When it was announced that a teacher was to be chosen to go up in space, I got very excited. Why couldn't it be me? Surely I would be found acceptable. Eldon was not happy about my applying, but he went along with it. The application was lengthy and required many recommendations from important people. Some people I asked seemed to think I was a bit arrogant even to try. I persisted and was disappointed when I didn't get the position. As things worked out, we were in London when we saw the newspaper headline that the shuttle had crashed. I can never forget that day. I was grateful I didn't get what I wished for, and at the same time sad for those who lost their lives.

Another near miss for me happened as I drove to school one morning. I was stopped at the front of a long line of cars waiting for the red light to change to green. When the light turned green, the car stalled. Embarrassed at holding up that long line, I restarted the car just as a large truck came barreling down the cross street in front of me at about ninety miles an hour, obviously trying to beat the light. If the car had not stalled, I would have been T-boned and killed. The car had never before stalled nor did it ever stall again. It seemed to me to be a miracle, and I was grateful.

The Children

Sharon took ballet lessons and loved them. She was in the high school drill team, along with the German, French, and Biology Clubs. She and her friend Sue Moss were both National Merit Scholars. We were very proud!

Summer Employment

One summer Sprague Electric participated in a student employment program. Both Sharon and Elizabeth took part. They worked with many Vietnamese women who didn't appreciate the fact that the students didn't have to produce as many capacitors per hour as the regular workers. The work involved dipping wires into hot liquid solder, a procedure that resulted in burned fingers. One of the male workers was enamored of Sharon. We were concerned about these things, wondering if we'd made the right decision by letting them take part.

We said at least they knew why we wanted them to go to college, so they wouldn't have to depend on that sort of work ever again.

Sharon went to Rice University and got a degree in anthropology. She did very well on the LSAT and was accepted at UT Law School in Austin. After law school she married David Bowers, a boy she met at Rice, but this marriage didn't last. Sharon worked part time in Austin writing a column for a lawyers' newsletter summarizing the newest legislation affecting lawyers. A local lawyer told us those were the best-written, most helpful columns he had ever encountered. Sharon was hired to work as an aide to the Court of Criminal Appeals presided over by Judge Bleil in Texarkana. She invited us to come to the court to see her in action. We miscalculated the time it would take to drive to Texarkana and just missed seeing her in court. Her next job took her back to Austin to work in the legal department of the Texas Department of Human Resources. In January 1991 Sharon married Anthony Venza in Austin, Texas. We were prevented from attending the wedding by an unusual ice storm that made it impossible to drive to that area. Mother was then in Rolling Meadows retirement home in Wichita Falls and wanted badly for Sharon and Tony to marry in that building's foyer, but Sharon refused. They are still a happy couple and we are so glad of that.

We were astonished later when we returned from a semester of my teaching at a Moroccan university to be greeted by a hesitant Sharon, who later e-mailed us that she would stop all contact with us because she had been convinced by a therapist that we had tortured her in that basement in Delaware. We will never understand this, but believe this is a classic case of false memory syndrome. We mail her pictures of herself as a happy, smiling child periodically, but get no response. That therapist cannot know what pain she has inflicted. It is unbelievably sad to lose our beautiful, talented, creative red-haired daughter in this way.

Elizabeth

Elizabeth played the violin in the junior high orchestra. Her teacher was dismayed that she dropped out of orchestra when she reached high school. She was in the high school marching band, playing flute. She also worked on the high school yearbook and was a member of the Goal Post Decorators, a group of girls supporting the football team. She was assigned to go to a certain football boy's home to decorate his bedroom before a big game. When she got there, his mom told her he didn't have a bedroom. He slept on the living room sofa. So Elizabeth decorated the sofa!

Thyroid Problem

Always the quiet, sweet one, Elizabeth amazed us when she lost her temper in band one day. She had been to the pediatrician recently for her yearly checkup, during which he had noticed nothing wrong. Eldon was the one who noticed the swelling in Elizabeth's neck, which turned out to be a swollen thyroid gland that caused her heart rate to be quite high and made her nervous. The thyroid gland was not malignant but needed to be removed. We decided that radiation (I-131) would leave less scarring than surgery, so that's the route we took. Her heart rate came back down to normal, returning her to her usual calm, sweet self.

Elizabeth went to Trinity University in San Antonio. She had a weird roommate who invited boyfriends to spend the night in their shared room. Elizabeth had dated a nice young man in high school but had broken off with him to date a young man named David, who had been crippled in a car accident before moving to Wichita Falls. David was frustrated that the physical damage done by the accident prevented him from being the athlete he longed to be. Elizabeth was very sympathetic. She and David became engaged and would rendezvous at Hamilton, Texas, which was roughly halfway between San Antonio, where Elizabeth attended Trinity University, and Wichita

Falls, where David was a premed student at MSU. Elizabeth decided on a career in physical therapy not offered at Trinity, so she transferred to Texas Women's University in Denton to get that degree. She graduated in December of 1981 on one of the coldest days ever.

Elizabeth and David married August 14, 1982, at Faith Lutheran Church. It was our first time to put on a wedding. We were short of funds and foolishly thought we could do the reception ourselves. We discovered we could not accomplish even simple tasks in such an emotional state. David entered Southwestern Medical School that fall, and Elizabeth worked as a physical therapist at Methodist Medical Center in Dallas to provide financial support. Two beautiful baby boys were born to them, Daniel Warren on April 6, 1986, and Matthew Davis on October 10, 1988.

Divorce

A very sad time in my life came in 1997, when David decided to divorce Elizabeth to marry another woman, an aide who worked in his office. We felt as if we had given him an angel, and he had made her life hell. I could not fathom how he could justify deserting his precious family. He was not the man we had believed him to be. In 2000 the gallant and very talented Dan Vaughan came on the scene. He is an organist who builds and repairs organs and who also makes beautiful music. He and Elizabeth were married on April 22, 2000, in Rockwall, Texas, at the First Presbyterian Church, where Dan is employed. Elizabeth continues her work as a physical therapist.

Phillip

Phillip took on the job of delivering circulars and later the newspaper, as soon as he could qualify. He loved to earn money. He would get up before dawn to deliver his papers on his bike. Only if the weather was really treacherous would Eldon get up and drive him around.

Soap Box Derby

Phillip entered the Soap Box Derby. I was very surprised and impressed one day when I got home from school and heard Phillip on the phone asking the manager of a local pizza parlor to sponsor him in the derby. The man agreed, and Eldon and Phillip built a green derby car with the pizza parlor logo on the side. We all went up to Lawton, Oklahoma, to cheer him on in the race. He didn't win, but it was lots of fun. I was glad that the two men in the family had managed to work together on this project, no easy task!

A Cardinal for Mom

When Phillip was just a little tyke we went on a family vacation trip to Bellingrath Gardens in Mobile, Alabama. We visited a shop displaying beautiful porcelain birds crafted by the famous American sculptor Boehm. I oohed and ahhed over them and lamented that they cost so much. When we returned home Phillip took his allowance money and walked across Southwest Parkway, a major six-lane highway that was strictly off limits, to get to a store called Treasure City, where he bought a little ceramic cardinal for me. I treasure it still.

Sharon, Elizabeth, and Phillip all took piano lessons from a lady who lived near the school. She adored Phillip and wrote a piece for the local newspaper telling about this talented little boy who had composed a piece about a thunderstorm. Indeed, he loved to play his thunderstorm piece. It consisted mainly of his fists pounding on the bass keys.

Danish Student

We decided to have a Danish high school boy come to live with us for a year in 1976. Crazy me! I thought this would fulfill Phillip's wish for a brother. It did not go well. The boy bought a cowboy hat, and Phillip shot a hole in it with his BB gun. I told the Danish boy he should give his first name as John because everyone would understand that. His first name was Juergen, and when he pronounced it, it sounded like "urine." I thought he'd be teased. I never thought about John being another name for toilet. He pointed this out to me. After he left, we got a very sweet note from his parents, who said it had been a very good experience for their son. We got a nice thank you note from Juergen himself, so I guess it wasn't too bad, after all.

Phillip met Pam Mahon at the grocery store where he sacked groceries during his high school years. They married and had three beautiful and very intelligent daughters, Samantha Lauren on September 26, 1983, Emiley Kay on August 23, 1986, and Andrea Lea on February 15, 1991. Phillip graduated from Vernon Regional College in the field of Auto Mechanics and got a great job at a car agency in Wichita Falls. He was very proud of his daughters and a happy family man. He loved working in his yard and keeping everything in tip-top shape, just like his Daddy. He took his family on many car trips, one to see his grandparents and cousins in Wisconsin and Minnesota, and one to visit his sister Nancy in Charleston, South Carolina. He loved to fish and work on cars.

Phillip's Death

It was on Sunday, May 18, 2003. We were in church when Phillip's youngest daughter, twelve-year-old Andrea, came down the aisle to where we were sitting to tell us her daddy was sick. We left and followed the ambulance to the hospital. Phillip had had a seizure. The doctor on call at the hospital asked Phillip if he had been sniffing antifreeze at the car dealership where he worked. Phillip laughed as did the rest of us in the hospital room. Phillip was always very careful not to do anything that might harm his body. This doctor, not satisfied, kept repeating the question. I wanted to slap his face.

An x-ray showed a shadow on Phillip's brain, so we took him to Dallas to Zale Lipshy University Hospital at Southwestern Medical

School. The look on the surgeon's face when he came out of surgery told it all. Phillip, who had never been seriously ill, was diagnosed with an incurable brain tumor, glioblastoma multiformi. Even though we were told there was no cure, we tried everything and prayed for a miracle. We had been warned by a local doctor that in situations like this families often fall apart, and he was right. We all worked together for six months.

Then Phillip and Pam cut off all communication with us. We never knew why. An Angel flight took him to Duke University in hopes of a cure, but none was found. Phillip and Pam then spent time with Nancy and her family in Charleston, South Carolina.

I tried to keep in touch by scanning the slides we took of Phillip during his life and emailing the pictures to him. I got no response. Six months later we were leaving for a trip to New York City when Nancy called to say Phillip wanted to get the whole family together and reconcile. We shouted for joy and told Nancy we'd be back that weekend and to arrange everything. When we got to New York we called Nancy to see what had been arranged; she told us Phillip had just died, May 6, 2004. We were devastated. It took many years, but Phillip's three beautiful and talented daughters rejoined the family, one by one. That made us so happy.

Nancy

Nancy was a great competitor. In sixth grade she entered a contest that involved writing a theme on a certain topic. She worked and worked on it, and all that work paid off. She won, and to this day has her name inscribed on a plaque hanging in the hall at Fain Elementary School.

Hidden Frugality

Nancy surprised us one day while she was in high school. She needed new shoes. Money was tight, so she drove off to see what she could find at the Payless Shoe Store located on the main drag, Kemp Boulevard. Some emergency came up for which we needed to get in touch with her. This was before the age of cell phones, so we drove to the store. Her car was not there. "How could this be?" we thought. She had left the house only a few minutes before. We turned to drive around the block, and there we saw her car parked in the alley behind the shop. It turned out that she didn't want any of her friends to see her car and thus know she could afford only bargain shoes!

Nancy was a cheerleader at Rider High School and was elected Miss Rider Raider, a very big honor. On graduation she went to TCU in Fort Worth, Texas, where she majored in foreign affairs. She briefly joined a sorority but quickly dropped out. She did not care for the snobbery, the expense, and being told what to do when.

Nancy had gotten through high school with a winning smile. The result was she never really learned to write essays or themes. Her English professor at TCU was a former military officer. Nancy's first theme came back looking like it was bleeding to death and was given a low grade, so Nancy had to get busy and learn the right way to compose a complete sentence and other grammatical elements. Her letters home changed from little bits and phrases to very well-written complete sentences. She was up to the task! She graduated with a degree in foreign affairs. She met her future husband, Scott Thompson, in biology lab, where he was a student assistant. In Nancy's senior year she spent one semester studying in Paris through the TCU Study Abroad program. She studied horseback riding at the Sorbonne and had many adventures with the French family she lived with in the sixteenth arrondissement. She went skiing in Switzerland.

We got a phone call from her asking permission to buy a Louis Vuitton purse—on sale, great bargain. We said okay. When the credit card bill came, we noticed that the date of the purchase was prior to the date of the phone call asking permission. She was having such a good time we were afraid she might not come home, but home she came, and married Scott in Robert Carr Chapel, the chapel of Texas Christian University, on May 2, 1987.

Scott went to Southwestern Medical School in Dallas using military funds. Therefore, after he married Nancy, he had to go into the air force for four years. His first assignment was in Virginia Beach, where Nancy worked at a travel agency. Then came Alexandria and Shreveport, Louisiana, where their oldest child, Elizabeth Victoria, was born Sept. 3, 1992. Andrew Scott Thompson was born July 6, 1995, in Charleston, South Carolina, where Scott had set up practice. Annemarie Faulkner Thompson was born there Nov. 26, 1999.

Grandma with Grandsons

I prided myself on my ability to put babies in the church nursery to sleep by rocking them while softly singing a lullaby over and over. I couldn't wait to work my magic on Daniel, my first grandson. Daniel's name for me was "Popka." The first time I tried singing and rocking him to sleep, he opened a sleepy eye to peer up at me and murmured, "Be kite, Popka."

When Elizabeth needed to attend a course to keep her certification current, she asked if we would keep Matthew for a couple of days. Phillip and his wife Pam would keep Daniel. Elizabeth told me Matthew was in the midst of potty training, but I might want to keep him in diapers because he had this idea that to use the potty you had to be completely undressed. I said that was okay. I had plenty of time. Sure enough, when Matthew indicated he needed the potty, I took him there and watched while he took off every bit of clothing. He even took the shoelaces out of his shoes. The whole process took twenty minutes. Later we went through the whole operation again. The next time he alerted me to his need we were out in the yard planting a flat of flowers I had bought at the nursery. I really did not want to stop and take him inside. I had a brilliant thought. I told him these plants were really thirsty and he could help them by giving each one a little drink. His eyes lit up and he proceeded to lower his pants and give each plant a squirt. I said they were telling him, "Thank you." He then said "U welcome" to each one. Another thing Matthew learned at our house was the expression "You idiot," which Eldon had said to me. Elizabeth reported that when Matthew got home she heard him saying, "U welcome" over and over in the playroom. She investigated and found him "watering" the houseplants on the window sill and saying, "U welcome" to each one. He later relieved himself in the front yard and said "U idjit" to her when he was angry. She laughed and said she had sent us a sweet little child and we had returned a foul-mouthed exhibitionist. Ah, well!

Lost in White Mountain Fog

Eldon and I both loved to travel and enjoyed going together to chemical society and chemical education meetings all over the US as well as in Canada. At one particular conference—Gordon Conference in New Hampshire—a fellow chemist asked if anyone would like to go hiking with him in the White Mountains. We said we would. We followed him up the mountain, but he went much faster than we could. There were large crevices in the rocky terrain and no real markings, only a few vague blazes. A blinding fog came up, and the man we were following disappeared. We were terrified! We had to crawl on our hands and knees for fear of falling into a crevice. When we finally got down the mountain, we asked the ranger at the bottom if a man had come down earlier. He said yes, some time ago a man told him he had left two people stranded on the mountain in the fog because he didn't have time to wait for them. What an uncaring cad!

Terrible Tow

A very scary night was in store for us on one trip to Austin to attend a chemistry meeting there. About halfway on the drive down, we hit a large rock in the road, which left our car undrivable. We called AAA to get a tow back to Wichita Falls. By the time the tow truck arrived, it was dark. The driver loaded up our car and we rode in the front seat of the truck with him. A bit down the road the truck lights went out. We were driving in the dark at a good rate of speed. The driver said, "I've got to get those lights fixed. They keep going out on me. Don't worry. They'll come on again." He never slowed down. I don't know how he could see the road. I was terrified. The lights did come on again, but the saga was repeated several times on the way back to Wichita Falls. I thought we might die!

No Southern Gentleman

On one of our trips we stopped to see the sights in a small town in the hills of Tennessee. In a tourist shop there was an "end of season" sale in progress. The price of every item on a special table would drop one dollar each hour, as evidenced by the ringing of a bell. I was attracted to a ceramic soup tureen made in the shape of a chicken. It was white with a red comb, black eyes, and a yellow beak, very realistic looking. When I took it to the cash register a dignified older lady asked if I wanted it wrapped. I said no, at which point Eldon said to wrap it because he would not be seen carrying that chicken down the street. I explained to the lady that my husband was a Yankee. She turned her back to him, gave me a sympathetic look and said in a loud voice, "A southern gentleman would be honored to carry a chicken for his lady."

Hardin Professor Award

In 1975 Eldon was given the Midwestern State University Hardin Professor Award, which is announced each year at graduation to honor an outstanding professor. It carried at the time a $1500 stipend. I was notified in advance and told his parents, who came down from their farm in Wisconsin to see him get the award, as did my parents from Breckenridge. We were very proud.

Poster Paper in Dublin, Ireland

One meeting I attended by myself was the August 1979 meeting of the International Conference on Chemical Education at Trinity College in Dublin, Ireland. Sponsored by the National Science Foundation, I presented a poster paper entitled "Providing a Basis for Intelligent Decision Making in Today's World." It was about teaching chemistry to non-science-oriented students. I enjoyed chatting with chemistry teachers from all over the world. I was given a nice room in one of their dorms and had fun wandering around Dublin. There were lots of gypsy children begging on the streets.

In 1981 Eldon took a sabbatical to work under Dr. Edward C. Taylor at Princeton University for the spring semester. That left me alone at home, stressful for me but a great opportunity for Eldon.

Teaching Award

In 1983 I was the recipient of $2500 West Award for Excellence in Teaching at Wichita Falls High School, much to my surprise. The HVAC at our house went out of commission almost immediately after this award. It cost $2500 to replace, so we didn't hang on to my new-found wealth for long.

Second Fulbright Year

In 1985 Eldon and I applied for Fulbright teaching positions in England. Eldon was accepted for a position at Hatfield Polytechnic, and I was not. We both took "leaves of absence," he from his position as head of chemistry and premed advisor at MSU, and I from head of science and chemistry at Wichita Falls High School. Once in England I got a job at the Southbank American International School. In England at that time, female spouses of Fulbright professors were allowed to obtain jobs while male spouses were not, so it was fortunate that I was the one rejected for a Fulbright.

We exchanged houses with professor Tony Andrews from Hatfield Polytechnic and offered to exchange cars, but he chickened out at the last minute, saying he didn't think we could handle his Italian sports car. When Tony got to Wichita Falls, he attended our church, Faith Lutheran, and persuaded our friends, Gary and Linda Swenson, to lend him one of their cars. One of Tony's friends met us in London at Heathrow Airport and drove us to his house at 44 Crossfell in Hemel Hempstead, about thirty miles north of London. We bought a car that Eldon drove to his office at Hatfield Polytechnic (now Hertfordshire University). I took the bus to London to my school, located just around the corner from Victoria Station.

Commuting Into London

The bus ride into London was interesting. I awoke at 6:00 a.m. each school day to the strains of "Hail, Britannia" on the radio—called the wireless by my British neighbor, and lined up (queued) at the bus stop by 7:00 a.m. The bus would be almost full, so I had to walk to the back to get a seat. Almost every man on the bus had his copy of a tabloid open to the centerfold, which always had a nude woman on it. The one exception was a man who always had his Bible open. One day the bus was full, so it blinked its lights at our queue and drove on. We had to wait for the next bus, which stopped at Parliament before going to Victoria Station. The men on this bus were much the same, except many wore top hats.

Teaching at Southbank

I liked my job. I taught middle-school-level science. I was allowed to go to the bookstore to select the textbook I thought best for the class I was teaching. The headmaster told me that many of the students were from foreign countries, as their parents were diplomats, businessmen, or actors temporarily living in London. In order for them to take full advantage of London's many resources, he asked me to take them on as many field trips around London as possible. What a dream job! The museums and art galleries and other notable attractions had student exercise booklets the students could fill out on their visits, so that was a ready-made lesson plan. The students all had tube (subway) passes and knew how to use them. They took me places rather than the other way around.

On the first day of class I was amazed at the students' rapt attention. At first I thought I must be a very impressive lecturer but changed my mind when I noticed many of their mouths twisting as if they were repeating what I said. It dawned on me that it was my Texas accent that caught their attention. Many of these students were in London because either they or their parents were involved with the theater. To acquire a new accent was a bonus for them, and they loved it.

I embarrassed a student that first day. As I called the roll, I had difficulty with some of the foreign names and so was happy to come to one I felt sure I could pronounce correctly, St. John. I called out, "Saint John" and the class burst into laughter and stared at this slender slip of a boy whose body seemed made of mismatched parts. He blushed and looked at me with such distress in his eyes, then stood and limped up to my desk and whispered "Sinjun" in my ear. Having been wounded at birth, he was now re-wounded by my ignorance. I felt very remorseful!

One of my favorite students was Aisha. She was a dark-skinned little girl with soft black curls and eyes that shone like diamonds. She was from Mauritius and often told me how much she missed her grandmother, who lived where there was bright sand and sunshine, not like dark, dreary London. She told me I was just like her grandmother. After every class she came to me to say, "Thank you for the lesson, Miss." One day Aisha came to class very excited. She told me she had brought a picture of her grandmother, and now I would be able to see how I was just like her. She gave me the photo showing a very dark, wizened old lady standing barefoot in white sand under a palm tree. "She's lovely, Aisha," I said, "But we look so different." Aisha looked puzzled and replied, "The smile, Miss. Don't you see it? The smile is exactly the same!" That day I learned from Aisha, rather than the other way around.

At faculty meetings the staff was served wine and cheese and crackers. I knew I was no longer at Wichita Falls High School. On a field trip to the Lake Country I was assigned to drive a van of students to a farm where we would all spend the night in a barn. Eldon had done all the driving in England, so I was quite fearful that driving on the left side of the road would be too much for me. One of the students was the daughter of Joan Collins. I could picture the headlines in the paper saying an American driver had done in Joan Collins's daughter. But all went well.

Eldon and I joined the National Trust because that gave us free entrance to all the historical sites. We went somewhere almost every weekend. We attended the local Anglican Church.

Tea with the Queen Mother

Shortly after we arrived we were told that the Queen Mother had invited all the Fulbright professors and their spouses to tea on a certain date at her home in Clarence House. How exciting! We were told to dress up. The women were to wear hats. We were not to speak to the Queen Mother unless she spoke first. The people she would speak to were carefully chosen. When she arrived at the tea she came straight toward me with a big smile on her face. Her "lady in waiting" steered her toward the selected person instead. Anyway, I could tell she liked me.

We discovered it was easy to see the royalty. The *Daily Telegraph* newspaper always listed months in advance the functions the royalty would be attending. If you bought tickets to these functions you would see them. We got tickets to a concert at the Barbican theatre for that reason. I was hanging around in the lobby of the Barbican hoping to see them arrive. Just as I was about to give up, thinking they probably came in some secret door, a limo pulled up and six trumpeters dressed in red satin with gold trim came forward and blew their horns. In came Diana and Prince Charles, smiling at everyone. The few people still left in the lobby applauded politely. I nearly fainted with excitement as they brushed past me into the theater.

Prince William attended a preschool not far from where I taught in London. I asked one of the other teachers at my school if it would be all right if I stood on the sidewalk by the school in hopes of seeing the little prince arrive one morning. The teacher said, "Oh, they'd be happy that someone cared enough to do that. Some of us are not too keen on the royalty." So I went early in the morning and waited. A bobby (policeman) was standing nearby. Sure enough, up drove a limo and stopped in front of the school. Prince William scurried from the limo into the school while Diana went to the trunk of the car to fetch a sheet cake, which she carried in after the prince.

Please

One cultural difference I experienced in England was the use of the word *please*. The British hang a "please" after every request. We got in line at the Barbican cafeteria, where one can get a meal before attending a show or concert there. It was getting close to curtain time, so everyone was in a bit of a rush. I said to the young man behind the counter, "I'll have the ham." Long pause. He stared at me. I thought maybe he didn't understand my Texas accent, so I repeated the request. Still no action. People behind me in the line were getting anxious. Finally, the young man said, "I'm waiting for you to say, 'please.'" He was apparently trying to teach this American a lesson. He was probably what was called a "school-leaver" in England. At the age of sixteen students took their "O" level exams to determine if they should be allowed to go further with their studies or leave school to get a job.

In the spring Libya's dictator, Muammar al Gaddhafi, sent terrorists to bomb a Berlin nightclub frequented by Americans. President Ronald Reagan ordered the bombing of Libya in retaliation. The next morning when I got to Southbank American International School where I taught, there was a sign on the door saying that on the advice of the American Embassy the name had been changed, leaving out the word "American," for fear of retribution. Many Americans in London tried to dress more European after that. Some American men started wearing sandals with socks, a European custom at that time.

Edna Wimperis was a lovely lady who lived in Hemel Hempstead and attended the same parish church we attended. She was determined that I feel welcome in the community. She made sure that I was invited to afternoon tea by someone almost every week.

We went to see Parliament in action, the Tower of London, Rye, Oxford, Leed's Castle, Switzerland for Christmas, and then to the Isle of Wight. Later, we went to Stratford-upon-Avon, St. Albans, the Chelsea Flower Show, Cambridge, and Cornwall. We made great efforts to see the Severn Bore, but just missed it because we didn't allow for daylight saving time. Severn Bore is a large tidal surge wave that can be seen coming up the River Severn at Equinox, when the days are equal in time with the nights.

At Oxford we were given a lecture by a don. When I asked why they had no women students, he said women would not be able "to sit the exams," often four hours long. That has since changed, of course. We stayed overnight in one of the colleges, Keble College. The original of the painting *The Light of the World* by William Holman Hunt, showing Christ knocking on the door, is located there.

In London it rained so often that when it didn't rain, the TV weatherman predicted an "outbreak of brightness." We were so tired of it we just had to see the sun again, so we spent spring break in the Canary Islands. We went to Holland in May to see the tulips in bloom. In June we went to Greenwich; we saw the regiments Trooping the Colour at St. James's Park and the procession of the Order of the Garter at Windsor Castle. I also went to Wimbledon to see Martina Navratilova play. My students presented me with a huge bouquet of flowers at the final assembly at school. I think they hated to lose my Texas accent.

If we stayed away a whole year we were not required to pay US income tax for the year, so it was imperative that we not go home until mid-August. We went to Hampton Court, walked a canal, and then took off for Denmark to see Eldon's cousin, Henning Sund, and his wife, Lillie. We bought a railroad pass to tour Scandinavia and visited Oslo, Trondheim, Narvik, North Sweden, Central Finland, Helsinki, and Copenhagen.

In August Sharon came over to go with us on a week's bicycling tour through Denmark, starting in Aalborg. A tour company had provided us with maps and hotel reservations along the way. When we showed Eldon's cousin Henning the maps, he asked, "Have you considered the wind?" Indeed we had not. The wind off the North Sea is ferocious. The maps were not always accurate. We had to retrace our course several times. We were exhausted at the end of each day. At each hotel we were told that they had prepared a typical Danish meal for us: Danish meatballs and red cabbage. The first night, that was great. The second night it was okay, but on the third night, we said, "Oh, please, not again!" They gave us a different meal. A highlight of the trip was a visit to the church where Eldon's father had been baptized. We flew home August 16, 1986.

Back home I was honored to be a consultant for Addison-Wesley's 1987 high school chemistry text and pleased to have my name and Wichita Falls High School so listed.

History of Chemistry Tour

In the summer of 1989 we went on a History of Chemistry Tour under the guidance of Dr. Wotiz of the University of Southern Illinois. He had conducted several of these tours, and Eldon had heard great reviews about them. The deal was to fly to Paris where we would buy a car and meet at a small Paris hotel. We actually bought a car at the Paris airport with the guarantee that it would be bought back at the end of the tour. The charge for the tour was less if we agreed to buy the car (with a promised buy-back on return) and take passengers with us. The passengers who rode with us were a very nice chemistry teacher who taught at a private academy in Toronto, Canada, and a soccer coach from Chicago whose main interest was to see the soccer field in Prague, Czechoslovakia. We became great friends with the very witty Canadian, Jim Morwick, who kept us all in stitches when problems arose. He often cautioned, tongue in cheek, that we must not upset our driver, Eldon, or we might have to hitch a ride back to Paris.

Parking Tickets in Paris

At first we followed Dr. Wotiz's car, as instructed, but he drove too fast and jumped the curb to park on sidewalks in Paris. Our hotel in Paris was just across the street from a subway station that we could have easily used to get around Paris, but Dr. Wotiz would have none of it. We had dozens of parking tickets when we left Paris. We still have them. After Paris, we asked what each day's destination was and planned our own route.

Marie Curie and Louis Pasteur

In Paris we visited the labs of Pasteur and Curie. Marie Curie has always been a hero for me. She was Polish and taught an underground school in the Polish language in her home when the Russians controlled Poland and forbade the Polish language to be used in the schools. She earned enough money to send her brother to study at the Sorbonne in Paris and then saved money so she could go herself. She studied physics in the French language and sometimes fainted in class due to lack of food when her money was running out. Despite this, she graduated at the top of the class and went on to win two Nobel Prizes. It was easy to see that the French did not respect her nearly as much as they did Pasteur. Her lab was freely accessible. I was allowed to try on her lab jacket and read her notes. Very exciting for me! In contrast, Pasteur's lab was like a mausoleum: everything behind glass and set in marble. I asked a guide, "Why this contrast in the treatment of memorabilia?" The guide said, "Pasteur was French and Curie was Polish." We went through the Alps to Italy to see Alessandro Volta's lab and spent the night at a beautiful inn overlooking Lake Como. We had to drive up a narrow road to get to the inn, so narrow we had to park on a turntable to turn the car around to go back down the road the next day. Then we drove on into Germany to see Neuschwanstein Castle and then to Salzburg. We entered the East Zone controlled by Russia to go to Pribram, where Dr. Wotiz had relatives. He had told us his relatives would do our laundry for us. They charged a dollar a sock, so we declined.

The Failure of Communism

Pribram would cure anyone of thinking Communism might be a good idea. The hotel room had one bare light bulb hanging from the ceiling. The wallpaper hung in strips. The toilet flushed backwards. The lawn was not mowed. The garden benches were covered in weeds. When we questioned this, we were told that the Communist government paid the salaries of the employees whether there were any guests or not, so there was no reward for making it a pleasant place to stay. The ice cream shop sold ice cream only early in the morning, because then there were fewer customers and therefore less work. They got paid the same as long as they were open a certain number of hours.

Communist Prague

We then drove to Prague. The city was deserted, with only a few Russian tanks sitting around. Charles Bridge was empty. We didn't need a guide to tell us that this was a city with a glorious past. It was all too evident from such structures as the Charles Bridge, the Prague Castle, the palaces, cathedrals, theaters, churches, and museums. This had been a center of power and culture. Still, on this day, the past glory seemed to have been a long time ago. It was like looking at an old Southern mansion that the heirs had failed to keep up. Everything seemed to be in disrepair. We wondered what it must have been like back in the Middle Ages, during the reign of the Holy Roman Emperor, Charles IV, for whom the bridge and the university he founded are named. Or how it was when Mozart performed here.

There were no crowds or cars to be seen, just some soldiers and military vehicles, plus a few young people who appeared to be thoroughly soused, although it was early in the day. The air was gray with coal smoke. It was hard not to feel depressed and certainly wary as our footsteps echoed through the quiet streets. Most of the buildings were closed. We could look at them only from the outside. We did get to visit the alchemist museum and see the tiny houses along Golden Lane. We saw the window from which angry Protestants threw two Catholic royal governors to their deaths in 1618 to protest the coming of the intolerant Habsburg Archduke Ferdinand to the throne, thus precipitating the Thirty Years' War. We also saw the window where, in 1948 after the Communist Coup, Jan Masaryk, the only non-Communist in the newly formed government, fell or was pushed to his death. The word "defenestration," meaning to throw out the window, was coined here in Prague.

Students Predict End of Communism

We met with several chemistry professors from Charles University. They told us that they had been doing some very interesting research, but because they were not members of the Communist Party, they could not get grant money for their research, nor were they allowed to travel outside the country to present their work at scientific meetings around the world. In very guarded words they expressed their hope that the present system wouldn't last much longer. Many of the students at the university told us with great confidence that the Communist regime would be gone by fall. They proved to be correct. We were surprised, because this information had not been suggested in the US media.

Dvořák Visit

Between Pribram and Prague we turned down a dirt road, parked, and walked through a field to visit the home of the composer Antonín Dvořák's in-laws, where he had come almost daily to visit his sister-in-law, Josephine. The home had been donated to the state for a museum but was not well kept. A charming older woman met us at the door and served us tea around the dining room table while we listened to a scratchy recording of Dvořák's *New World Symphony* played on an old-fashioned record player. It was a magic moment in the midst of rather bleak surroundings.

After we left Prague, we went on to see the Meissen porcelain factory, then to Leipzig where we heard an American choir touring Europe sing in a church. We applauded and were told that in Germany one does not applaud sacred music. Then back into West Germany. It was scary crossing the border. The car in front of us was ordered into a garage for a thorough inspection. We were relieved when we were waved through.

When we reached Heidelberg, I told Eldon I could direct him, as I had studied there years ago. I got us in trouble because, unknown to me, the main street had been converted into a pedestrian mall. Several people screamed at us and some pounded on our car as we drove down what had formerly been the main street. Fortunately, our license plates made us appear to be French.

We continued on to visit the labs of Bayer, Cavendish, and Röntgen, the cities of Lancaster, Edinburgh, St. Andrews, Glasgow, Keele, Coventry, Cambridge, and Oxford in England, along with the Science Museum, the Maritime Museum, and the Greenwich Observatory. Jim Morwick was a fan of James Herriot, the veterinarian and author who wrote the book *All Creatures Great and Small,* plus several others.

Jim asked that we drive to Herriot's home in Skeldale, Yorkshire, so we did.

With this experience behind us, we wondered in the following years what changes might be occurring in post-Communist Prague. In 2000 the Elderhostel organization, now called Road Scholar, gave us the opportunity to find out. We jumped at the chance. This travel group for seniors offered a tour of the capitals of Central Europe, spending a week each in Warsaw, Cracow, Prague, and Budapest. We wanted to see how things had changed since we were there in 1989. Wow! They have changed, all right!

Post-Communist Prague (Capitalist Prague)

On this visit the traffic in Prague was comparable to any large US city, complete with rush-hour slowdowns and headaches. The streets were crowded with people, and I think the majority were tourists. Everywhere we saw umbrellas pointed skyward, not for protection from rain but to help groups of tourists locate their particular guide. Our guide used her umbrella to stop the heavy traffic for us to cross the street, like Moses at the Red Sea. For a small sum one is allowed to enter the palaces and cathedrals, but once inside, the problem is to maneuver your body through the throngs of tourists at the most popular sites.

Charles Bridge, which had been deserted on our previous visit, was now packed with people. This stone bridge, ordered built in 1357 by Charles IV, was the only bridge over the Vltava River (Moldau) until 1741. It is an inspiring sight, with large Gothic towers at each end and eight statues along each side. One statue is that of St. Nepomuk, a priest who was said to have displeased the king by refusing to tell him the secrets the queen told him in confession. His tongue was cut out and he was thrown off the bridge into the river. Touching his statue is supposed to bring luck, although he had rather bad luck himself.

Free-market entrepreneurship abounds in the form of shops selling souvenirs, Czech crystal, pottery, embroidery, toys, jewelry, and other tourist items. The prices are very reasonable. People stand on the sidewalks handing out leaflets telling of concert venues and ticket prices. The Czechs sincerely love their music. Almost every church, cathedral, museum, castle, and palace in the city has a concert every day. We chose to hear a string quartet play Mozart in the garden of Bertram, the former home of the composer Dusek, where Mozart finished writing the overture to his opera *Don Giovanni* just hours before its premiere at the Estates Theatre in 1787. We also attended a concert in the Klementinum Chapel of Mirrors featuring Mozart, Vivaldi, Bach, and Handel. We saw *La Traviata* performed at the Lichtenstein Palace.

The Elderhostel program includes lectures by local experts, so we heard talks from a retired economist/lawyer and various professors. I asked one professor, a social historian, how his life had changed since the fall of Communism. His face lit up and he said, "Now I can speak freely and I love doing just that, although some of my colleagues at the university have expressed the wish that I keep my lunatic ideas to myself." We noted the return of free speech also in the form of the ubiquitous graffiti. Many war-damaged buildings had been restored to their former splendor, only to be defiled by graffiti. I do think it's great that the old buildings are restored rather than torn down and replaced by modern buildings.

I'm happy to report that the food we were served in Prague this time around was excellent, well-seasoned, and beautifully presented, from the supper on the cruise down the Vltava to the gourmet farewell meal at the Zofin. The big surprise was the ice water. In times past when I've been in Europe, asking for a glass of ice water was like asking for the moon. The waiter would look at you puzzled, as if he could not possibly have understood you correctly. Then he might suggest that you perhaps wanted to swallow a pill. Otherwise, why would you want a glass of water? On this trip, at every meal, there was a pitcher of ice water waiting on each table.

Restrooms, or WC's, as they are called in Europe, were plentiful and sparkling clean, instead of scarce and dirty as they were back in 1989. About half of them require payment of a few coins to the cleaning lady in charge. I was glad to do so. One thing had not changed. The hotel beds come with a featherbed that is supposed to cover your body but doesn't quite. Sleeping under these giant, pillow-like objects is too warm, but with no other sheet or blanket, we had no choice. I tried baking half my body at a time, hoping the body temperature would somehow even out.

We visited the Bohemian Crystal Glassworks in Svetia Nad Sazavou, where beautiful lead crystal is made for a good price. We watched craftsmen blowing and molding the glass. The lack of safety measures was appalling, but the company puts out a nice product. We bought some crystal and discovered that airport security does not like it because the lead is opaque to their x-ray machine. Security stopped us and searched our carry-on bags both in Zurich and Chicago. Eldon had stuffed his dirty socks around the crystal to protect it, so the search was a pretty smelly operation. The security guards earned their salary that day.

We went to the Jewish ghetto where we visited the Pinkus Synagogue and saw written on the walls the names of 77,297 Jews who did not return from the Nazi extermination camps. We were reminded of our visit to the Auschwitz concentration camp in Poland the week before. There we had walked through the infamous gate with the slogan "Arbeit Macht Frei" (Work Makes You Free). Perhaps this slogan was meant to give those imprisoned here false hope. We saw the ovens where innocent people were cremated and piles of eyeglasses of all sizes that had belonged to the adults and children murdered there. There were pictures of starving men who were forced to do field labor on very little food.

This evidence of man's inhumanity toward his fellowmen is hard to fathom. How could a so-called civilized society live with the knowledge of the pain they caused innocent people whose only "crime" was being Jewish? Unbelievable! Even as I write this, it brings tears to my eyes.

Transition from Communism to Free Market

The various lecturers gave us their opinions on Communism and the transition to a free market. One thing was emphasized by the lecturers in all three countries. They resent being called "Eastern Europe" and being treated like second-class humans. They attribute this designation to Churchill's statement, when Stalin started taking over the area, that there was an iron curtain coming down over Eastern Europe. They point out that the people of this region have made great contributions to science, literature, and music. In 1938 the Czechs had the fifth highest per capita income in the world, with six car factories and an airplane factory. Their land and treasure has been attacked, plundered, and ruled by outsiders over many decades. Yet Austria, which lies to their south, is considered a western country, while the Czech Republic is dumped into the east. It doesn't make sense or seem fair to them.

Another comment often heard in the lectures is that Communism was doomed from the start. It was only a matter of time before Communism would self-destruct. Lecturers pointed out that Communism did not fall out of the sky like a dragon. It was an alternative economic plan or more like a religion that appealed to people who felt as if they had nothing to lose by trying it. It came as a reaction to a capitalist tragedy. There was great poverty, workers working up to sixteen hours a day in factories, children working at age five, mothers nursing babies while working, no safety measures. Inflation was soaring. Communism offered security.

The state took over all property and then gave everyone a job. It might not be the job they were trained for, but it was a job. There was zero unemployment. Anyone who refused a job was labeled a shirker and could be imprisoned. Employees could not be fired. Education, health care, and childcare were all free. At retirement, workers would receive a pension that was eighty percent of their working salary.

The children were organized into athletic clubs, taught patriotic songs, and encouraged to be helpful to others and to serve their country. They were told that the Communist Party would always care for them. We saw a Communist statue that showed gigantic bronze hands holding a world globe. I immediately thought of the Negro spiritual "He's got The Whole World in His Hands." Of course, the Communists meant it to mean the Communist Party would always be there to protect you. When I commented on this to our guide, she said that Communism is a religion.

In the Czech Republic citizens were not required to join the Communist Party. They were encouraged to and could get special favors if they did, but only about 10 percent of the people did. They were not allowed to oppose the party in any way, however. One lecturer noted that the only way someone could be excused from work was to get a doctor's notice affirming illness. Since visiting a doctor's office was free, many people showed up there on Fridays to try to get an excuse for a long weekend. The Communists announced a big investigation into this practice until it was discovered that most of the people going to the doctors' offices were party members. The investigation was dropped.

As the economist pointed out, if the state is going to provide all these things, it has to have a source of income. It has to earn money before it can give it away. Income wasn't happening. The people were not motivated, as was obvious in the hotel and ice cream shop in Pribram in 1989. Many jobs were redundant in order to have full employment. Two or three people would be doing a job that needed only one. All management decisions, from how much should be produced to where the raw materials should be acquired, were made by the state, without consulting the manager at the job site. These practices could not and did not work. The whole system went bankrupt.

So how was the transition to a free-market economy accomplished? In the Czech Republic we were told that the decision was made to give private property back to the original owners, take it or leave it. All unclaimed property would be auctioned off. This redistribution was 85 percent complete by 1995. Then each citizen was given four vouchers, worth one thousand koruna each. These vouchers were to be used to invest in any company, just like buying stock. The people were not used to this idea, so most of them sold the vouchers to buy cars or washing machines. Those in the know made money and were often the people who had been high-ranking members of the Communist Party. Several stock-managing companies sprang up, offering to manage the vouchers. Some were fraudulent. It was then decided to try to attract capital investment from outside the republic.

Hawaii

After our 1989 History of Chemistry Tour in Europe, our next great adventure came when Eldon was appointed to be Visiting Professor at the University of Hawaii in Honolulu for the year 1989-1990. At the time I had risen to Head of Science at Wichita Falls High School.

I took a leave of absence to go with Eldon, of course. We arranged for the new Spanish professor at MSU to live in our house for that year. Just as we arrived in Honolulu, we got word that Mother had been hospitalized and needed help. It was determined that I should be the one to help her, so I flew right back and left Eldon to find a place for us to live in Hawaii. When Mother got better, she put her house on the market and eventually moved into Rolling Meadows in Wichita Falls. I stayed with her awhile and then joined Eldon in Honolulu. He had found us an apartment, two bedrooms, on Wilder Avenue within walking distance of the university and very close to Punaho, the school President Obama attended. I got to substitute at

Punaho and found it to be a dream school. It had a long waiting list of students wanting to get in, so if a student misbehaved or didn't keep up in the work, the student could be expelled. The administration of Punaho offered me a job at the end of that year, but I needed to return to MSU with Eldon and to care for my mother.

Substituting at the public schools was not fun in Hawaii. They were pretty much run by those of Japanese heritage, who seemed to feel non-Japanese teachers could not possibly be as neat, orderly, or intelligent as the Japanese. With few exceptions, they treated me like dirt. I did enjoy teaching one semester at Kapi'olani Community College. Many of the students there were worried about the rising cost of taxes on property that had been in their families for generations. They feared they would have to sell their property and move to the mainland.

Wind Surfing Class

As the spouse of faculty I was allowed to audit any class for free. Eldon and I signed up for a PE class in wind surfing. It was great. When the instructor thought we were ready, he let us go out on our own. He cautioned us not to go beyond a certain perimeter. I was immensely pleased when I managed to stand up and fly over the waves on a surfboard. When I got close to the edge of the perimeter assigned, I discovered to my dismay that I could not turn around. Every time I tried, the surfboard would flip around and go straight on. As I passed one ship, a man stuck his head out a porthole and asked, "I say, would you like to come aboard for a spot of tea?" I'd probably have gone on to China if I hadn't had the good fortune to get hung up on a coral reef. The instructor came in a motorboat to rescue me. I'm sure he was grateful I didn't show up for the next class.

6

ROBERTA
NEW CHALLENGES ·

Back to Wichita Falls

When we returned to Wichita Falls, I was not given my old job back. A new principal had been installed at my high school. She didn't believe what degree one had should determine what one taught. She believed anyone could teach anything with the right textbook for the subject. I was asked to teach three classes of Physical Science and German (two levels in one class) and one class of Chemistry II. The other chemistry classes were taught by a man who had no degree in chemistry, while I had both the BA and MA. This new principal cared only about discipline. Very bad news. I lasted one year, then resigned and took an adjunct job teaching freshman chemistry classes at Midwestern State University where Eldon taught. I enjoyed those classes.

Mother seemed pretty happy at Rolling Meadows. She liked to play Bingo and to chat with the other residents and the attendants. I enjoyed visiting her every day after school and taking her on walks in her wheelchair around the grounds. I even took her to Lucy Park to see the waterfall there. One day she said to me, "Buddo, you like the outdoors. I do not." That was the end of those excursions. I should have known better.

Tornado

We had bought a lake lot on Lake Wichita in 1976 with the intention of building our retirement home there. Then the tornado of

April 10, 1979, destroyed a fourth of all houses in Wichita Falls. The tornado destruction made building a home at the time impossible because of the demand to rebuild houses lost in the storm.

We had been to a chemistry conference in Hawaii and had just gotten home after driving from the DFW airport when the siren sounded. Nancy and her friend Melanie were baking cookies in the kitchen. They were seniors in high school, and Melanie had driven over to show Nancy the new car her parents had just given her. After the second siren sounded, Melanie decided to drive back to her home, as her parents might be worried. She did, and she and her parents ended up hiding in a ditch across from her home. The tornado completely destroyed her home and her new car. It missed our house, only pulling up one tree. Despite my urging them to seek shelter, Eldon and Nancy watched the tornado's progress from our front yard. I hid under a mattress in a closet. Phillip, who sacked groceries at the grocery store, sheltered with others in the freezer. The store was partially destroyed. Sharon and Elizabeth were away at college. It was 1990 before we started to build our retirement home on Lake Wichita.

Our house on Marsha Lane sold very quickly, so we had to move into a rent house on Danberry in the Sikes Addition until our house on the lake could be completed. Most of our belongings were packed in boxes and left in the upper room of the rental house. The house was burglarized one weekend while we were away. Newspaper personnel had left a note on the stack of newspapers for our neighborhood, telling the paperboy which houses had temporarily stopped delivery. This is how the burglars knew we were gone. We recovered some things when the police arrested the burglars. After that, if we couldn't find something, we would suppose the burglars took it. This was our third burglary experience. The house on Marsha Lane had once been burglarized, but only the silverware was stolen. Insurance replaced that. The house in Hemel Hempsted in England was burglarized when a band of gypsies came through.

Life on Lake Wichita

Our new home on Lake Wichita has greatly increased our scope of wildlife watching. In spring, mother turtles toil slowly up the back yard from the lake to bury their eggs in our flowerbeds. Sadly, the skunks often dig them up. Armadillos dig for grubs. Robins, doves, bluejays, finches, and cardinals vie for food at our feeders. Mockingbirds defend their territory. Cedar waxwings invade to eat the yaupon berries. Canada geese survey our territory for nesting sites.

The white pelicans are fascinating to watch. They spread out evenly over the lake, looking like white polka dots on the blue water. All at once, maybe on some sort of signal, they come together and herd fish into a shallow spot on the edge of the lake. The water grows frothy with flopping fish. The pelicans gorge on the fish, their heads bobbing up and down in a frenzy of eating.

One Easter morning we lined up the grandchildren in the front yard for a picture. As I started to take the picture I saw a snake raise its head right next to the children. I called to the children to come on the porch and then walked toward the snake. I expected it to retreat. It popped its head up and made a rattling sound. Thinking it was an unusually aggressive rattlesnake, I called the sheriff, who arrived with a shotgun and declared it to be a bull snake, beneficial for keeping down the rat population. He walked toward the snake, which repeated its rattlesnake imitation. Boom! The sheriff shot it, then identified it as truly a bull snake. We decided the rattle was a defense mechanism that backfired.

Our other encounter with a bull snake happened sometime later. We were standing under the mesquite tree in the front yard when we heard furious squawking above our heads. There followed a tremendous thump on the ground before us. It was a very large bull snake. The force of the thump caused it to burp up a baby bird, which went staggering off into some bushes.

University Teaching

I was amazed at how easy teaching at Midwestern State University turned out to be. I had classes in a large lecture hall with more than a hundred students who listened attentively with almost no discipline problems. I taught at MSU for three years before a faculty bulletin advertising a job in Morocco caught my eye. It said that the King of Morocco had built a new university in Ifrane in the Middle Atlas Mountains and was looking for professors from the US to teach there. It seems that many top Moroccan students were going to the US or France for college, so the king wanted to set up a college in Morocco that would be just like an American college. All classes would be taught in English, and half the professors would be American. It was hoped that this would keep the top Moroccan students home and therefore not tainted with Western ways. The name of the university was Al Akhawayn, which translates "The Brothers." The reason for the name was that the Saudi king had helped financially in the building of the university. He wanted to make up to the king of Morocco, Hussan II, for a potential oil spill from a Saudi tanker in trouble off the coast of Morocco. The oil spill didn't happen, so the money was used to build this university.

I was intrigued. What a chance for a new adventure! Eldon was ready to retire and could go along if I got accepted. Why not give it a try? I applied and was very surprised to be accepted for the spring 1996 semester.

Morocco

I was told that I must be there by January first. It turned out that the university was not in session until the second week of January, but Dr. Rossini, my Moroccan boss, liked to give adamant orders. He was a real control freak. He required me to come to him for the key to the lab every time my classes met there.

Eldon retired from MSU and came with me. We were met at the airport in Rabat by a chauffeur who did not speak English, only French and Arabic. He drove us to the university, stopping on the way at a bakery where he indicated we should buy something to eat. All along the road we saw men in robes riding donkeys. I felt as if I had fallen asleep and awakened in a Christmas pageant, but I didn't know my role or my lines.

Luckily I had brought along two instant dinners in my suitcase, and that kept us going until we found English-speaking fellow professors who clued us in on our surroundings. The apartment we were given was brand new, two bedrooms with a kitchen.

The town of Ifrane was a good walk away. It had a bank, a pretty good restaurant in a hotel, and a grocery store. The post office opened and inspected all mail. Telephones had to be applied for; we never received one. Renting a car was impossible. Our only communication with the outside world was through the computer that all professors were given. Eldon had not used the computer at MSU, but in Morocco he quickly learned how to use one.

Our best friends turned out to be the Clarks. Jan was a business professor and Al was concerned with the university finances. They had been in Morocco a year and had bought a used Jeep Cherokee from an American Embassy person who was headed home. They took us into Meknes, the closest big town that had a Sam's Club-type store. We paid for the gas, so after that they asked us to go with them whenever they took a touring trip within Morocco. The university had a cafeteria, open whenever students were around. You had to be careful anywhere in Morocco about eating uncooked food. Otherwise your tummy would get upset, big time. Eldon got to be a pretty good cook in the apartment kitchen. His specialty was green pea soup made from dried peas. We bought canned Danish hams at the Meknes store.

I taught chemistry for non-science students, plus a lab for science students. In my lecture for non-science students I discussed kitchen chemistry and such things as not mixing toilet cleaners that could produce toxic chlorine gas. A young man said, "Which of us will ever clean a toilet?" I replied that he might not, but his wife might. He said he certainly hoped his wife would never clean a toilet. I quickly learned that the wealthy Moroccans considered physical labor degrading and beneath them. The students arrived at the dorms at the beginning of the semester in chauffeur-driven Mercedes. When some of the girls invited me to tea in their dorm room, they phoned their chauffeur to go to the market for more donuts when we ran out. There were a few scholarship students, but not many. The rest of the universities in Morocco were free. Classrooms in them were crowded and instruction questionable.

Language Problems

The students at Al Akhawayn were supposed to know English and to have passed an English test to prove it, but it soon became apparent some were less proficient in English than others. Perhaps they were friends of the examiner. On the first day of lab I gave my usual safety lecture. One rule was always to replace the lid of the reagent bottle after getting a chemical out of it. When I noticed the lid was not being replaced, I stopped the class and reminded them. They smiled and nodded but continued not replacing the lids. Then I spoke sternly, and the class got very quiet. A voice from the back of the class said, "Please, Sir, what means lid?" I knew then that English might be a problem. I explained what a lid was and that only men were addressed as "Sir," a comment that caused students to giggle at their mistake.

Eldon and I were strolling in the village of Ifrane near some shops and across from a school one day when a group of little girls came rushing out of the school toward us. "Bonjour, bonjour, bonjour," came from every girl's mouth. These children must have just come from their French lesson. French was taught in all the public schools in this part of Morocco because the country had been occupied by the French not too long ago. I said, "Bonjour" back, but when they continued the conversation I had to say, "No *parle* France. Parle *English*." Sudden silence. Looks of consternation. Much consultation. Then one small voice said hesitantly, "How—do—you— do"? I reached toward this child and shook her hand, saying, "How do you do?" back to her. Then all the little hands went up along with a chorus of "How-do-you-dos." A shopkeeper came out and asked us to leave. He thought we were blocking potential customers.

Maintenance work was not done to any extent at the university. We were told that the campus and buildings were designed to resemble an American campus. Everything was brand new. The buildings looked like a series of Swiss chalets, very pretty. This was the second year of the university's existence, but little things like loose doorknobs had not been tended to. There was beautiful green grass, unusual for this area, but it was hand clipped because the lawn mower had stopped working and no one fixed it.

A Visit from Prince Charles

Prince Charles of England came to the campus for a visit. It caused quite an uproar, but I was told it paled in comparison to the visit of Arafat the year before. Prince Charles had made a speech at Oxford entitled "Islam and the West," and the university had a contest for students to write an essay in English in response. The winner would get to spend a semester at Oxford as a prize. I was on the panel of judges, so I got to attend the reception and meet Prince Charles. He asked me where I was from, and I said, "Texas." When he spoke he said, "I am surprised to come to Morocco and find myself knee-deep in Texans." I wasn't sure how to take that.

In preparation for Prince Charles's visit, all the doorknobs were tightened, toilet paper appeared in the restrooms, and all the books in the library were stashed in bookshelves lining the hallway down which the prince would proceed to the reception. It was a snowy day, and all the marble sidewalks were lined with Arabian carpets. After Prince Charles's visit everything went back to normal.

Prince Charles chatting with Roberta

Eldon and I were invited to one of my student's homes in a medina in Meknes. Her father had five daughters and was active in Moroccan Girl Scouts. Her mother showed me how to make couscous from scratch. The girls took us shopping in the local souk. They coached me in how to bargain with the merchants. If I wanted to buy something I should tell the merchant I was poor and then offer a low price. Then the merchant would counter with a very high price and eventually come down to about half his first offer. I tried this out, and when I explained to the merchant that I had four children to feed and very little money, he replied, "Is that my fault?" I had to chuckle at that.

A Cultural Difference

An interesting difference in cultures quickly became apparent. Moroccans are loyal to friends and family. You are their friend if you do anything to help them, maybe just lending them a pencil when they need one. If your friend needs help on a test, it is your duty to help him or her. What we would call cheating they would think was the morally right thing to do. For that reason, Eldon had to help me monitor tests.

With the Clarks we visited Marrakech, Erfoud, Azrou, Rabat, Ouarzazate, Zagora, Taroudant, Fez, and Volubilis. We saw tree-climbing goats on Argon trees and were told that each tree was owned by a specific person, so your goats had better not be climbing the wrong trees. In Erfoud a movie was being filmed. Several German would-be actors thought we must be part of the crew. They kept pestering us to give them bit parts in the movie.

On one adventure Al Clark turned onto what he thought was a road to an interesting village. It was very bumpy. After we had driven awhile, a woman came running towards us waving her arms, her burka flapping out around her. She was screaming, *"Eau, eau, eau!"* Silly me, not knowing French, I thought she was saying, "Oh, oh, oh!" Al recognized she was saying "Water, Water, Water!" We were driving in a creek bed, not a road, and she was warning us that we were about to reach the main river. Good for her! We turned around and went back.

The buildings at Al Akhawayn were brand new, with many having long marble stairs leading to the entrance. The frequent snowfalls made the stairs slippery. I commented to one of my students that the university should install railings to hang on to. She replied, "Don't you know, Mrs. Sund, if Allah wanted you to fall, you would? Otherwise, not." Several students asked me to consider converting to the Muslim religion because they liked me and wanted to see me in Paradise. One lecturer who came to the campus spoke about recruitment in America. He said that if students went to America as missionaries for the Muslim religion, they should go to the prisons, as they had been shown to be fertile fields for recruitment.

7

ROBERTA
RETIRED BUT NOT RETIRING

At the end of the semester I was asked to stay at the Moroccan university, but I said no. One semester of adventure was enough. This was the end of my teaching career and the beginning of my quest for meaningful volunteer work. I tried several things before I hit on those that felt right for me. Interfaith Ministries, Kemp Center for the Arts, No One Dies Alone, Meals on Wheels, Democratic Women, Silver-Haired Legislature, and, finally, writing a column for the local paper, the *Times Record News*.

I had always considered myself an independent voter until George Bush took us into what I felt strongly was an unnecessary war in Iraq. We ordered a peace flag from the Mennonites, and I waved it on the side of Kemp Boulevard one cold February day. I joined the local Democratic Women's Club and was president for two years. At one meeting the editor of the local paper spoke. Several people asked why their letters to the editor were never published and why the Republican point of view was so prominent in the paper. She replied that if we wanted our say, we should apply to be on the community editorial board. She left application forms. The next morning she wrote in a newspaper editorial that she had spoken to the Democratic Women who challenged her to print more examples of their point of view, and she had left forms for them to apply for the editorial board, although not a single person took one. That challenged me. I applied and was accepted. I wrote a column almost every week for two-and-a-half years. Then the paper decided to rotate the community members off the board, replacing them with new people. This was fine with me. I had had my say. I treasure the many compliments I received and was not ruffled by the rude remarks of some Republicans who disagreed with me. Eldon kept a scrapbook of all my columns and of some of the replies I got.

Eldon's favorite volunteer work is with the Wichita Falls Adult Literacy Council. He loves to teach adults how to read. Many of the students are graduates of the local high school, where they were enrolled in special education classes either because they had learning disabilities or because they were class clowns and their teachers wanted to be rid of them. Thus they graduated without being able to read. Eldon is very proud of his successes. After Eldon's tutoring, one young man went to a junior college and passed English with an A. He enrolled in a welding course and had a job waiting for him. Another has just started classes at a junior college. Eldon enjoys advising his students on life problems as well as reading.

Our togetherness volunteer work has been delivering Meals on Wheels and serving on the board of the League of Women Voters.

Cuba

We have never quit traveling. Those adventures continue. One of the most interesting trips we made was to Cuba just after US visitors were once more allowed to go there. Rogene, Eldon, and I went on a visit sponsored by the Road Scholar program, formerly known as Elderhostel. It was explained to us that when the Russians were there and paying high prices for the Cuban sugar crop, things were fine. The government had plenty of money and paid everybody a decent salary. When the Russian economy tanked, the Russians left and ceased to buy the sugar. Now the government paid workers one-fourth of what was needed barely to survive. "The government pretends to pay us and we pretend to work," we were told. The Cubans were very proud of their excellent public schools and free medical care, with clinics within walking distance of every home. The medical school produced fine doctors who went to Venezuela to train doctors there. But the doctors could not live on the money paid them by the government. They could earn more as bellhops in a hotel. Tourism was the money pot. Mainly Canadians came to enjoy the climate and beauty of Cuba and added a lot of money to the economy.

We were amazed about the ingenuity of the Cuban people in finding ways to earn money. Old cars were kept running because Cubans made their own parts for them if something wore out. We visited a bed and breakfast for tourists. Very nice paintings and jewelry were for sale. Obviously the government was allowing some private enterprise.

The Russians had been in the process of building a subway system in Havana before they left. "Be careful not to step in any holes in the sidewalks in Havana. You might fall through to underground tunnels that were to be a part of a subway system," we were told. A nuclear power plant was also under construction. "Thank heaven the Russians left before they finished that," our guide exclaimed. The Russians did build a four-lane highway across Cuba. At one point our bus veered into the left-hand lane because a farmer was using the right-hand lane to dry his wheat crop. We saw many horse-drawn carts and people riding on benches in the backs of trucks along this four-lane expressway.

Having read about the sad fate of anyone who criticized the communist government in some countries such as North Korea, we were amazed at the jokes we heard spoken openly in Cuba. For example: If a Cuban died and was told he was going to hell but could choose between a socialist hell and a capitalist hell, he would choose the socialist hell because in the capitalist hell, the pot of boiling oil would be ready for him to be thrown into, but in the socialist hell, they would not be able to locate enough oil for the pot, or if they did, no one would know where the matches were.

8

ROGENE
ROGENE AND RICHARD

Richard and I married at the end of our second semester in graduate school. It was a double wedding with my twin and her husband, and I have never seen my father so happy. His two youngest daughters were marrying responsible young men, and his responsibility for their care was over. There is a picture of us leaving the church. Richard and I are in front, and Roberta and Eldon are just coming out of the door behind us. I am looking back at them over my shoulder. My elderly maiden aunt, Aunt Bob, upon seeing the picture said, "There goes Rogene. Always looking out after Roberta." I was deeply hurt by her remark and claimed it was not a valid statement. But, in truth, she was right. I was indeed looking back to see if Roberta and Eldon were okay. When this fact dawned on me, I resolved never again to play that role. It was Eldon's turn to take the responsibility to see that Roberta was okay. So, like our father, I gave up that care and resolved to move on in my married life without my twin.

My doctoral mentor was a man interested in the biochemistry of invertebrate organisms. My study was of the biochemical mechanisms of control in regenerative activity in the flatworm *planaria*. This little creature, which can be found under rocks in flowing cold water streams, has the interesting property of being able to regenerate either its tail or its head if it is cut in two. When cut in two, the head end grows a new tail and the tail end grows a new head. I kept the worms in a physiological saline medium and fed them bits of raw liver. But to obtain the creatures, I enlisted my husband, Richard, to help me collect them from under rocks in nearby Barton Creek. He complained mightily about the bruised shins he got from this activity, but it was a big help to me. I could, of course, increase the number of worms I had by cutting them in two. My studies involved developing hypotheses about what controlled the regrowth of the animals and then testing the hypotheses by adding various biochemicals to the solution in which the wounded flatworms lived. I can still think of things I would like to test.

Children

With time, the babies started to come. My husband liked to tell people that I got a husband, two children, and a PhD, all in four years. Those were busy years. We lived in a small apartment over a garage and had a bedroom with bath, a living room with a dining area, and a small kitchen. It was adequate for our needs. The birth of our children seemed to be timed by our major exams. All new graduate students in chemistry had to pass a major written exam at the end of two years of study, to determine if they would be allowed to continue in the doctoral program. The exam would ordinarily be in the late fall, but the faculty decided to move it up to late September so that I could complete the exam before the birth of our first child. This shift was thoughtful on the part of the faculty, but our first-born, Tim, decided to come on the exact date of that exam. My poor husband had to balance his time needed to study for the exam and the time he wanted to devote to being with his wife in labor. In the end, we both passed the exam. I was given a special dispensation to take the exam a week later if I promised not to discuss the questions with my husband. I had always been thorough in my studies, but that first week of motherhood curtailed my studying quite a bit. My mother came and stayed in our small apartment to help. But then my husband's mother and brother arrived, unannounced, to see the first baby their family had seen in decades, so my mother had to leave to stay with Roberta and Eldon in their apartment. My mother-in-law slept on the couch and Uncle

Johnny slept fitfully on the baby mattress on the floor. It was tough, but we made it. Our second child, Edith, was born just as my husband and I were both finishing our doctoral degrees in chemistry. I recall that I was about eight months pregnant when I went before my committee for my major oral exam. It was only a few months later that I had a meeting before the same group for my final defense of thesis. Many remarks were made about my change in appearance.

Arkansas School of Medicine

My husband's first job after we both finished our doctorates was with the Biochemistry Department of the Arkansas School of Medicine in Little Rock, Arkansas. He was an assistant professor, and I took a position as a research associate in the same department. When we first moved to Little Rock, I seriously considered staying home as a full-time mom. After discussions with my husband, we decided that I would work part time (9:00 a.m. to 3:00 p.m.) and hire household help to stay with the children and to do housework. I wanted to work only part time, so I could be with my children more. It had been painful for me in Austin to have to hand Tim over to a woman caregiver during the day. She kept a few babies, mostly of university students, in her home. Tim seemed happy there, but I missed him. So I was determined to keep Tim and Edie in our home in Little Rock and bring in help to do the housework and care for the children while I worked.

This arrangement turned out to be a wise choice, and we had two very fine people who worked for us. One was an African American woman who was very proud of the fact that none of her brothers had ever been in jail—quite an accomplishment. She was an excellent cook and made lunch for all of us every day. The house was just across the street from the medical center, so coming home for lunch was easy. The second helper we had was from the hills of Arkansas and almost scared me to death the first day she came. She spoke with a heavy

The Henderson family in Little Rock. From left,
Edith, Richard, Rogene, Tim, Lucy

backwoods accent and had many interesting sayings that were new to
me. After I came home on the first day, we talked over how things
had gone, and all seemed well. Then, just as she was leaving, she announced, "See y'all tomorrow, the Lord be willin' and the creek don't
rise." I gasped and said that I surely hoped she'd make it. She replied
that she would be there, "the Lord be willin' and the creek don't rise."
I held my breath the next day, and sure enough, she appeared. Every
day she left with the same message, but I knew to trust her after that
first day. Her other quaint saying was that anything made of cloth was
a rag. A scarf was a head rag, a pretty dress was a glad rag, and a handkerchief was a snot rag.

I was fortunate to be able to get that type of part-time work at the
beginning of my career. As the children prepared for school, I was
home to get them off and was back about the time they returned. The

arrangement also allowed me to keep up with my field so that when the children were older I could expand my career to full time.

Lucy, our second daughter, was born in Little Rock. She was a pleasant baby who was easy to care for. Our fourth child was a tragedy. Little Bobby was born prematurely and died shortly after birth because of poorly developed lungs. I think his death was the worst event in my life. But we had a happy family with Tim, Edith, and Lucy. They were all exceptionally bright children who learned quickly, learning to read well before they started school. Tim taught Edie to read and Lucy learned from her older siblings. Each had their own personality, of course, and that was illustrated by how they faced a common crisis, such as when they arrived at school without their lunch money. Tim would skip lunch and arrive home very hungry and angry that I had forgotten to give him his lunch money. Edie would not dream of missing lunch and would go through the lunch line as usual, but then at the cashier station, she would break down in tears and say her mother had forgotten to give her lunch money. The cashier would say it was all right, she could bring it tomorrow. Lucy would just ask her friends to share lunch with her, and they always did.

I was able to be a den mother for the Cub Scouts when Tim reached that age. It was interesting that the instructions given to den mothers by the Boy Scouts of America emphasized that all craft projects should be such that they could be taken home by the boys to be finished in collaboration with their dads. This was to ensure that male bonding was established. In my den, only my assistant den mother and I had male spouses at home. In fact, one single mother told me that she wanted to have her son in the Cub Scouts so he could have some male bonding. I wondered at the time if she was confused as to my gender.

I also taught Sunday school for two- to three-year-olds at my church. One Sunday a man whom I knew to be a prominent lawyer in town, and who was the father of twin boys, rushed in to drop the boys off for their class. As soon as I saw them, I suspected they had chicken pox, because the disease was going around and the boys had obvious red spots on their faces. I asked the father, who seemed to be in a hurry, "Could the boys have chicken pox?" He assured me, "No, they had that last year." With that, the father was gone, and I had two apparently infectious boys on my hands. The next week the father apologized and said it was mumps the boys had had last year, and the boys were now home recovering from chicken pox. Needless to say, many of my other charges were also home with the chicken pox.

Tim, Edie, Lucy

Tim grew up loving history and reading. He was never aggressive, as illustrated by a story he told me one day. He said that the cafeteria lady and he had a special signal. As he approached the checkout spot, the cashier would raise her eyebrows and Tim would nod yes. This was their secret code for saying he was the last in line. It seemed he was almost always last in line.

Tim was also very sensitive to any injustice he perceived, perhaps more so than I realized. After supper each night, my husband and I had a nightly ritual of discussing who would do the dishes that night. We both knew that I would end up doing the dishes, but my husband liked to offer to do them. This ritual occurred before the children were old enough to wash dishes. One night, after hearing our nightly ritual, Tim burst into tears and sobbed, "Mom, you should let Daddy do the dishes tonight. It's his turn!"

One reason Tim might have appeared passive is that he loved to daydream. One day he came home from third grade with an exercise sheet marked F-. The grade was the only mark on the sheet. Tim had been told to show it to his parents. I gasped when I saw it and Tim brushed it off as unimportant. "Gee Mom," he said, "it's only an F, it's not a Z."

Another time I visited Tim's class and the teacher discussed my husband as if he were a farmer. I was puzzled until the teacher told me that when she asked the students to tell what their fathers did, Tim said his dad worked with chickens. Tim was correct. His father was using chickens as an animal model for his Vitamin B_{12} deficiency research.

Edie caused a little more trouble in grade school. I knew she read very well before she went to school and wondered what the teachers did with her when the other children were learning to read. So I visited one day and found Edie in the far corner of the classroom reading the King James Version of the Bible. The teacher explained that that was her solution to keeping Edie busy. In the second grade, her very fine teacher sent a note home saying Edie had a behavior problem. I visited and found that when the teacher gave an assignment, Edie often rolled her eyes in apparent disgust. I said I would talk to her about it. On my next visit, the teacher was most apologetic and said she had discovered that Edie's eye rolling meant the assignment was too easy for her and now the teacher was giving her more challenging work.

I also had fun leading a Brownie troop for Edie and Lucy. The Brownies were for the younger girls (seven to eight years old) before they became full Girl Scouts. The funniest event I remember was when one of the little eight-year-old girls kept fidgeting with the top part of her Brownie dress. Finally she looked disgusted and said, "I just can't keep my bra down!" There was a good reason for that. She had nothing to impede her bra from sliding up around her neck. Her mom was apparently over-anxious on the subject.

While Tim and Edie were both on the shy side, Lucy was not. Lucy always had lots of friends and also made good grades in school. She was in the band. In high school, she had to be at school early for band practice. She also washed her hair every morning. Many a morning I remember her dashing out the door for school with her wet hair flying behind her. Sometimes, on cold mornings, the hair nearly froze.

Camping

In both Arkansas and later, when we lived in New Mexico, my husband and I loved to go camping, sometimes with fishing added as a special treat. One spring we headed for the Grand Canyon, planning to walk down the Bright Angel Trail to the bottom of the canyon, spend the night in sleeping bags, and then walk back up. This was during the Easter vacation when our children were six, eight, and ten years old. When we arrived at the camping ground at the top of the canyon, we were surprised to see the ground covered with snow, but we were told the temperature at the bottom of the canyon was in the seventies. We spent our first night in our pickup camper at the top campground, then proceeded to walk down the trail. The children carried their sleeping bags on their backs and my husband and I had backpacks filled with our own sleeping bags, food, and supplies. The first part of the trail was snowy and icy. My biggest fear was that our children might accidentally slide off the trail. But we walked very carefully at first and soon got past the snowy part of the trail. It was a fun walk after that, but I did notice that some of the hikers we met coming up out of the canyon had a curious yellowish/green color to their faces. I think they must have been short of oxygen. There were signs saying that donkeys were available for the trek down, with the restrictions that you must be over twelve years of age and under two hundred pounds in weight. Since I was the only one of our group to fit those restrictions, we did not consider taking the donkeys.

We had lunch on the trail and reached the bottom in time for supper, spreading out our sleeping bags for the night. The temperature was indeed in the seventies, and sleep came quickly to our crew. My husband was a bit of a noisy sleeper, and the sound of his snoring, which I found rather soothing, filled the air. Suddenly Tim appeared at my side. "Mom," he said, "there's coyotes out there." I reassured him that it was only his father snoring. "No," he said, "I am old enough to know the truth. I know that there are coyotes out there." It took a while to convince Tim that we were safe, but eventually, we all had a good night's sleep and walked out the next morning. It was a beautiful camping trip.

We had many weekend camping trips to local lakes in New Mexico. We often went to the Zuni lakes to fish. My husband and I would catch a lot of trout, and it was my job to cut off their heads, clean them, and store them in the ice chest. The children loved to use the fish guts and heads as bait to catch crawdads on the ends of lines made of string. They would end up with large bags of crawdads that we took home in the ice chest. Then it was my job to boil the crawdads and meticulously pick out the small amount of meat in their claws and use the meat to make a crawdad salad to serve the next day. I did not do that often, as it was too much work!

One time we had special visitors with us when we fished in the Zuni lakes. Our St. Andrew Presbyterian Church and the local Jewish community at Temple Albert formed an interfaith discussion group. Each family in the Presbyterian Church had a partner family at Temple Albert, and the two families did things together. We attended religious services together on Friday night and Sunday morning and ate a Sabbath dinner on Friday, then a Sunday noon meal together also. It was a very moving group for me, and I learned a lot from the interaction. When it came time to do an activity together, our family took our Jewish friends fishing with us at the Zuni lakes. As the Jewish mother watched me clean the fish, she saw that I first cut off their heads and then pulled out all the innards. She looked at me and said something I have never forgotten: "Do you know what those fish are thinking, Rogene? There is no God! There is no God!"

One of our camping trips was to see Disney World in California. We camped in our pickup camper in a location across the street and walked over to the site. On the way we passed a large sign saying, "No Pedestrians Allowed." Lucy, who had just begun to read, cautioned the family about the sign, saying they did not want any Presbyterians there. To this day, Lucy claims that she knew what the sign said but just did not pronounce it right, but it was too good a family story not to tell.

Lovelace Foundation

After five years in Arkansas, Richard got a job as a biochemist with the Lovelace Foundation in Albuquerque, New Mexico. I was again hired as a research associate on the same part-time schedule I had had in Arkansas. Lovelace was a great place to work. The Lovelace family had established a medical center that was well known for its medical work, especially on the lung. The original Doctor Lovelace had been at the Mayo Clinic in Minnesota when he was diagnosed with tuberculosis, a disease that physicians were exposed to in their care of their tuberculosis patients. Dr. Lovelace moved to the dry climate of New Mexico and eventually set up a large medical practice in Albuquerque. It was thought that the Lovelace Clinic would eventually become the state medical school, but that did not come to pass. The clinic was famous, however, for its respiratory research, and the National Aeronautics and Space Administration (NASA) used the clinic to perform medical exams on the first astronauts. After the atomic age began with the dropping of the atomic bombs on Japan, there was a great need for information on the effect of inhaled radionuclides on the body. The Atomic Energy Commission (AEC) asked for bids for medical research institutions to study this problem. A Rhodes Scholar named Sam White submitted the winning proposal for the work to be done at Lovelace, and a large facility, originally named the Fission Products Inhalation Laboratory, was built on the nearby Kirtland Air Force Base. The facility had state-of-the-art inhalation testing facilities. As the AEC later became the Energy Research and Development Agency (ERDA) and later the Department of Energy (DOE), the mission of the facility was broadened to include research on the health effects of inhaled air pollution products from any source of energy production. The name of the facility was changed to the Inhalation Toxicology Research Institute (ITRI) and later to the Lovelace Respiratory Research Institute (LRRI). My husband and I arrived at about the time the facility was ITRI when the main emphasis was still on radiation toxicology.

Change in Culture

The move from Little Rock, Arkansas, to Albuquerque, New Mexico, marked a change in culture. In Little Rock, there was a right

The Hendersons in Albuquerque.
From left, Edith, Richard, Tim, Rogene, Lucy

(expected) way to do things. You either followed those mores or you were considered an outcast. Our family fit the mold pretty well, so we were not too much bothered by the restrictions that were part of the culture. When we got to Albuquerque, we found a whole new world. There were at least three fully acceptable cultures (Anglo, Hispanic, and Native American), and no one right way to do things. I felt it as a breath of fresh air. But it also meant that my husband and I had to be careful to teach our family values to our children; we could not depend on society to take on that task for us.

Sarah and Isaac

My husband had been reared on a farm and wanted us to settle in a semirural area. After several years in Albuquerque, he bought a two-acre plot with a house on the edge of town. One day he announced that we needed an animal for our two-acre farmette. He said he would go to the local livestock auction and buy a calf that we could raise and later slaughter for meat. When he discovered the price of calves, he decided to buy a "butcher ewe," a sheep that was too old to breed and whose only value was to butcher and use for mutton. Thus our backyard became the home of an old snaggle-toothed beast headed for slaughter. After a few days, I noticed what looked like a white towel on the ground. With much fussing at my children for being so careless as to leave a good towel in the yard, I marched out to find not a towel, but a sweet little newborn lamb. We named the mother Sarah after the biblical character and the lamb was, of course, named Isaac. Sarah had not been too old to breed after all, but she was too old to nurse her son. So Isaac was bottle-fed by willing children and was used in a children's play at our church to represent the Lamb of God.

Ghost Ranch

In New Mexico we discovered an almost magical place called Ghost Ranch, where our family loved to vacation. This large acreage was once a dude ranch owned by the Pack family and was given to the Presbyterian Church for use as a conference center. There were many stories about the old days when cattle rustlers roamed the area and sometimes ended up hanging from trees in a ghostly manner— thus the name of Ghost Ranch. The ranch offered many lively one- or two-week courses that ranged from science (geology, paleontology, archeology, geology), to courses on social issues, to religion studies, to backpacking adventures. Sometimes our whole family went for different courses, and sometime I went alone or with the children. I truly enjoyed Ghost Ranch. When we drove through the gates to Ghost Ranch, I always felt a great sense of relief, as if my blood pressure went down twenty points. My husband shared this love of Ghost Ranch. When he died at the age of sixty-nine, his ashes were scattered there, as he had requested.

Many notables have come to Ghost Ranch, both as guests and as leaders of the conferences. Early on, our family came in our pickup camper to stay in the campground because it was too expensive for us to stay in the cabins. Also camping one summer was a family from Denmark, whose adult male member was consulting at nearby Los Alamos National Laboratory. He told me his family name was Bohr.

Rogene's family at Ghost Ranch. Back row, from left: Mark, Lucy, Catherine, Maryanne, Tim. Front row, from left, Nathaniel, Joe, Vivienne, Genny

"Oh," I said. "Are you the famous Neils Bohr, the Nobel Prize-winning physicist?"

"No," he replied. "I am his brother, Hans." I wondered how many other nuclear physicists working at Los Alamos came to vacation at Ghost Ranch.

At another time, when I was helping dig up an archeology site, the man digging with me chatted about how he had invented Pringle potato chips when he was working at Procter and Gamble. You never knew what your fellow students had been doing in their other lives.

One course that attracted a sell-out crowd was led by Dr. Karl Menninger of the Menninger Clinic in Kansas. The name of the course was What Ever Happened to Sin?, which was the title of Dr. Menninger's latest book. A thesis of the book was that our whole judicial system was based on trying to deny the responsibility of a criminal for his/her crime and to delay punishment as long as possible. The book pointed out that the benefit of immediate punishment was so the person at fault could move on to improve his or her life. He was hoping to meet with "movers and doers" who could influence prison reform in New Mexico. When he found out that we were just ordinary folk, he was not happy. The sponsors of the course were standing with Dr. Menninger on a porch outside the classroom, so we students could hear every word of their conversation. Dr. Menninger openly and loudly objected to teaching us, while the sponsors of the course pleaded with him to proceed. "These folk have come from all over the country to hear you talk. We can't let them down." Finally, he agreed to come in.

He sat down in front of us and asked, "Well, what do you want to talk about?"

We all held up his new book and in unison called out, "What ever happened to sin?"

He replied, "Have you read my book?" There was much nodding of heads. "Well, I said everything I had to say on that topic in the book. What else do you want to talk about?" Despite this rough start, we had a good week with Dr. Karl.

Another popular lecturer at Ghost Ranch was John Nichols, the Taos author of *The Milagro Beanfield War*. It was a powerful book and we enjoyed chatting with John about it. Part of the book's appeal was that it described the people of northern New Mexico so clearly. One local Hispanic man in the class asked, "How did you know my uncle so well? I know one of the characters must have been him." But John did not think so well of the book. He had written it quickly when he needed money. He then took his time to write two more books to complete a trilogy; he thought the last two books were his best. The class did not agree. I could not even read enough to finish the last two books in the trilogy. But John was a great storyteller. His class consisted of a morning and an evening lecture, but there was no agenda. John started each session with a story. Before the class realized it, the time for the morning or evening session had passed. No wonder he was a successful author!

Horse Tales

I recall two adventures at Ghost Ranch concerning horses. In one course we were to ride into a campsite in the mountains of northern New Mexico. I had had very little experience in horseback riding, so I asked the wranglers for a gentle horse. "Oh, yes, ma'am," I was told, "We'll get you a real gentle one." When the horses were distributed, my horse was named Terminator! I thought there had been a mistake and protested that I did not think I could handle a horse named Terminator. Again I was assured, there was no mistake, old Terminator was just the right horse for me. So off we went. I immediately noticed that "old Terminator" did not seem to like the fact that I was sitting on his back. As the column of horses headed up the trail, he would pause, and I had to encourage his forward movement with a little kick in the side. With each of my encouraging nudges, Terminator would buck up as if he wanted to get rid of me. This pattern continued all during the morning ride up to the top of the mountain where there was a campsite. By the time we stopped for lunch, I was exhausted from the constant struggle with Terminator and from the high altitude. I asked the wrangler what I was doing wrong that caused this "gentle" horse to act up so. "Oh," replied the wrangler, "Did Terminator get upset by the new saddle we put on him? We had a new saddle, and we needed to break it in. I thought old Terminator was the best horse for the job. Sorry if he acted up." Needless to say I rode a different horse and saddle going back down the mountain.

The other adventure with horses occurred much later. A young fellow named Bill, who was working under my supervision in the lab, came to me very excited about a forthcoming horseback ride in the Colorado mountains the next weekend. He was very proud of himself for having signed up for what seemed to him to be a fairly treacherous adventure. I was going on a similar trek that weekend but didn't tell him. I didn't want to belittle his bravado. After all, I was an older woman who he apparently would not expect to be strong and daring enough to do such a thing.

The trip I had signed up for out of Ghost Ranch was a week's horseback ride into the southern mountains of Colorado. Our group was hauled to our starting point in Colorado in vans, and then we and all our gear were loaded on horses for the trek up the mountain. When we came to our campsite, we each set up our own tents and settled in. Each new day was glorious. We ate our breakfasts in camp, packed our lunches, and then headed off on horseback for various beautiful mountain sites. On one of those days we met another group on horseback coming down the trail beside us. I looked up, and to my surprise, I saw that Bill was one of the group. As we passed on the trail, Bill looked shocked to see me. I casually said, "Hi, Bill" and he nodded and said, "Hi, Dr. Henderson." Suddenly Bill's famous trip became more down to earth and somewhat similar to what his old-lady boss might do.

The last night of our campout was filled with packing in expectation of an early morning ride down the mountain. We were to leave early so we could return to Ghost Ranch for lunch and check out for the journey home. During the week, we had asked about the fact that the wranglers only tied up one horse at night. The other horses were left loose. It was explained to us that the horse that was tied up was the lead horse, and the other horses would always stay with the lead horse. The morning of our last day we awoke to a strange silence. There was only one horse at our campsite. During the night, apparently, a new lead horse had emerged and led the other horses back to their ranch home below. To say that the wranglers were upset is an understatement. I learned some new words that day, words I hope I never have to hear again. The wranglers had to go down the mountain, some on foot, and bring back the errant horses. We were stuck on the mountain with not much to eat for lunch. It was growing dark when the horses returned. We finally got on the road to Ghost Ranch. We stopped at a restaurant for our evening meal, so it was quite late when we got back to Ghost Ranch. I threw my stuff in my car and headed for Albuquerque. All the way home, my car radio was announcing that a prisoner had escaped from the state prison, which I had to pass on my way home, and that no one should pick up any hitchhikers. What an end to a long, long day!

Among the famous people who came to Ghost Ranch was an elderly gentleman who helped me when I decided to go on a week-long backpacking trip out of Ghost Ranch. I was in my fifties and concerned that perhaps a week-long backpack would be too much for me. I wanted to go on the trip, but I did not want to slow the group down. At the beginning of the trip, we had a group meeting to establish camaraderie and to get our basic instructions. I was relieved to see that a seventy-two-year-old gentleman was to go on the trip. *Ah ha!* I thought. I will just walk with the older man and perhaps take care of him a little and all will be well. The next morning, I observed the older man running like a little jackrabbit around the two-mile loop that surrounded the alfalfa field in front of the dining room at Ghost Ranch. *Oops,* I thought to myself. *Perhaps I have misjudged the situation.* And truly, I had misjudged the older man. He had been a runner in the two-mile race in the 1932 Olympics. He and I did walk together on the hike, but he was looking after me, not vice versa. He always liked to be the first person to get up in the morning and to make the coffee. He would serve each of us, but his vision was no longer good. When he poured coffee, you had to be agile and move your cup to meet the flow or else the coffee might end up on the ground, or worse still, on your arm.

Medical Supplies

One summer our family was packing in Albuquerque for our traditional one-week vacation in Ghost Ranch when we got a call from the Ranch. "Would you mind stopping by Presbyterian Hospital to pick up some medical supplies for Ghost Ranch?" Of course, we said, we would be glad to. On our way to the hospital I imagined what the supplies might be. Hypodermic syringes? Bandages? Antibiotics? When we opened our trunk for the hospital attendant, he brought out boxes containing cases and cases of only one thing—Kaopectate!

Whoa! Before we left, the hospital attendant told us that we should stop off at a certain pharmacy in Española on our way and pick up some more kaopectate. Oh, my gosh! To top it off, when we stopped in Española, the pharmacist said they had had a run on this item, and now he had only two bottles left to give us. Oh, whoa! Should we perhaps just drop off this huge supply of kaopectate at Ghost Ranch and come back home? No, we were looking forward to a good time and would continue with our original plan. We were glad we stayed. The Ranch guests had had an unusually high outbreak of gastrointestinal upsets the week before we came. But the episodes had declined, and fortunately we had a great week with no ill health in our family.

Archeology and Paleontology

I loved to take archeology and paleontology courses at the ranch, where a major phytosaur (dinosaur) site was located. In the courses, archeology and paleontology sites on or near the ranch were studied under the leadership of people from the New Mexico Museum of Natural History. A famous explorer, Dr. Florence Ellis, was one of our teachers. One year, a site a little way outside the ranch was chosen for study. It had lots of tower structures. It had been studied the year before, and we were a follow-up crew. I held my breath when Dr. Ellis read off the assignments for each of us students to explore different locations on the site. I was in a group of three people who were to continue digging down in a tower that had been studied by another group the year before. Dr. Ellis told us, "I am sure the group last year did not reach the bottom of this tower. There must be valuable artifacts below the currently cleared level." And so we had our marching orders. Dig on! Digging in the tower was no easy task. It was already about twenty feet down, so the routine was pretty arduous. First, we gingerly dug up a layer of dirt and filled a bucket attached to a rope leading to the top of the tower. One of our group stayed on top and pulled the filled bucket to the top. The dirt was then put through a sieve to look for any artifacts that might be present. This routine was followed for five days. Even though there were many signs we were digging in virgin dirt, we eventually found some digging tools that had apparently been left in the tower in the past year. Ah, well. At least we had answered Dr. Ellis's query. Last year's crew had truly gotten to the bottom of the tower.

High School in Albuquerque

For high school, my husband and I felt our nerdy children would benefit from going to a private school in Albuquerque called the Boys Academy. It had recently become coed, so we had all three of our children take the entrance exam. All three passed and were admitted, but only Tim and Edie actually accepted the admission. Lucy had too many friends she did not want to leave, so she remained in public school. We found that some perceptions were left over from the old boys' school. Tim, who was okay in math, but did not excel, was placed in advanced math classes. Edie, who was a math whiz, was at first placed in a remedial math class and only later placed in the advanced class.

Tim loved the swim team; it was a sport in which he could compete well. Edie liked the choral group. Lucy was in her high school marching band.

College for Our Children

All of our children went to college. Tim did exceptionally well on the SAT exams and was accepted at Pitzer College, one of the Pomona Colleges. However, he was not offered scholarship money, so he accepted a Presidential Merit Scholarship to the University of New Mexico, where he began his college career. He later switched to the University of Cincinnati and, earning his own way, got a degree in journalism, which led to a job on a newspaper in Nyack, New York. He later worked for the *Miami Herald* and was part of a Pulitzer Prize-winning team for that paper. In New York he met the love of his life and his future wife, Maryanne McTernan, a registered dietician. This marriage was a great blessing for Tim and our whole family. They have one beautiful and talented daughter, Genevieve. Tim is still a journalist and works for the *Stateline* news agency of the Pew Charitable Trusts. Maryanne is a highly capable registered dietician who specializes in dietary counseling for people on dialysis.

Edie turned down a full scholarship to Washington University in St. Louis to attend Caltech in Pasadena. We drove her there to enroll. Edie had always printed her name as a signature and was challenged on this at the bank in Pasadena. My husband went with her to buy a car for transportation, but the only car within our price range had a standard shift, which Edie did not know how to drive. We left her with one of her male classmates offering to teach her to drive. Ah, the trials of taking a somewhat socially naïve daughter to college! She majored in applied math at Caltech and began dating. Edie finished her course of study as an undergraduate at Caltech and has earned her living since as a software engineer. She had two marriages that did not succeed, but is now happily married to Gene Brooks, in a more blissful union. She has had a highly successful career as a software engineer, doing classified work for federal agencies. She is and always was a good problem solver in writing software. She has been active in the community, especially in her church, where she is a leader and sings in the choir.

Lucy had a scholarship to Rensselaer Polytechnic in Troy, New York. She had an adventure getting to Troy. The distance was too far for us to drive her, so she took a plane with a transfer at New York's Kennedy Airport. She had a very heavy trunk and had never flown before. I held my breath and told Lucy to call as soon as she got to Troy or first thing in the morning after she got some sleep. She left on Friday. By Monday I was frantic—no word—so I called the college; they told me there were no private phones in the dorms, only phones in the hall. But an employee volunteered to check if she had registered. She had. What a relief! She was alive. It was two weeks before she actually called, after I sent her a postcard with two checkboxes, one marked alive, one marked dead. She explained that she knew she was all right, so why call? Lucy had an excellent time at Rensselaer. After four years and with high recommendations, she was admitted to the University of Pittsburg where she earned her PhD in physics. Lucy met her future husband, Mark Clemen, during her PhD studies. He was also finishing his doctorate in physics. They now have four children—Catherine, Nathaniel, Vivienne, and Joe—and live near Seattle, Washington, where Mark works for Boeing Corporation. Lucy occasionally teaches physics at a local community college and is very active in her church.

Grandchildren

There are many stories that could be told about our grandchildren, but one in particular I remember was about racing with Catherine in Washington State. It was a family reunion with Lucy and Mark in Bremerton, Washington. The rain forest was to the east, and the Pacific Ocean was to the west. It was a time of chatting and eating and bonding among my three children, their spouses, and my five grandchildren. When we could no longer stand being all together any longer, groups began to split off to do their thing. I joined my daughter, Lucy, her husband Mark, and the oldest of my grandchildren, Catherine. Catherine was thirteen, tall, willowy, and beautiful, but pleasantly unaware of her beauty and allure to the opposite sex. She was the first of the grandchildren to reach puberty. The four of us drove down the highway to a park and discovered a beautiful lake, so calm compared to the Pacific Ocean. We divided into two teams and rented small, flat, two-person kayaks. I was pleased that Catherine picked me as her teammate. I loaded into the back seat of our kayak, with much solicitous help from the owner and all my family members. They did not want the elderly grandma to get dunked in the water. But once on board, Catherine dared me to race her mom and dad, and off we went. Oars dipped smoothly into the water, pushing us ever faster over the calm lake. At first I tended to paddle against Catherine at times, but then I learned to coordinate my strokes with hers. We raced over the water with complete abandon, and I was no longer Grandma, but the rugged teammate of a beautiful young goddess determined to win. We easily beat Mom and Dad, who seemed somewhat startled by the ferociousness of our competitive spirit. It was good to be young again!

My goal, as a grandmother, was to take each grandchild on an exciting overseas trip. When Catherine reached the age of fifteen, I took her with me to Lyon, France, where I was working with the International Agency for Research on Cancer (IARC). Because I was working most of the time, Catherine was on her own a lot. She did not speak French and was a little shy, but she joined with the spouses of other scientists doing work for IARC on visits to various places near Lyon. The highlight of the trip for her was when I was able to take the weekend off from my IARC work and take her by train to Paris. There we attended mass at the famous Notre Dame Cathedral.

Nathaniel and I took a marvelous trip to the Galapagos Islands. I did not realize that Nathaniel suffered from seasickness, but he looked after himself and got some pills from the ship's doctor. He enjoyed all the swimming, hiking, and kayaking.

Vivi and Genny were about the same age, so I took the two of them together on an intergenerational Elderhostel trip having to do with the theater in London. A group of elders from the site told stories about their past, and the young people acted out the stories for evening performances. In addition, we attended three musical or theater performances in London. It was fun!

Finally, I took the youngest grandchild, Joe, on an intergenerational Elderhostel to Peru. It turned out that of the ten young people on the trip, only two were boys. Joe was at the age when he liked the attention of girls, while the other boy was not yet that interested. Joe was fifteen and already six feet three inches tall. I had no trouble locating him in the group of young people. He had a great time entertaining the girls. The trip involved three microclimates: the dry desert on the coast, the cold, high Andes in the center, and the hot and humid rain forest further inland. It was a great trip for both of us.

Catherine and Rogene in Lyon, France

Nathaniel and Rogene on Galapagos Island

9

ROGENE
MY CAREER IN SCIENCE

Research at Lovelace

When I first came to Lovelace, I still had a couple of years of funding on a National Institutes of Health (NIH) grant that I had gotten while in Arkansas looking at the effects of vitamin B_{12} deficiency in chickens. Chickens were one of the few animal models available for such studies, because mammals had too many intestinal bacteria that produced B_{12} to allow an animal to become deficient. In Arkansas I had had facilities in which I could house chickens and feed them a special diet deficient in B_{12}. This procedure proved difficult at Lovelace, where, at the time I came, there were no facilities to house chickens. So they set me up with cages in an old shack. When I came in to observe my chickens eating their special diet, there were mouse droppings all over the feed. So much for a B_{12} deficient diet! I struggled on as well as I could with other parts of my NIH work that did not require the chickens, but it was obvious I could not do the work at Lovelace, and I did not renew my grant. It was time to switch to work more appropriate to the goals of my new institute.

Broncho-Alveolar Lavage Technique

I became interested in the broncho-alveolar lavage technique that was being developed to wash out the lungs of dogs that had been exposed to radionuclides to help reduce the dose of insoluble radioactive material that had deposited in the lung. The lavage procedure consisted of gently filling the lung (one-half lung at a time) with a saline solution and then gently retrieving the solution. The Lovelace laboratories were known to have skilled procedures for the use of the broncho-alveolar lavage procedure in beagle dogs, an animal model that has a lung structure similar to humans. These skills were put to good use when a worker at the Rocky Flats Plant of the Department of Energy accidentally inhaled an aerosol containing plutonium oxide. This compound is poorly soluble, and the portion of the material reaching the alveoli in the deep lung would be expected to remain there for some time. Thus it was felt necessary to wash out his lungs to remove as much of these alpha-radiation-emitting particles as possible to reduce the dose to his lungs. A physician from Duke University was brought in to consult with the Lovelace veterinarians on their technique and to perform the lavage on the worker. The most surprising finding was that although the lavage fluid removed a small portion of the inhaled plutonium from the lung, the procedure stimulated a much larger portion of the dose to be excreted in the urine. The reason for the excretion is not entirely clear. I was allowed to analyze a sample of the lavage fluid for any biological markers of disease, but in the dilute solution, the markers were not detectable.

Medical personnel were already using this technique in patients to assay the cellular content of lavage fluid for cellular markers of lung disease and indicators of the stage of the disease. But I was interested in examining the soluble biochemical markers, such as enzymes and cytokines, that might serve as indicators of lung injury due to inhaled air pollution. This topic became my research niche for the next several years, as I studied the biochemical and cellular content of lavage fluid from animals on various studies of the toxicity of inhaled air pollutants. I established a publication record as my children were growing up.

Earthquake

In addition to the importance of biological markers of disease, there was also a great need for biological markers of exposure that could be used in epidemiological studies to link the occurrence of a disease entity to an exposure that might have caused the disease. I was invited to give a talk on this broad topic at a conference held near Athens, Greece. The site was a beautiful one, with the hotel on the side of a cliff overlooking the ocean. During one morning session, a slight rumbling could be heard. Some in the audience looked apprehensive. I had no experience with such rumbling and continued to concentrate on what the speaker was saying. Then the room began to shake and the rumbling became louder and louder, much like an approaching freight train. Now many people began to flee the room, heading for the outside area surrounding the hotel. I stood up and began to head outside also. But the speaker, who had no doubt spent a great deal of effort preparing his talk for this international meeting, just kept right on talking. This was my first, and so far only, experience with an earthquake. I did not know how to react. When I got outside, I felt sorry for the local people, who were trying to call their families to see if they were all right. One small group of attendees gathered on some nearby rocks and tried to continue the conference. I thought they were nuts and did not join them. My room was on one of the lower floors. I wondered if I was safe, especially if there were aftershocks. That night I was so tired I decided to risk it. I was awakened in the middle of the night when my son called from the US to see if I was all right. What excitement!

About the time Lucy reached junior high, the head of our institute called me in one day to discuss my future. I could tell he was pleased that I was being rather productive even though I was a part timer. But he was trying to decide if perhaps I was willing to go full time, now that my children were older, if he gave me a supervisory position. He wanted me to supervise the analytical chemistry/biochemical toxicology group, about fifteen people. I agreed and went to full time. There were many productive researchers in the group, and I benefitted from participating in many of their studies.

It was not long after I became a supervisor that the National Society of Toxicology pushed to establish a licensing exam for all toxicologists. The license meant that if we wanted to have credibility for our work, we should all take the exam. The leader of our institute did not tell us to take the first exam, but he, himself, did take it and passed. The second year he encouraged the rest of us to take the exam, and we set up a study group to prepare. The director told me privately that he knew I was a chemist and had never studied toxicology formally. He said he would not expect me to take the exam if I did not want to. Nothing he could have said would have made me more determined to take the exam. He was right in that I had never had a formal toxicology course in my life, but he was wrong in thinking I would not take up the challenge to pass the licensing exam. How could I supervise a group of toxicologists who had passed the exam if I had not taken it? With the help of the study group, I and most of my group passed the American Board of Toxicology exam the second year it was offered.

Our work was ideal for my interests. As someone who was interested in both chemistry and biology, I enjoyed doing research that used chemistry to understand the biological changes induced in animals by air pollution. The National Institute of Environmental Health Sciences was conducting studies on the ability of chemical exposures to induce cancer in rodents. If the chemical was administered by inhalation, it was important to know the dosage the test animals (rats and mice) were getting. We conducted toxicokinetic studies in the rodents to determine how much inhaled vapors or gases reached the target tissues, how the compounds were metabolized, and what the rates and routes of clearance were.

Another research problem I participated in was the effect of diesel exhaust on health, using a rat animal model. The Department of Energy was interested in the potential public health effect of increasing the use of diesel engines in light-duty vehicles, a prospect that was brought about by a gasoline shortage. My role was to quantitate the inflammatory response in the lung by analysis of broncho-alveolar lavage fluid for biochemical markers of damage. The study offered me many opportunities to meet and discuss issues with researchers from all over the world who were also working on this problem. The gasoline shortage problem did not last, but a major result of the research was that engine manufacturers were motivated to improve the diesel engine so that emissions were reduced to negligible amounts. With time and the turnover of existing diesel vehicles to those using the newer model engines, the emission of the traditional large black cloud of pollutants from diesel engines became a thing of the past. I felt good about that.

As supervisor of the Chemistry and Biochemical Toxicology Group, I ended up going on many field trips as we received funding to monitor the emissions from different kinds of energy production facilities. I considered these field trips as great adventures because I could see inside plants I would normally never visit. One of the first trips was to Morgantown, West Virginia, to visit the fluidized bed combustor there. I embarrassed myself by my naivety on this first trip. I happened to be the only female along. We flew into a nearby airport and then rented a car to drive to the motel where we were to stay. Now at this point in my life, the only time I had traveled by car and stopped at a motel was with my family. My father or husband always got out and got our rooms for us. So when we got to the motel, I asked the leader of our group to get a room for me. He looked at me in disbelief and replied, "Rogene, unless you want to sleep with one of us guys, you had better get in there and get your own room."

On another trip, we were at a facility making ammonia from coal. I remember walking down some steps on the side of what I think was a fermentation vessel. There was a faint smell of ammonia in the air and I remember thinking, "What is a lady from a small West Texas town doing walking down the side of this vessel?" But I considered it a great adventure and was grateful that I was privileged to participate in such interesting venues.

Texaco Visit

Later I learned the realities of industrial concerns. Our group received funding from the National Institute of Occupational Safety and Health (NIOSH) to monitor emissions from a coal gasification unit at a Tennessee Valley Authority (TVA) facility that had been built by Texaco. Our institution was mostly funded by the Department of Energy (DOE), so four major agencies were involved. After we got the funding, we were anxious to spend it, because we had budgeted salaries based on the new funding. As time passed, we negotiated with more and more people. We were invited to visit Texaco at their corporate headquarters in White Plains, New York. An aerosol scientist, George, and I visited with them. We were ushered into a very large conference room with a huge conference table at which many Texaco personnel were seated. I learned later that most of them were lawyers. Two were toxicologists whom I knew. Everyone was cordial. George gave a presentation on exactly what we wanted to do. There was a little discussion and then each person there was asked if we should be allowed to do the work. I have never heard so many clever ways of saying no. Even my toxicology friends said they did not think so. Then we were all taken to lunch. As an aside I noticed a picture on the wall of Dr. Loreen Rogers, my helper in graduate school, who was now on the Texaco Board. Amazing! She had gone from being the assistant to a major professor at the University of Texas to being president of all of UT, to being on the Board at Texaco.

We came home discouraged but kept pushing for entry into the TVA facility. Once we were told that we would be welcome, but we had to keep all our data in a lock box at the gasifier and could not take any information home with us. That sounded like a new form of "no" to me. After a bit, George remembered that he had a friend who worked at the same TVA facility. He called him up and asked, confidentially, what was going on. The friend explained that the Texaco gasifier had had a lot of good publicity. It was written up in *Time* magazine as the latest and greatest energy tool. Then it hit a glitch. It was not performing well. The friend assured us that as soon as it was up and running again, we would be welcome. Sure enough, a few months later, we were called and asked to come on down. What were we waiting for? They would be glad to see us. No lock box required. So, at last, after eighteen months, we went on our monitoring mission for NIOSH. The facility was clean as a whistle, with little to no emissions. Live and learn!

Gulf War Syndrome/ Nerve Gas

Some of my research related to military concerns. Veterans returning from the Gulf War in the early 1990s complained of a poorly defined malady that came to be called the Gulf War illness. One hypothesis for the cause was possible exposure to small, subclinical amounts of the nerve gas sarin. A lot was known about the effects of high doses of sarin, but there had been fewer studies on the effects of low doses. We were funded to shed some light on this topic. We designed a study in which rats were exposed by inhalation, under normal and heat stress conditions, to enough airborne sarin to result in one tenth the dose required to cause nervous symptoms. The experiment required a high level of safety measures to generate the sarin exposure atmospheres safely and to expose the animals without exposing the technical staff to any danger. We only needed, and indeed were only allowed to receive, an "exempt" amount of sarin for our studies. The term exempt meant that it was too little for us to cause much harm with it. We calculated that if we dropped the vial containing all the sarin we had on the exposure room floor, a person standing in the room without respiratory protection would suffer only constricted pupils. Nevertheless, the technical staff was rightfully concerned about handling the nerve gas sarin. One fellow put it bluntly, "We've been taught how to handle plutonium, but we don't know how to handle nerve gas."

We instituted a more intensive training course. I learned that one concern was that the respirators worn might not prevent exposure to the sarin. The technical staff had excellent skills, so I told the members to design their own experiment to test the efficiency of their respirators in blocking their exposures to sarin. They designed a rigorous test, and the results convinced us that the respirators were protective. So the experiment went on. During the time of concern, one technician who had an air force friend assigned to Kirtland Air Force Base where our laboratory was located (at the courtesy of the Commander) told her friend that we were working with sarin. She apparently did not mention that the amount was "exempt." This information resulted in a message from the office of the base commander asking for information about our planning to receive "agent on base." The phrase "agent on base" seemed to govern the mode of delivery of sarin to our laboratory. I received a call saying a team of Air Force personnel would visit our laboratory to inform us of the protocol for transfer of the sarin to our laboratory. We were told that a plane would bring the sarin to our local airport and a truck with an accompanying convoy of armed personnel would bring the sarin from the airport to our laboratory. Someone would inform me of the progress on a regular basis. Thus, on the day of delivery, I got a call saying the agent would land at a specific time; this information was followed by a call saying the agent had landed and was in a truck headed our way. A third call told me the agent had arrived at our laboratory. By that time I and the technical staff were all lined up at the previously designated parking spot, ready to receive the agent. The truck, which was the size of a middle-sized moving van, and the accompanying convoy of cars drove up and parked in an area close to, but not exactly where, we had agreed to receive the sarin. Immediately, the driver of the truck and all drivers of the convoy cars jumped out of their vehicles in their army uniforms with rifles in their hands and formed a circle around the truck, arms at the ready. I naively ran toward the truck to let them know they had parked in the wrong place. One of the young soldiers jumped in front of me with his rifle, blocking my way. A soldier who seemed to be in charge and who had attended our earlier planning meeting, yelled out "Don't worry! She's the PI (Principal Investigator)."

After this bit of excitement, we decided the truck was parked just fine. The back of the truck was opened, and I saw a rectangular wooden box, about four feet by two feet in size, that was dwarfed by the large size of the otherwise empty van. The box was moved inside and opened. In the box was a small vial about the size of a lipstick tube, which contained the few milliliters of sarin that we were allowed to have under the exempt category. This vial was promptly put in a safety vault and closed by a special lock provided by the army. Once the agent was locked up, the soldiers visibly relaxed and asked us about good places to eat in Albuquerque. Thus began our studies on the inhalation toxicity of low levels of sarin. Our findings, which were interesting but did not fully explain the symptoms seen in the Gulf War illness, are published in the toxicology literature.

Committee Service

As I grew older and more recognized in my field, I began to be asked to serve on advisory committees. These were mainly for the National Institutes of Health (NIH), the National Academy of Sciences/National Research Council (NAS/NRC), the Environmental Protection Agency (EPA), the World Health Organization (WHO), and the Health Effects Institute (HEI), plus a few state committees.

National Institutes of Health

The NIH was a primary funding source for studies in biochemistry and toxicology. There are several institutes that are a part of the NIH, and the institute that funded work in my field was the National Institute of Environmental Health Sciences (NIEHS), which was located in Raleigh Durham, North Carolina. Their external review process for funding research was headed by a highly capable woman, Anne Sussman. She was a pleasure to work with. I served two terms on their Toxicology Study Section, which reviewed research proposals submitted for funding. I then served on the NIEHS Council, chaired by the then director of NIEHS, Ken Olden. The council performed a programmatic review of the proposals that were ranked highly for their science in the first review group, the study section. By law, there must be one member of the council who represents the business community. One year, this person suggested that we not recommend funding for anyone who had a long history of NIH funding, which included some of the best researchers. The businessman felt that if they had not finished their work after years of funding, they did not deserve continued funding. NIH staff quietly advised him on the value of long years of successful research. It was an honor and a privilege to serve on both the study section and the council.

Inhalation Toxicology Workshop/Textbook

Once I worked with Faye Calhoun, the NIEHS person in charge of our study section, to develop an Inhalation Toxicology Workshop at our institute in Albuquerque. The workshop was sponsored by the NIEHS, and a book with the same title was published with all the presentations made at the workshop. The hands-on demonstrations required quite a lot of commitment of time and equipment from the Lovelace Institute. I am grateful to R. O. McClellan, the director, for coordinating the work. He and I served as editors of the book, which came to be used as a classroom text.

How One Sentence Torpedoed a Rather Large Research Grant

I was once asked to participate in a review group for a site visit at a major research facility doing a study on the use of analysis of human broncho-alveolar lavage fluid for biomarkers to stage a pulmonary disease process and to determine the effectiveness of intervention treatments. Site visits are used by NIH to review major research projects, so a great deal of funding was at stake for the research group. The biochemist who was the principal investigator presented a solid case for why the study should be done and indicated the time sequence required for the conduct of the broncho-alveolar lavages. On the last day of the review, at almost the last hour, the medical doctor who was to conduct the broncho-aveolar lavages and who was internationally known for his clinical work, arrived for our questions. His arrival was a dramatic scene. He processed into the room, dressed in a long white coat with a stethoscope swinging from his neck, followed by several of his fellows, who stood behind him like a muted Greek chorus. The chair of our review group expressed our gratitude to him for taking time from his important clinical duties to come and talk with us. Then came the key question. Was the good doctor willing to conduct the lavages on the schedule planned by the biochemist? The answer was immediate and firmly stated. "I will perform broncho-alveolar lavage when it is clinically efficacious and at no other time." Ah, the power of a single sentence. Whether he knew it or not, the medical doctor had just put an end to all consideration of what might have been a very valuable research project. It was obvious that the biochemist had not consulted with the pulmonologist about his research plan. If I had been a patient of the pulmonologist, I would have been grateful for his stand.

Research Project Rescued

I am a strong supporter of the NIH review process, but occasionally, human nature interfered. When new people came on the study section, it was only natural that they wanted to prove themselves in some way. I happened to be the primary reviewer of what I considered to be an excellent proposal. I gave it a glowing review, which was followed by a supportive, but somewhat less glowing review by the secondary reviewer. We were about to vote when a brand new member of our group, who prided herself on her knowledge of statistics, said that the proposal could not be approved because of the faulty statistical plan. I was caught flat-footed, because I had thought the statistical plan was adequate and therefore had not spent much time planning to defend it. The secondary reviewer was in a similar position. The debate ranged back and forth, and it was finally decided to hold off funding for six months until the head of the study could explain. In the end it turned out that the statistical methods were not only acceptable, they were state-of-the-art. To this day I regret that I was not able to defend the methods adequately. The person who had raised the objections that led to delaying funding for six months merely stated she was sorry; she guessed she had not read the statistics properly.

National Academy of Science/National Research Council

Quite early in my research career at Lovelace, one of the senior investigators in the radiation toxicology field told me he wanted me to consider serving on a National Academy of Sciences (NAS) committee. He had been asked to serve but did not think he had the time and had suggested me as a replacement. I was totally shocked. A committee of the National Academy of Sciences was to me the pinnacle of scientific prestige, and I felt unworthy to be a member of such an auspicious group. After asking the advice of several colleagues, I decided to accept the challenge, beginning a long and fruitful interaction with the National Academy of Sciences and its National Research Council (NRC), for which I served on twenty-eight committees, chairing eight.

I quickly learned that the members of academy committees were just like the rest of us but with special knowledge that was required for the report that was being developed. That first committee was on the epidemiology of air pollution, chaired by Maureen Henderson of the University of Washington. Because of the similarity of our names, I sometimes got memos meant for the chair by mistake. She was a great chair and served as a good role model for me. Subsequently I was asked to serve on many NAS/NRC committees, sometimes as chair. I worked on committees addressing the air quality on submarines, on spacecraft, and on aircraft carriers. Other committees were on biological markers of lung disease, risk assessment methodologies, guidelines for estimating acceptable acute exposures, permissible exposures for jet fuels and for military smokes and obscurants, the toxicity of zinc cadmium sulfide, risk-based criteria for non-RCRA hazardous waste, public health benefits of proposed air pollution regulations, human health risks of trichloroethylene, the hidden costs of energy production and use, and an Institute of Medicine (IOM) committee on assessing the science base for tobacco harm reduction. These were not paid positions but well worth the effort because of the fascinating people I was able to work with and because the problems we were addressing were real-world problems, in need of the advice of committee members. This real-world connection was especially strong in the case of the NAS/NRC Committee on Toxicology (COT), a standing committee that met about three times a year and gave advice to the military. The staff person for COT was Kulbir Bakshi, a great person to work with. In contrast to the EPA, which was usually predicting potential toxic events for the future, the military had immediate, acute problems that needed solving.

The Yellow Submarine

A great example was what I called "the yellow submarine" problem. Submariners on nuclear-powered boats found that when they arose from their bunks, a yellow image of their bodies was left behind, which was disconcerting. What was the source of the yellow substance in the air? It turned out that the electrostatic precipitator that was part of the air clean-up system was catalyzing the interaction of trace airborne organic matter with the nitrogen in the air to form nitrophenols, which are bright yellow in color. Once this information was known, the Navy quickly solved the problem.

Germ Warfare Experiments

Another exciting problem was when information regarding the Army's studies designed to protect the US from potential germ warfare attacks was first declassified and made public in the 1990s. It turned out that the Army back in the 1950s had used a simulant for germs to determine how broadly such material could be dispersed from an airplane. The Army had first used a bacterium, *Serratia marcessans*, which was considered not to be harmful. But when a few people seemed to be sensitive to this bacterium, the Army had to consider alternatives for its studies. It chose to use a tiny ceramic bead of zinc cadmium sulfide that had been sintered (heated to a high temperature) to harden it into respirable-sized particles. The chemical was useful because it could be manufactured to be the size of a bacterium and would fluoresce under black light (uv light), making it easily detectible. Army personnel at the time were not too concerned about the potential toxicity of the particle, since they had apparently asked George Merck if he thought it was toxic, and he said he did not think so. So toxicity testing had been suboptimal, to say the least. The Army used the zinc cadmium sulfide to determine the disbursement characteristics of such a particle if it was released at different altitudes over our nation. Thus the test particles were spread over a good deal of the US, from Mexico to Canada. One specific spot that was studied in depth was Minneapolis, Minnesota. Planes released the particles over an elementary school and then a black light (UV light) was used to detect the particles and determine if they had entered the school. School children were lined up and scanned with a black light.

When this information was declassified and made public, there was naturally some public concern about the potential health effects of spraying these particles over such a wide area of the country. The Army asked the NAS/NRC to form a committee to evaluate the situation. The committee fell under the aegis of the Committee on Toxicology, so I chaired the subcommittee on zinc cadmium sulfide. It was perhaps the most interesting committee I was ever on. Because of the public concern, the committee had a diverse membership including not only physical, chemical, and health scientists, but also public and environmental activists and ethicists. We had three public meetings, and I was quite impressed with the local public speakers we heard.

Some of the children who had been scanned in Minneapolis, now forty years older, had organized into a group called Children of the 50s. They spoke before our committee and said they feared that the black light was a radiation detector and that they had been exposed to radiation. Among other members of the public, concerns were wide ranging, covering everything bad that had happened to them in the past forty years. But none of them directly accused the zinc cadmium sulfide of causing their problems. They just seemed to want information on whether members of our committee thought there was any possibility of a connection. We noted all concerns and published two reports. One report was for the public, to address its concerns. The other report was more technical and included all the scientific data on potential exposures and health effects. After much study, the committee concluded that the particles, which were used in small amounts as tracers, were not released in an amount that would be expected to cause health effects.

Board on Environmental Studies and Toxicology

Finally, after all this committee work, I was asked to become a member of the Board on Environmental Studies and Toxicology, or BEST. The Academies of Sciences have about sixty to seventy boards that provide oversight for the many academy committees, but BEST was one of the most active. The Academy Director of BEST was and still is Jim Reisa. BEST was Jim's life; he devoted all his many talents and his many contacts in Washington, DC, to keeping BEST as fully engaged in the nation's scientific problems as possible. Funding for the BEST projects came from federal agencies, sometimes as the result of congressional mandates. The scientific experts who served on the various committees were not paid, but their travel expenses were reimbursed. Also the BEST had a talented staff of scientists who worked full time at the Academy and whose salaries had to be paid. It seemed as if Jim was tuned in to just about every potential source of funding and knew how to keep the BEST advisory body busy doing the nation's work. If funding was available, we met three times a year to discuss current and pending projects.

Song and Dance with Twin

At the end of each member's three- or six-year term on BEST, the group had a farewell "roast" of retiring members at a lovely old home on Cape Cod, a home that had been donated to the Academy by the original owners. I especially remember my "roast" at the end of six years. I asked my twin sister, Roberta, and her husband to come as my guests. As a surprise, she and I performed a singing act, called "We had to be two." We danced together, singing a song about deciding to clone ourselves, then split apart for the grand finale. It was quite a hit!

Now at the end of my career, I was asked to serve two terms as chair of BEST. It remains a highly viable and productive group that is available to meet the special scientific problems in our country. I was also asked to assume the honorary title of National Associate of the National Academies. This is sort of a prize for doing a lot of work for the Academies, even though you are not an official member of the Academies.

The Environmental Protection Agency

The EPA funded some of my research on biological markers of pulmonary disease, so in 1989 I was asked to be a member of an Ad Hoc advisory group on biological markers for the Environmental Health Committee of the EPA Science Advisory Board. I later became a member of the Environmental Health Committee, but it was not an active committee, meeting only twice in my four-year term. In the same time frame, I was asked to serve as a member of the Advisory Search Committee for a Director of the Environmental Toxicology Division of the EPA. This was an important responsibility. I especially remember taking part in a swearing-in process in which I pledged allegiance to the USA. I had not done that since I was in grade school.

There followed other EPA committees. I was a member of the EPA Ad Hoc Advisory Group on Applications of Specimen Banking, Biological Monitoring, and Biological Markers for Exposure Assessment (1993); a member of the International Life Sciences Institute/EPA Committee on Dose Selection for Chronic Bioassays (1993); a member of the EPA Advisory Panel for Revising the Ozone Criteria Document (1993); and a member of the EPA Review Panel for providing guidance on setting acute exposure reference standards (1995). In 1995, I also served as an author on the EPA revision of the section on biological plausibility of the revision of the PM_{10} regulations.

One state committee I enjoyed serving on was related to the EPA. The committee was the New Mexico PCB Expert Advisory Panel. A furnace in the basement of a state public building had overheated and hydraulic fluid containing PCBs was distilled upwards into all parts of the building, with the material condensing first on the upper floors and relatively less material condensing on the lower floors. Our panel was to advise on the degree of cleanup required to allow reentry into the building. This was a practical use of my training in chemistry and toxicology. We met with representatives of the EPA several times. Each time we met, our panel would make recommendations, but the representatives of the EPA were not able to make any decisions until they had gone back to headquarters for consultation. So it was a slow process. For the final monitoring of the cleanup, the EPA at first proposed dividing all surfaces of the building, including floors and ceilings, into small squares, and taking swipe samples from each square to be monitored for PCBs. This would take a tremendous amount of time and money. A member of our panel suggested that the number of samples to be taken from a surface should depend on the likelihood that the surface would be touched by occupants. Thus only a few samples needed to be taken from the ceiling, but more intensive sampling should be taken on doors. This plan was ultimately accepted. By the time the cleanup was completed, I think the building was so much cleaner than the outside air that just opening the doors to the building probably contaminated it a bit.

In 2002 I accepted an invitation to join the EPA Board of Scientific Counselors (BOSC), which gave scientific and administrative advice to the EPA. Jim Johnson chaired the BOSC, and I became his vice chair. In 2004 I chaired the BOSC Symposium on Risk Assessment Practices of the EPA, and in 2005 I chaired the BOSC Review Panel for the EPA PM/O3 Research Program. My experience on BOSC was an important learning process for an even more important task that I was to begin in 2004.

The Clean Air Scientific Advisory Committee (CASAC) of the EPA is a congressionally mandated committee that by law (the Clean Air Act) is to advise the administrator of the EPA on the scientific bases for setting standards for the criteria air pollutants (lead, ozone, particulate matter or PM, carbon monoxide, sulfur oxide). The CASAC is to inform the administrator on the scientific bases for setting standards that will protect human health (primary standard) and the environment (secondary standard) without regard for either the cost or the ability to implement the standard. The committee membership includes some of the best air pollution and medical scientists in the country. As you might guess, there is considerable pressure on the committee from stakeholders whose interests are affected by the setting of the standards. I had a great deal of respect for the CASAC.

Chair of CASAC

Thus I was startled one day in 2004 when I received a phone call from Vanessa Vu, the head of the EPA Scientific Review Office, asking me if I would consider becoming chair of the CASAC. I was as startled as I had been early in my career when a colleague asked if I would join my first Academy committee. First of all, I had never been a member of CASAC, and the chair was usually selected from the membership. Second, I had just retired from active laboratory work and was concerned about the workload for the chair of CASAC. I asked Vanessa why she was asking me. I could tell she was not wholeheartedly enthusiastic about asking me. But she explained that the CASAC had been on dead center for a while and could not seem to move forward. The hope was that a neutral person such as myself could get things moving again. I later learned that a person at the Academy of Sciences had strongly recommended me because of my ability to chair committees that included cantankerous members. I suppose I was a sort of peacemaker. I told Vanessa I would think about it and get back to her in a few days.

I first talked to the man who had been my boss for a short time before I retired and who had served as chair of CASAC fairly recently. I asked about the amount of time it took and whether he found it a rewarding experience. I think I have never seen a man as surprised as he. He did not, at first, answer my queries, but just exploded with reasons why I should not accept this invitation. It was fairly obvious that he did not think I was up to the job. As usual in my life, I was inspired to meet the challenge. I knew right then that I would accept the invitation. He later said he had given it some more thought and guessed I would be acceptable in the job. He also gave me some idea about the amount of time it would take.

A New Challenge

The next real challenge I had was the first committee meeting with me as chair. I was praying for guidance as I walked into a room with a huge table at which sat some of the most brilliant and self-assured scientists in the world. These people had strong ideas. They not only thought they were right, they knew they were right. Also present in the room were reporters and EPA staff members and stakeholders who wished to speak to the committee. No one looked especially happy to see me. The general process was that the EPA staff prepared a large review of all the scientific information available pertinent to the setting of a standard for one of the criteria pollutants. Then another part of the EPA prepared a document suggesting how this scientific information could be applied to implementing a standard. The job of the CASAC was to review both documents for scientific accuracy and completeness. The CASAC review of the first document was usually fairly routine because the document was exhaustive in its inclusion of all possible scientific data on the subject. But the second document, in which actual possible standards were suggested, could be quite controversial. It turned out that the holdup that had caused EPA concern was that the CASAC was continually delaying sign-off on the second document; therefore, they were effectively delaying the setting of the standard. Some members of the committee felt that they should be in charge of how the standards were set; instead of just advising the administrator, they wanted to tell the administrator what to do. In other words, they wanted to set policy. That was not the intent of the Clean Air Act. We were to advise the administrator on the scientific basis for setting standards, and the administrator was to set the standards based on science and his policy decisions. If the administrator did not follow our advice, the administrator should explain why he/she did not.

Feisty Chair

So we got the committee moving again, and sure enough, the administrator did not set the next standard within the range of values suggested by CASAC. This move resulted in a strong, precedent-setting letter of protest from CASAC to the administrator. I felt this was the appropriate approach for CASAC because, in the letter, we emphasized the scientific basis for our recommendations and our concern for the public health. That letter earned me the moniker of "the feisty chair" of CASAC, as I was referred to by a reporter for *Inside EPA*. I took this as a compliment.

The next major conflict that occurred on CASAC was when, for the ozone standard, we recommended a separate form for the secondary standard (to protect the environment) from the primary standard (to protect health). In the past, there had never been enough information concerning the setting of the secondary standard to allow setting it any differently from the primary standard. The experts at the CASAC meeting on ozone in 2008 provided convincing evidence that we now knew enough about how ozone affects vegetation that we should use a different form for the secondary standard. It was not to set a different level, but to monitor the levels to protect against damaging ozone levels during the growing season. This was a new approach that we felt was a pioneering step in making the secondary standard more meaningful. The EPA staff was in agreement, and we heard rumors that the administrator was supportive. The last step in setting a standard is that it must be reviewed by the White House through the Office of Management and Budget (OMB). To our dismay, the OMB review came back negative, stating that by law the secondary standard had to be the same as the primary standard. This was not true. The EPA wrote back a lengthy, scholarly response pointing out that it was not against the law to follow the suggestion of a new form for the secondary standard.

President Bush Prevents Setting of
New Ozone Secondary Standard

Hours before a press conference had been called to announce the new ozone standard, a message came from OMB saying that it had asked President Bush for his opinion, and he had recommended not to use a separate form for the secondary standard. This decision caused EPA staff members to have to delay the press conference until they could quickly change all the documentation and drop the section on changing the form of the secondary standard. No valid reason was ever given for not being able to implement the new standard. A tremendous amount of work by many scientists went down the drain in what must have been a snap decision by those who had not fully considered the science behind a need for the altered form. This situation resulted in a letter of protest from CASAC signed by all its members.

Speaking Truth to Power: Testifying Before House Committee

As a result, I was called to testify before the House Committee on Government Reform chaired by Congressman Henry Waxman. At the witness table were Administrator Stephen Johnson, the OMB lady, and myself. My testimony was simple. I only had to tell the truth, and I felt it important to speak truth to power. The other two had to explain their actions. I remember the OMB lady turning to me afterward and saying that I should not be concerned because they were not talking about the level of the standard, just the form. I replied that the form change was the part that required scientific knowledge of how ozone affects vegetation, and the CASAC was the best source of that scientific information. Nevertheless, the recommendation of Administrator Johnson, President Bush, and the OMB remained in place.

I was honored to be able to work in an advisory role for the EPA. I consider our country to be most fortunate to have an agency such as the EPA to look after the quality of our environment. I was only involved in the work to keep our air clean, but the EPA is responsible for the total environment, including our water. I observed that the EPA staff were hard working, devoted public servants who took very seriously their roles in providing the information needed by policy makers to maintain a healthy environment. This was done with full regard for sound science and with no regard for current political pressures. The EPA is truly a valuable resource for our nation.

World Health Organization (WHO)

Part of the great pleasure of working on international advisory groups is the ability to meet and exchange ideas with people from different cultures. I served on the WHO Advisory Group on the Use of Biological Markers in Risk Assessment and on the WHO Advisory Panel on Biomarkers in Australia. The trip to Australia was fascinating all by itself, as I had never been "down under." It was 1993, and cell phones had just begun to be used in the US. But at our meeting in Australia, I think every single Australian citizen in our workshop must have had a cell phone. At our breaks, they would line up in a circle around the rest of us, all talking earnestly on their phones. It was a sign of what was to come in the US.

There was another memorable event in our Australian meeting. In the US, we were exploring all types of biomarkers that were early indicators of a disease process as a means of developing therapeutic interventions to slow or stop this process. One of the Australian physicians gave a talk emphasizing death as an indicator of disease. Well, he was certainly right that death was an indicator of disease, just not an early indicator that would allow intervention.

Benzene

I also participated in a WHO Task Group on Benzene. We met in Germany with representatives of countries from all over the world. We in the West were concerned about allowable limits of the carcinogen benzene in the air, be it in the workplace or confined spaces such as submarines or spacecraft. As we discussed the very low levels that might be allowed, a man from Egypt explained that, in his country, the concern was to keep workers from washing their hands in benzene, because it was a good solvent to remove grease. We certainly came from two different worlds.

Later, I cochaired a WHO Task Group on Environmental Health Criteria for Bentonite, Kaolin, and Selected Clay Minerals that met in England. These materials were not very toxic, so the meeting was routine.

Twin Mix-up in France

A productive activity of the WHO is the publication of volumes on the ability of various chemicals or processes to cause cancer, and the sponsoring group is called the International Agency for Research on Cancer (IARC), located in Lyon, France. This organization was originally founded soon after World War II by the then leader of France, Charles De Gaulle. He wanted France to devote a major effort to fighting cancer. The IARC volumes are devoted solely to documenting evidence for the potential carcinogenicity of a substance or process. The volumes do not deal with regulatory levels of exposure—a much easier task than trying to set "safe" levels of exposure. I have enjoyed working on several of these volumes, including those on butadiene, trichloroethylene, and outdoor air. An amusing thing happened when I was in Lyon for work on the trichloroethylene document. I asked my twin sister, Roberta, to come along on that trip just for fun. I invited her to have lunch with us at the IARC cafeteria, and she came and waited in the lobby for us to have our lunch break. I was upstairs working when Vince Calgliano, the IARC person responsible for leading our group, happened to notice her. He, of course, assumed that she was I and that I was goofing off in the lobby when I was supposed to be working. The IARC does not pay its committee members, so Vince politely asked her what she was doing. She replied that she was waiting for lunch. He then probed a bit deeper, and, as he told me later, she did not seem aware of the major issues under discussion. He eventually gave up and went upstairs to our work area where, to his surprise, he observed me hard at work. Vince still tells me that story every time he sees me.

Health Effects Institute

I spent eight years on the Research Committee of the Health Effects Institute, an organization that funds research on the health effects of automobile emissions. It is most unusual in that it receives half of its funding from the regulator (the EPA) and half from the automobile industry—the regulated. I consider it an excellent paradigm. It was headed by Dan Greenberg, who had experience in Massachusetts state in public health. I mentioned earlier the research I participated in at Lovelace on the health effects of diesel engine exhaust. The HEI funding for this project made possible the conversion of diesel engines to cleaner devices, which was a major contribution to improved public health.

Detained by Airport Security

A long trip from Albuquerque to Boston for our HEI meetings resulted in an infamous event on one of them. I had had a church group over for a potluck dinner the week before one of my trips. After the dinner I discovered that someone had left a fair-sized knife at my home, so I wrapped it in paper and put it in my purse to take to church on Sunday to seek the owner. I did not find the owner and forgot about the knife in my purse. On Monday, I began my trip to Boston. I had an intermediate stop in St. Louis. My purse came through the screening in Albuquerque with no questions asked. In St. Louis, there were problems with the plane to Boston, so I had to spend the night and take an early morning flight out. I called HEI and said I would be late. It turned out that I was much later than expected. After my overnight stay, I, of course, had to go through airport security again. This time the knife did not go undetected. I was pulled aside and "detained." Our family still argues over what the word "detained" means. Some say I was arrested. I say I was detained. I was taken to a jail area in the airport and questioned in depth. Of course, I missed my plane. Eventually a person who appeared to be a supervisor came by and asked the questioner about me. When he explained, the supervisor said in a firm voice, "Get her out of here NOW!" So I was released in time to catch the next plane to Boston and was told that I might have to return to St. Louis to appear in court. Thank goodness I did not have to do that. But I received much ribbing from my fellow committee members about the time I was detained by the police on my way to our meeting.

10

ROGENE
MORE ADVENTURES

After my husband passed away in 2001, I began to travel, either with Buzzy and Eldon or with another member of my family. I enrolled in a Ghost Ranch-sponsored class with Phillip Newell to be held on the island of Iona, off the coast of Scotland. The course was entitled Iona: A Celtic Journey—Listening for the Heartbeat of God. I don't like to travel alone, so I asked my daughter, Lucy Clemen, if she would like to come along. We had a relaxing week and were given a boat ride to a cave on an adjacent island where the sound of the winds in the cave were said to have inspired a musical composition by Mendelssohn.

In 2006 I took an excellent Elderhostel (later called Road Scholar) trip to Turkey. Buzzy and Eldon were along. I rank this trip among the best I ever took. So much of the history of the territory relates to biblical events. When we came to Ephesus, one could envisage Paul speaking to the crowds. The public toilets there were for men only, and the multi-seat marble toilet covers were fascinating. One could imagine elderly men with constipation sitting there discussing world problems. But where did the women go? That was unclear.

At Cappadocia we took a hot-air balloon ride over the soft-rock chimneys marking the underground hiding places where persecuted people hid from their oppressors. We also witnessed whirling dervishes at a religious ceremony. One of the participants spoke with us afterwards. We were impressed by his sincerity. As scientists, we know the whole world is in constant motion, from the smallest atoms to the planets above us. These men sincerely believe since God created a world in constant motion, that whirling brings them closer to God. When they are not whirling they are businessmen who do charitable works in addition to running their businesses, much like our Rotarians or Lion's Club members.

We visited the famous site at Gallipoli where the Turks defeated the British and many men died. There we saw a plaque of a statement made by Ataturk abhorring the madness of war and offering sympathies to all who lost family members there. In 2004, on another Elderhostel, we had visited the War Memorial in Melbourne, Australia. It was explained to us that, at the beginning of World War I, the Australians were pleased that the British expected them to help in the war effort. Their boys went proudly to fight in Gallipoli. The Australians were put on the front lines. The battle was fierce, and many died. The bodies were never returned home, hence the memorial. This poem is written on the wall:

> They shall not grow old
> as we that are left grow old.
> Age shall not weary them,
> nor the years condemn.
> At the going down of the sun
> and in the morning
> we will remember them.

Here in 2006 at the site we saw a copy of Ataturk's moving letter to the grieving mothers in Australia after the battle:

> Those heroes that shed their blood and lost their lives . . .
> you are now lying in the soil of a friendly country. Therefore
> rest in peace. There is no difference between the Johnnies
> and Mehmets to us where they lie side by side here in this
> country of ours. . . . You, the mothers, who sent their sons
> from faraway countries, wipe away your tears; your sons are

now lying in our bosom and are in peace. After having lost their lives on this land they have become our sons as well.

A modern Turkish woman was our guide in Istanbul. She was very proud of the secular government that Ataturk had brought them. She was worried about all the money the Saudis were sending to Turkey to build mosques with very conservative imams to preach in them. She told us to look around at all the mosques already there. "Do you think we need more mosques?" she asked. She pointed out groups of young women who wore floor-length raincoats and scarves on their heads. Underneath the coats their dresses were beautifully embroidered—very fashionable. These women, whom our guide called "The Raincoat Brigade," were reverting back to something like the Muslim dress for women. Our guide was annoyed by them and said, "These girls do not know what it was like in the old days when strict Muslim dress was required. I have a twelve-year-old daughter, and I fear she may be told she has to wear such things." She was a great admirer of Ataturk and the more secular government he had established.

In September 2006, a widow friend and I took an Elderhostel trip to the Baltic nations (Lithuania, Latvia, Estonia) and St. Petersburg, Russia. Joanna's relatives came from Lithuania, so she was thrilled to have a chance to visit the "homeland." We started in Vilnius in a wonderful old hotel with huge rooms and gold-ornamented bathrooms. We had lunch at a local café that featured folk music played by a violinist, a drummer, and a woodwind instrumentalist. We observed that most Lithuanians were fair, blond, and blue-eyed. On the outskirts of Vilnius we saw a beautiful memorial to fourteen young people who died trying to keep the Russians from capturing the TV station located there. The next day we drove by bus to Trakai to see the restored castle there. The courtyard had a stable, and you had to cross a moat to get to the part of the castle where the duke and his family lived. We ate lunch at a café that served traditional Karaites food. These are the people the duke brought back from the Crimean area. They do

Rogene in Africa

Women in Nelson Mandela's church in Johannesburg

not consider themselves Jewish but follow the traditions of the Jewish faith. We learned that eight percent of Lithuanians are Russian and have full rights as citizens; Russians make up forty percent of Latvia's population and twenty-five percent of the Estonians, but they cannot be citizens of either of those countries and have no passports. We were told that Lithuania has a high rate of alcoholism, suicide, and divorce.

Our next stop was in Riga, Latvia. The forty percent of people who are Russian must learn the history, language, and constitution of Latvia to become citizens. Latvians are mainly Lutherans, not Catholic. We had another concert near a moving memorial at a former concentration camp. Next day we drove to Sigulota, a castle in an area that looked like upper New York state, then on to Tallin, Estonia, via the Ganja National Park. Buzzy has a friend named Peg who lives in Tallin and who took us to lunch with good local food. I had a delicious mushroom, onion, and cheese casserole. On the drive to Russia the next day we saw oil shale mining sites, the inlet to the Gulf of Finland, lots of birch forests, small wooden houses with garden plots, and long stretches of prairie. It took a while to get through the Estonian border, but we quickly went through the Russian border. Our visit in St. Petersburg was brief but fruitful. We saw a ballet at the Maarinski Theater and spent a lot of time visiting the Hermitage. Then we were on our way back to the USA.

I once joined Buzzy and Eldon for an Elderhostel trip to Africa. It was an exciting adventure in viewing animal life in the wild. We visited Zimbabwe, the Chobe Game Reserve in Botswana, and the TETSI Water Lodge on the Zambezi River. We stayed in three different hunting camps, each of which had cabins open to the forest and its inhabitants. In all of these camps it was required that we call security guards if we left our cabins at night to go to the dining room for dinner. In one of the villages, a distinguished medicine man talked us about his medical powers. He looked directly at me and said he had something to get rid of my winkles. Later I asked if I could buy some of this product. He said, "No, God gave me this knowledge, so I would not charge for the information." But he would give me a prescription of herbs that I should take home and soak in oil, then rub the oil on my face. Quite a generous offer! In the evenings in our cabins we had many animal visits that brought excitement to our lives. One place supplied us with slingshots to scare off the monkeys. We saw beautiful views of Victoria Falls and took canoe trips down the Chobe and the Zambezi River to view wildlife along the banks of the river and hippopotamuses jousting with each other. When Buzzy arrived at her cabin, she found a smiling houseboy who pointed out he had prepared a bubble bath for her. When she let the water out after her bath, she discovered many small creatures on the bottom of the bathtub. She had not bathed alone!

At one elephant farm we observed a pitiable sight. Each of us was riding an elephant and mine was named Miss Ellie. She was a twenty-four-year-old female who had never been bred, and had no children. But she adored all the children around her. We came to a place in the trail where there was a huge mud hole that the elephants used to cool off. A large elephant, stuck deep in the mud hole, was crying in a pitiful manner. The other elephants just walked on by, but not Miss Ellie! She stood by the mud hole and would not leave. She began to sway from side to side, a sign of sympathy according to her handler, but it felt to me as if she was trying to get rid of me. Eventually the handlers got Miss Ellie to move on, but she continued to look back at her suffering friend. What a show of animal empathy! We were told later that they managed to pull the elephant out using large straps, but she was too far gone and had to be put down. Poor elephant!

Our final visit was to Johannesburg with its Apartheid Museum, Mandela's former home, and the church where many refugees sought safety during the freedom struggles. The museum was interesting, and Eldon lamented that we didn't have such a museum in the USA. His wish was granted in 2016, when a museum dedicated to African Americans opened on the mall in Washington, DC.

Early in 2009, I took an Elderhostel trip to explore Costa Rica. Costa Rica seemed very stable and prosperous. I wondered why they were doing so much better than other Central American countries.

A lecturer told us that it was because they had a sizable middle class. Also, the culture was much more influenced by Europe than by the US. Its citizens sent their brightest students to Europe for college rather than to the US. They had no army, and their main industry was ecotourism. And what a beautiful ecosystem they had! We saw an abundance of spectacular wild life, including howler monkeys that sounded like lions, colorful Toucan birds, gorgeous butterflies, cacao and cinnamon trees, and the wonderful quetzal bird. In addition to wildlife, the country had active volcanos and frequent earthquakes. One earthquake while I was there was rated at 6.1 and knocked out our lights for a while. The quake also changed a nearby river from a beautiful, shallow, clear waterway to a tumbling muddy waterway that was hard to navigate. While on this trip I discovered a different way to handle minor illnesses. I developed a sore tooth and had a swollen jaw. I was taken to a local pharmacy and was surprised at the difference from what we had in our local drugstores in the US. A pharmacist asked me what I wanted. Our guide and I explained, and the pharmacist went into another room to discuss the matter with a man I thought must be an MD. Back came the pharmacist with three options in terms of antibiotics: one was very strong and should be taken only once, one was medium in strength and should be taken daily over three days, and a third was relatively weak and should be taken daily for two weeks. Which did I want? I was so used to a doctor making such a choice that at first I did not know what to say. But I chose the medium strength antibiotic, which did the job.

Later in the year, I suggested that we three (Buzzy, Eldon, and I) take a highly rated Elderhostel trip to Patagonia and the Andean Lake Region. It turned out to be a really great tour. One interesting aspect was the trip from Puerto Mott, Chile, via bus and boat, through the beautiful Andes Mountains, ending up at Bariloche, Argentina, a world-famous winter ski area. We had lectures on the Mapuche Indians and the Europoean immigrants of Patagonia.

Next day we heard about the Patagonian estancias, which are large ranches established by Welch settlers. In the town of Gaiman we learned that one of the early settlers was named Rogers. He was captain of one of the ships that brought settlers there from Wales. He was from Pennsylvania and decided to live in Gaiman after bringing over a shipload of settlers. Our guide was the great-granddaughter of one of the settlers. She bore a striking resemblance to our mother, Lenoma Rogers Faulkner, so Buzzy and I wondered if we might be distantly related. There was a monument to Captain Rogers in the graveyard, but the gate to the graveyard was locked, so we could not read what was on the gravestone. These settlers developed into small communities with their own school and institutions that continue to this day.

From there we traveled by bus to Trelew with its exceptional paleontology museum and a beautiful view of the Andes. Then on to Buenos Aires for a tango show, tango lessons, good food, and interesting street performers. Our final museum visit before leaving for home was the Evita Museum. The Argentinians seemed to be quite fond of Evita.

In the fall of 2010, I took one of my favorite trips. I went to India with a group called Overseas Adventure Travel. We arrived in Calcutta, whose streets were chaotic. There were six lanes of heavy traffic on a four-lane highway filled with all sorts of cars, trucks, and two-wheelers, plus cows and monkeys. Traffic signs were totally ignored, and each truck or bus had a sign on the back saying, "Please honk." This meant one should honk before passing, and the noise was deafening. Poor people lived under small tarps on the sidewalk. After a restful night in our nice hotel we visited the home of Mother Theresa. There we attended an Anglican Church service before catching a plane to Paro, Bhutan. We had a week in Bhutan and I loved the people there.

They seemed very happy and peaceful. In fact, the national goal of the country was "happiness." We had a charming young man as our guide whose name was Tshering Penjor. He was a devout Buddhist and told us how lucky we were to be there during a season of ceremonies. We were taken to a temple where a ceremonial dance was to be performed. The polite young man carefully explained that the men could enter the ground floor where the dancers were, but the ladies must go upstairs to the balcony to observe the dance. Of course, we modern ladies asked why. The young man blushed slightly and said that everyone knows that women are impure. It turned out that we ladies got the best deal. The men had to sit cross-legged on a concrete floor, and we ladies had an excellent view of the dance sitting on benches in the balcony. Perhaps the ladies of Bhutan were cleverer than the men knew. We saw a place that made paper out of mulberry tree bark and attended a festival on another temple square. The festival dancing reminded me of pueblo dances in New Mexico. There we got acquainted with betel nut chewing, which is almost universally done in Bhutan. Betel nuts for chewing were handed out to the young monks and the dancers we saw at ceremonies. The routine was that you took a leaf, added a betel nut and some lime to enhance it on the leaf, and then chewed it. It is a mild stimulant. The people then spit it out on the street, so the streets and buildings are covered with the foul-smelling stuff. It is legal and encouraged despite the fact that betel juice is carcinogenic to the mouth and esophagus. We heard some of the older monk doing "throat singing," a highly guttural sound.

We broke into small groups and visited a family in their home. It is traditional to bring a gift when you visit, and I had forgotten to bring something. So I searched desperately in my purse. I came up with a family photo, and the lady of the house we visited seemed especially pleased with it. She stared at the picture a long time and then put it away. There is a beautiful trout stream flowing through Bhutan, but the local people were not allowed to fish there because of their religious belief that they should not kill any living thing. Once on our drives, a member of our group swatted a mosquito. Our guide laughingly cautioned the man that if he killed a mosquito he might have to spend two or three of his next lives as a mosquito.

We left Bhutan for Delphi and northern India with a guide named Sanjay Sethi. The local school there had poor lighting, and the children sat on the bare dirt floor. In the family home it was evident that the family was well off. The father, who had recently died, had been a high-ranking police officer, and his widow had two servants to help her. She served us a wonderful dinner. But by far the most interesting place we visited was the holy city of Varanassi on the Ganges River. That night we took a terribly bumpy ride in a rickshaw from the center of the city to a spot near the river. The sight was macabre, with jams of people pushing to get to the river to see a Hindu ceremony or to carry a dead member of their family to a crematorium. We walked though throngs of people to the river and got on a barge that went out into the river for a good view of the Hindu ceremony being conducted on the stadium-like steps leading down to the water. We then came back in the barge to sit on the steps and watch the activity There were men standing in the river bathing and even drinking the filthy water. Our guide swore that the water had been tested and was found to be potable. I frankly did not believe him. There were crematoriums spaced out along the river, and people brought their dead covered by a white cloth on a stretcher to be placed on stacks of wood on one of the crematoriums. Hired "drones" handled the placement of the body on the wood and lit the fire in the wood. Then more wood was placed on top of the body and was also lit. The cremation took about four hours. We observed people pawing through the ashes of completed cremations looking for any gold or other precious metals that might have survived the fire, On our way out we were nearly knocked over by a family carrying a corpse on a stretcher rushing to get down to a crematorium. It was all very macabre. I was glad to get back to the hotel and a more normal life.

Our group traveled on to Nepal, flying into Katmandu. We had one day of seeing many temples. One morning we were standing on one side of a river when we heard loud sobbing. Looking across the river we saw several cremation sites. At one site a body in a white robe was lying on top of a pile of wood. A man was lying across the body and sobbing loudly. Other family members (I assumed) were standing by. One man pulled the sobbing figure off the corpse, and more

Rogene and guard outside hotel in India

branches were piled on the body and lit with fire. Because it was early in the day, children in school uniforms were chatting happily while walking to school. Businessmen in suits were headed for their offices, and shop keepers were opening their doors. Everyone was going about their business while "grandma" was burning on the corner. What a sight! The family had no privacy at all.

The final trip in 2013 was the most important of all. To celebrate Buzzy's eightieth birthday, Eldon suggested a family boat trip to Alaska, and I asked if I could come along with my family. Thus the families of both twins got together for a cruise to Alaska with almost all members of the immediate families present. It was a week of joy and a chance for almost all our offspring to get acquainted with each other.

The combined families on the twins' eightieth birthday cruise

An early picture of the twins' children.
From left, Nancy, Lucy, Phillip, Edith, Elizabeth, Tim, Sharon.

11

AFTERWORD

W e come, not to the end of our story, by any means, but to the present. Who would imagine that two little girls from a small town in rural West Texas would experience lives of such travel and adventure, mingling not only with ordinary folk but with royalty, rubes, and rulers, teaching and consulting around the world, and making significant contributions to environmental health? The "undecided" young ladies who entered TCU in the fall of 1951 never regretted the choice to go into the field of science as a future career. Rogene saw it as totally consistent with our deep religious faith. In addition to satisfying our curiosity about the chemical and physical laws of nature, we found, as our faith matured, that the study of the laws of science was really the study of the laws of God. We thus considered ourselves fortunate to be allowed to study scientific problems which, in an important sense, was a holy calling. Roberta feels she is fortunate to have had the opportunity to teach children and young adults from all over the world, at Hirschi and Wichita Falls high schools, at Midwestern State University in Wichita Falls, Texas, at Southbank International School in London, at Capiolani College in Hawaii, and at Al Akhawayn University in Morocco. These experiences have helped her realize that she could find goodness as well as heartache among all people, no matter their religion or country of origin.

Through it all, together and separately, Neany and Buzzy have romped their way across the world, throwing flowers as well as studying them, learning and loving their world.

ACKNOWLEDGMENTS

ROBERTA would like to acknowledge with gratitude the encouragement and help on this project from her friends Lynn Hoggard and Ann Hunter.

ROGENE would like to acknowledge the persistent encouragement of her twin, Roberta, to see that this project was completed.